CHINA

Marxist Regimes Series

Series editor: Bogdan Szajkowski,
Department of Sociology, University College,
Cardiff

Further Titles

CHINA

Politics, Economics and Society

Iconoclasm and Innovation in a
Revolutionary Socialist Country

Marc Blecher

Frances Pinter (Publishers), London
Lynne Rienner Publishers, Inc., Boulder

First published in Great Britain in 1986 by
Frances Pinter (Publishers) Limited
25 Floral Street, London WC2E 9DS

First published in the United States of America in 1986 by
Lynne Rienner Publications, Inc.
948 North Street, Boulder, Colorado 80302

Printed in Great Britain

British Library Cataloguing in Publication Data

Blecher, Marc
   China: politics, economics and society.
   —(Marxist regimes series)
   1. China—Social conditions—1976—
   I. Title   II. Series
   951.05´8   HN733.5
   ISBN 0-86187-402-1
   ISBN 0-86187-403-X Pbk

Library of Congress Cataloging-in-Publication Data

Blecher, Marc J.
   China, politics, economics, and society.
   (Marxist regimes series)
   Bibliography: p.
   Includes Index.
   1. China—Politics and government—1949-   .
   2. China—Economic conditions—1949-   .   3. China—
   Social life and customs—1949-   .   I. Title.
   II. Series.
   DS777.75.B547   1986   951.05   86-555
   ISBN 0-931477-80-8
   ISBN 0-931477-81-6 (pbk.)

Typeset by Joshua Associates Limited, Oxford
Printed by SRP Ltd, Exeter

Editor's Preface

This comprehensive and penetrating study of Chinese politics, economics and society is a major contribution to scholarship in general and Chinese studies in particular. China, with its huge size both in terms of population and space, ancient civilization and dramatic swings of policies, programmes and personalities, has been the subject of many academic and popular books—most of them, however, tended to be distant and impersonal in character. In addition, in the main, studies of contemporary China, suffered from the lack not only of an adequate conceptual framework, but also of evidence.

This book breaks the mould. It frankly and eloquently discusses the many complex and perplexing questions both old and new that face China as it moves into the 1990s. In using historical perspective, this book provides a solid base for contemporary analysis of issues such as the type, scope and speed of economic and social reforms needed, or how to redirect the nation's massive energies towards the construction of a modern and more productive society. Furthermore, this book analyses important questions not only about the central issues of rural development but also about the nature of socialism in China and its future for the developing world.

The study of Marxist regimes has commonly been equated with the study of communist political systems. There were several historical and methodological reasons for this. For many years it was not difficult to distinguish the eight regimes in Eastern Europe and four in Asia which resoundingly claimed adherence to the tenets of Marxism and more particularly to their Soviet interpretation—Marxism-Leninism. These regimes, variously called 'People's Republic', 'People's Democratic Republic', or 'Democratic Republic', claimed to have derived their inspiration from the Soviet Union to which, indeed, in the overwhelming number of cases they owed their establishment.

To many scholars and analysts these regimes represented a multiplication of and geographical extension of the 'Soviet model' and consequently of the Soviet sphere of influence. Although there were clearly substantial similarities between the Soviet Union and the people's democracies, especially in the initial phases of their development, these were often overstressed at the expense of noticing the differences between these political systems.

It took a few years for scholars to realize that generalizing the particular, i.e. applying the Soviet experience to other states ruled by elites which claimed to be guided by 'scientific socialism', was not good enough. The relative simplicity of the assumption of a cohesive communist bloc was questioned after the expulsion of Yugoslavia from the Communist Information Bureau in 1948 and in particular after the workers' riots in Poznań in 1956 and the Hungarian revolution of the same year. By the mid-1960s, the totalitarian model of communist politics, which until then had been very much in force, began to crumble. As some of these regimes articulated demands for a distinctive path of socialist development, many specialists studying these systems began to notice that the cohesiveness of the communist bloc was less apparent than had been claimed before.

Also by the mid-1960s, in the newly independent African states 'democratic' multi-party states were turning into one-party states or military dictatorships, thus questioning the inherent superiority of liberal democracy, capitalism and the values that went with it. Scholars now began to ponder on the simple contrast between multi-party democracy and a one-party totalitarian rule that had satisfied an earlier generation.

More importantly, however, by the beginning of that decade Cuba had a revolution without Soviet help, a revolution which subsequently became to many political elites in the Third World not only an inspiration but a clear military, political and ideological example to follow. Apart from its romantic appeal, to many nationalist movements the Cuban revolution also demonstrated a novel way of conducting and winning a nationalist, anti-imperialist war and accepting Marxism as the state ideology without a vanguard communist party. The Cuban precedent was subsequently followed in one respect or another by scores of regimes in the Third World who used the adoption of 'scientific socialism' tied to the tradition of Marxist thought as a form of mobilization, legitimation or association with the prestigious symbols and powerful high-status regimes such as the Soviet Union, China, Cuba and Vietnam.

Despite all these changes the study of Marxist regimes remains in its infancy and continues to be hampered by constant and not always pertinent comparison with the Soviet Union, thus somewhat blurring the important underlying common theme—the 'scientific theory' of the laws of development of human society and human history. This doctrine is claimed by the leadership of these regimes to consist of the discovery of objective causal relationships; it is used to analyse the contradictions which arise between goals and actuality in the pursuit of a common destiny. Thus the political elites of these countries have been and continue to be influenced in both their ideology and their political practice by Marxism more than any other current of social thought and political practice.

The growth in the number and global significance, as well as the ideological political and economic impact, of Marxist regimes has presented scholars and students with an increasing challenge. In meeting this challenge, social scientists on both sides of the political divide have put forward a dazzling profusion of terms, models, programmes and varieties of inter- pretation. It is against the background of this profusion that the present com- prehensive series on Marxist regimes is offered.

This collection of monographs is envisaged as a series of multi-disciplinary textbooks on the governments, politics, economics and society of these countries. Each of the monographs was prepared by a specialist on the country concerned. Thus, over fifty scholars from all over the world have contributed monographs which were based on first-hand knowledge. The geographical diversity of the authors, combined with the fact that as a group they represent many disciplines of social science, gives their individual analyses and the series as a whole an additional dimension.

Each of the scholars who contributed to this series was asked to analyse such topics as the political culture, the governmental structure, the ruling party, other mass organizations, party-state relations, the policy process, the economy, domestic and foreign relations together with any features peculiar to the country under discussion.

This series does not aim at assigning authenticity or authority to any single one of the political systems included in it. It shows that depending on a variety of historical, cultural, ethnic and political factors, the pursuit of goals derived from the tenets of Marxism has produced different political forms at different times and in different places. It also illustrates the rich diversity among these societies, where attempts to achieve a synthesis between goals derived from Marxism on the one hand, and national realities on the other, have often meant distinctive approaches and solutions to the problems of social, political and economic development.

University College
Cardiff

Bogdan Szajkowski

This book is for Ian, Jacob and Joel Blecher—brothers in our arms—with all a father's love.

Contents

List of Illustrations and Figures

Map

Figures

Tables

Preface and Acknowledgements

As part of a series of volumes on socialist experiences throughout the world, this book emphasizes themes of comparative analysis. This approach is important both to advance theoretical understanding of socialist reality and also to shed light on China's own experiences. As the most iconoclastic of socialist countries, China was long isolated from comparative study. Sinologists were happy to stick to their bailiwick, and comparativists, puzzled by the peculiarities of what appeared to be going on there, were equally happy to leave China to them. Its rural-based revolution was itself a puzzle which gave it 'special' characteristics. The Great Leap Forward and the Cultural Revolution confirmed suspicions that something unusual was afoot in Chinese socialism. The changes in China since Mao Zedong's death in 1976 have made evident the fact that China has encountered some of the same problems as other socialist countries, an insight which Sino–centred analysis may be prone to miss.

China's approach to them is as heterodox as ever. Yet China's refusal to conform to the Soviet-style orthodoxy is an opportunity, not an obstacle, to comparative analysis. The Chinese revolution, with its rural base, has been an inspiration to more socialist revolutions than the urban-based Russian revolution and will probably continue to be so (as the contemporary struggles of the New People's Army in the Philippines suggests). Therefore the reasons for the greater success of rural-based revolution need to be better understood, as do the implications for the forms of socialism that emanate from them. Because it tried out but then systematically rejected the Soviet model of socialist organization and development, the Chinese case reveals much about the former's contradictions and problems. It also has much to teach about the possibilities and dangers of alternative routes, for which the world's increasingly diverse group of socialist countries is increasingly on the lookout.

Chapter 1 examines the Chinese revolution, seeking to explain it in the context of the specific social formation within which it appeared. It asks why urban-based bourgeois revolution failed, and why a revolution with a rural base and a broadly popular participatory politics—both significant departures from the Russian revolutionary model—could succeed. It also suggests some of the theoretical and practical implications of these specific qualities of China's revolution. Chapter 2 traces the history of China's socialist transition

and development from 1949 to the present. Chapter 3 presents an interpretation of that history, emphasizing the differences from the Soviet model
(and suggesting the reasons for them), while also taking issue with the
widespread conception that Chinese development has essentially been
cyclical or repetitive. Chapters 4–7 address topical questions concerning
politics, society, economy and policy.

My greatest scholarly debt in this study is owed to my students at Oberlin
College over the past decade. The high level of intellectual ability which they
have brought into my classrooms and office has provided the crucible in
which many of the ideas in this book were catalysed and then refined. They
have also made a teacher's work rewarding and thrilling. Their constant
search for complex understanding has informed the approach taken in this
volume, and has helped provide much of its substance. It is my deepest hope
that this book, drawn so much from them, will help sustain and develop such
enquiry among their successors.

My debts to colleagues whose work I have read and studied, and with whom
I have conversed and debated on so many of the issues treated here, are also
very great. Collectively, they have opened up new modes of enquiry about
China and other socialist countries. They have somehow managed, against
great obstacles, to set aside the strong ideological charges that always go with
the territory, and found ways to look at socialism in China and elsewhere
objectively and in a balanced way. They have provided inspiration and ideas
too numerously and diffusely for me to be able to mention them all by name.
They will have to content themselves, then, with the words of Fernando:
'You know who you are'.

My special thanks go to Bogdan Szajkowski, editor of the Marxist Regimes
Series, for honouring me with the opportunity to contribute this volume
to it, for being such a helpful and sympathetic critic, and for being so
understanding and supportive at crucial moments. He is a model editor with
a wonderful touch for finding precisely the right mix of deference and
guidance. Peter Moulson and Heather Bliss, editors at Frances Pinter
(Publishers) Ltd, have given new meanings to the words patience and
efficiency, despite my repeated efforts to frustrate them. Mark Selden did a
heroic job of making extended comments on the manuscript. Susan MacLean
and Phil Steinberg, my research assistants at Oberlin, were of great help in
tracking down sources, compiling data, and giving their critical comments
from the student reader's point of view. Thanks also to the Dana Foundation
and Oberlin College (especially David Love) for providing and arranging the
funds to employ them.

And finally to my wife Sharon, who, while managing her own busy career, had to take much more than her share of household duties and hours of lost companionship, and to my children, who have suffered because 'Daddy's in his study again'; apologies and thanks will not suffice. I hope you'll accept a promise not to do it again very soon, or at least to write this message again when I do.

Marc Blecher

Oberlin, Ohio, 1985

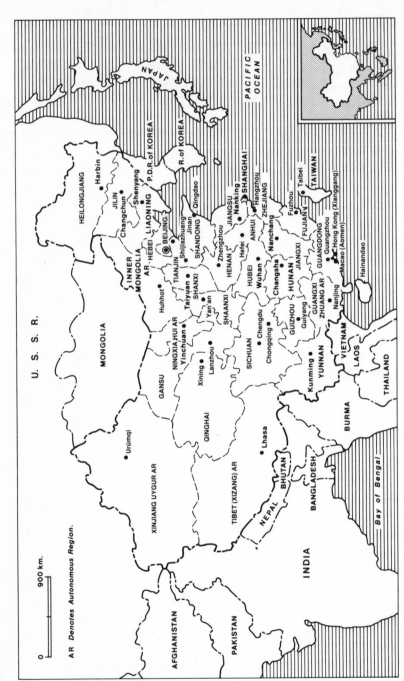

People's Republic of China

Basic Data*

Official name	People's Republic of China
Population	1,024,950,000
Population density	107 per sq. km.
Population growth (% p.a.)	1.154 (over 1982)
Urban population (%)	23.5
Total labour force	460,040,000
Life expectancy	67
Infant death rate (per 1,000)	38
Child death rate (per 1,000)	2
Ethnic groups	Han 94.79%; ethnic minorities include Mongols, Hui (Moslems), Tibetans, Uygurs, Miao, Yi, Zhuang and 48 others
Capital	Beijing (pop. 9,340,000)
Land area	9,600,000 sq. km., of which 33% mountainous, 26% plateaux, 19% basins, 12% plains and 10% hills
Official language	Chinese
Administrative divisions	30 provinces and provincial-level municipalities and autonomous regions, 286 municipalities, 552 rural districts under city administration, 2080 rural counties
Membership of international organizations	UN since 1971; 21 governmental and 71 non-governmental international organizations (1981)
Foreign relations	Diplomatic relations with 129 countries (1984)
Political structure	
Constitution	Fourth (September 1982)
Highest legislative body	National People's Congress
Highest executive body	State Council
Prime Minister	Zhao Ziyang
President	Li Xiannian

Trade and balance of payments

Exports	US$22.226 billion
Imports	US$21.390 billion
Exports as % of GDP	8.09
Main exports (%)	Light industrial products (including textiles and metal products) 36.8; oil products 21; food products 12.8
Main imports (%)	Light industrial products (including textiles and metal products) 33; machinery and transport equipment 18.6; food products 14.6; chemical products 14.9
Destination of exports (%)	USSR and East European socialist countries 5%; industrial capitalist countries 42%; developing countries 52%; high-income oil-exporting countries 2%
Main trading partners	Japan, Hong Kong, USA, Germany, Canada
Main natural resources	Coal reserves 727.6 billion tons; iron ore reserves 46.76 billion tons; forest stock 10.26 billion cu. m.; hydropower resources 676 million KW
Food self-sufficiency	12,380,000 ton net foodgrain imports; RMB 529,000,000 net value of imports of all food
Ruling party	Chinese Communist Party
Secretary General	Hu Yaobang
Party membership	40,000,000 (1985)
Armed forces	Over 4,000,000 (approx 6.3% of population between 15 and 65 years of age)

Education and health

School system	10 years (5 primary, 5 secondary), entrance age 7
Primary school enrolment	93% of age cohort admitted
Secondary school enrolment	50% of age cohort admitted
Tertiary education	805 institutions, enrolling 1,206,823 students (16.24% of population aged 20–24)

Adult literacy	66%
Population per hospital bed	483
Population per physician	759

Economy

GNP	US$305.73 billion (1982)
GNP per capita	US$300 (1982)
State budgetary revenue	25.9% of national income
Defence expenditure	18% of state budget (1979)
Monetary unit	*Renminbi* (RMB) (approx. US$0.35)
Main crops (% of sown area)	Rice 23, wheat 20, corn 13, tubers 6.5, soybeans 5.3, cotton 4.2
Land tenure	Collectively-owned farmland contracted to households
Main religions	Animism, Buddhism, Islam

Transport

Rail network	51,600 km. (2,300 km. electrified)
Road network	910,510 km.

*All statistics are for 1983 (unless otherwise noted), and do not include Taiwan Province.

Growth indicators (av. % p.a.)

	1952–78	1978–83
National income	5.98	7.13
Industrial output (gross value)	11.26	7.88
Heavy	13.64	5.13
Light	9.14	11.21
Agricultural output (gross value)	3.25	7.91
Foodgrain production per capita	0.40	3.60

Population Forecasting

The following data are projections produced by Poptran, University College Cardiff Population Centre, from United Nations Assessment Data published in 1980, and are reproduced here to provide some basis of comparison with other countries covered by the Marxist Regimes Series.

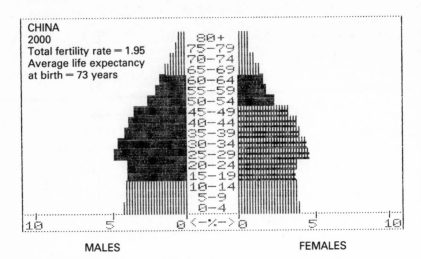

CHINA
2000
Total fertility rate = 1.95
Average life expectancy
at birth = 73 years

80+
75—79
70—74
65—69
60—64
55—59
50—54
45—49
40—44
35—39
30—34
25—29
20—24
15—19
10—14
5—9
0—4

10   5   0 <—%—> 0   5   10

MALES   FEMALES

Projected Data for China 2000

Total population ('000)	1,257,298
Males ('000)	638,265
Females ('000)	619,033
Total fertility rate	1.95
Life expectancy (male)	70.6 years
Life expectancy (female)	74.6 years
Crude birth rate	17.3
Crude death rate	6.8
Annual growth rate	1.05%
Under 15s	24.34%
Over 65s	7.33%
Woman aged 15–49	27.69%
Doubling time	67 years
Population density	131 per sq. km.
Urban population	38.6%

Geographical Setting

Physical Geography

Two geographical facts of overriding importance shape Chinese affairs. First, the country is huge but its population even huger, creating deep and perennial problems for China to feed itself. Its land area of 9,561,000 square kilometres—7.3 per cent of the world total—is exceeded only by the Soviet Union and Canada; overall it is slightly larger than the United States. But China ranks second to none in population: in 1983, 102.5 billion people—22 per cent of the total on the planet—lived there (exclusive of Taiwan Province). The food problem is compounded by the fact that only 1,400,000 square kilometres (around 15 per cent) of China's land is arable. With 0.0014 square kilometres of such land per person, China faces food self-sufficiency problems more serious than most countries.

Second, China's vastness encompasses a great breadth of physical and climatic diversity. One-third of the country is at elevations of over 2,000 metres, most of which is in the far west and inhospitable to any agriculture at all. In central and southern China, comprised of plateaux and hilly areas, up to half of the land can be cultivated. Some of this—in Sichuan, and in the east and south-west—is very rich, supporting paddy rice which Chinese farmers grow at yields that rival those anywhere in the world. The most important secondary crops there include sugar cane and tea. Other places, such as the north central provinces of Shaanxi and Shanxi, and the north-eastern provinces of Liaoning, Jilin and Heilongjiang, concentrate on millet, corn, wheat, sorghum or soybeans. On the North China Plain, comprising Henan, Hebei and Shandong Provinces, almost all the land is cultivated, mostly to corn, winter wheat and sorghum; cotton is a major industrial crop there. These major crops aside, China also supports a wide range of agriculture, including almost everything from an enormous variety of fruits and vegetables to luxury crops like tobacco, coffee and spices.

Concomitantly, climate is highly variable over different parts of the country. In the vast expanses of the north-west and some of the central-north, rainfall averages under 250 mm. per year, while in the south-east it exceeds 1,500 and even 2,000 mm. over large areas. Mean January temperatures range from $-19°$ C in Harbin, the capital of Liaoning in the north-east, to over $10°$ C in Fuzhou in the south-east. More serious are the erratic variations in the weather. Historically and at present, China has been prone to frequent and often disastrous drought and flood. The country is endowed with a complex system of rivers that aid agriculture and transport but can also cause great damage when they overrun their banks or even change course, as they have often done and continue to do. Construction, reconstruction and maintenance of water-conservancy infrastructure—including dams, river banks, canals, drainage channels and reservoirs—have been a major activity for Chinese governments throughout history. While the very impressive and persistent efforts of the People's Republic to pour resources and energy into agricultural infrastructure have diminished the difficulties significantly, there is still much to be done to 'weatherproof' Chinese agriculture.

China is also well endowed with natural resources. It is self-sufficient in most minerals, with large untapped reserves and probably many as yet undiscovered ones (since geological work is not up to world levels). It has tremendous hydroelectric potential and enough coal reserves to last 1,700 years. Oil reserves are ample for China's needs for the foreseeable future.

Human Geography

Over three-quarters—76.5 per cent to be precise—of the Chinese people lived in the countryside in 1983, a figure which has been dropping rapidly in recent years (from 82.6 per cent in 1976, for example) with the forward march of urban industrialization and the relaxation of the population-control regulations that had prevented townward migration. China's pattern of urbanization is different from that found in so many countries, especially those in the Third World, where there are often enormous primate cities but a poor articulation of smaller urban settlements between them and the countryside. Of course, China has its giants, like Shanghai (which in 1983 contained 11,940,000 people (a figure which is overstated since it includes the farmers living within the metropolitan Shanghai administrative zone)) and Beijing (9,430,000 (likewise inclusive)). But even Shanghai contains only 6 per cent of China's urban population, compared with an average of 38 per cent (for urban population in the largest city) in the rest of the Third World. Only one-quarter of China's urban population lives in cities with populations over 2,000,000, while half lives in cities with populations between 100,000 and 1,000,000. This greater development of small and medium-sized cities is no accident. Based historically on China's well-articulated hierarchy of administrative and commercial centres, it is also the result of conscious efforts by the People's Republic to restrict the growth of large cities (largely by closing them to immigration) and to expand the growth of smaller ones (through development of decentralized, rural and medium-sized industries).

Because so much of the country is comprised of a basically self-provisioning peasantry, patterns of settlement in the countryside correspond closely to those of land cultivation and quality. Population densities are highest on the North China Plain and the rice-bowl areas of Sichuan and the lower Yangzi River, and lowest in the west and north-central wastes. In 1983 they ranged from 598 people per square kilometre in Jiangsu to only 1.6 in Tibet. At the grassroots, most Chinese have traditionally lived in towns, villages and hamlets rather than isolated settlements, a feature of China's human geography which facilitated immeasurably its rural revolution and the collectivization of agriculture, as we shall see.

The Han Chinese—the dominant ethnic group—comprise 95 per cent of China's population. The remaining 5 per cent consists of a stunning variety of ethnic and national groups. The Chinese government's 1984 *Statistical Yearbook* lists no fewer than fifty-five, of which the largest are Mongols, Moslems and Tibetans (State Statistical Bureau, 1984, p. 37). Five provinces (of thirty (17 per cent)), thirty-eight cities (of 289 (13 per cent)), and 590 counties (of 2,080 (28 per cent)) are formally designated as 'minority nationality autonomous areas'. Minority groups in China attain an importance disproportionate to their size because most of them live in sensitive border regions. In fact, almost the full length of China's land borders is peopled by minority nationalities.

International Aspects of China's Geography

China dominates the Asian land mass. Accordingly, it shares borders with no less than twelve countries, including politically important ones like Korea in the north-east, the Soviet Union there and in the north-west, Afghanistan, Pakistan and India in the west, and Vietnam and Laos in the south. Its land borders run to almost 15,000 kilometres, of which about one-third face the Soviet Union (and another one-quarter the People's Republic of Mongolia, a Soviet ally). This lengthy border with rival and sometimes hostile countries presents China with a perpetual security problem. Since 1949 the country has experienced armed conflict along most parts of it. It fought the United States and its allies in Korea, had skirmishes with the Soviet Union in the late 1960s, fought a war with India in 1962, was bombed by American warplanes during the Vietnam War, and later fought the Vietnamese themselves in 1978 and in skirmishes since.

China's coastline, too, presents security problems. For many years the United States' Seventh Fleet patrolled the Taiwan Straits. A continuing state of civil war with the Nationalist government on Taiwan, an American-supplied island fortress, led to the shelling of offshore islands in the late 1950s. China also lays claim to a vast archipelago in most of the South China Sea, as far south as Borneo and as far east as the Philippines.

Historically, China dominated Asia economically as well as politically. It was the leading trading country in the region and regularly received tribute from the smaller countries there. Chinese emigrants came to dominate business in most of South-East Asia. With China's economic decline starting in the mid-nineteenth century (as well as the rise of Western colonial influence there even earlier), its regional economic hegemony waned. Even after the establishment of the People's Republic, China's international predominance in Asian politics has not been matched in the economic realm, since it maintained low levels of trade for so long. But with the opening to the West in the early 1970s this has at last begun to change.

Beginning in the 1960s and 1970s, East Asia has become the most economically dynamic part of the Third World. Small countries with little in the way of domestic markets or natural resources, such as South Korea, Taiwan, Hong Kong and Singapore—the latter two hardly countries at all in geo-political terms—have experienced rapid economic growth based on export-orientated production of manufactured goods using imported raw materials. (Hence, production for re-export would perhaps be a more accurate term.) China is seen by many observers as possessing the same attributes that these countries drew on for the export-led growth: a skilled, inexpensive, disciplined labour-force; a tradition of entrepreneurship; a strong, developmentally-minded state; and a political culture and structure with propensities toward stability. But it also possesses the vast domestic natural resources and, potentially, home markets that its East Asian neighbours lack. China's potential power in the regional and even the world economies, therefore, far outstrips that of other East Asian countries, including even Japan.

1 Imperial Legacy, Capitalist Failure and Socialist Triumph

Why did China fail to develop into a successful capitalist country? This is a paradox. Culturally, the Chinese people are well known for their business acumen and entrepreneurial bent. And, comparatively, other parts of East Asia—such as Hong Kong, Japan, Singapore, South Korea and Taiwan—with various similarities in historical social structures, states, economic bases and cultures have produced some of the most vibrant structures of capitalism in the world.

Why did China produce instead one of the world's most massive and far-reaching socialist revolutions, and why did this revolution have a peasant base and a more popular (or at least populist) character than any others? This, too, is paradoxical. Marx, of course, predicted that socialist revolutions would be the product of contradictions of developed capitalism, which China has never experienced. He also predicted that the proletariat would provide the social base of the revolution when it did break out. Moreover, China's long history of imperial authoritarianism and bureaucratic centralization hardly presaged the popular democracy, orientation to local specificities and anti-bureaucratism that were distinctive features of the communist-led revolutionary movement.

In this chapter we shall explore these paradoxes. This inquiry will help us address three analytical problems. First, how can the triumph of socialism in China, with its specific characteristics, be explained? Second, how did China's history affect its socialism once it did triumph? And third, what does the Chinese case tell us about the general theoretical and practical use of the preconditions and bases for socialist revolution and transformation?

Imperial China and its Failure

Not only did the Chinese empire collapse in 1911. It also failed to provide the basis for China to make a smooth transition to a new social formation. It would take nearly four decades for China to re-establish political unity and coherent governance under the Chinese Communist Party (CCP). Why did the empire, which had succeeded better than any state in world history in establishing continuous rule (for nearly two thousand years!), and which had presided over the development of the most advanced economy and culture on the planet for a millennium or more, finally collapse in the late nineteenth and early twentieth centuries? Why did it not prepare the ground better for its succession?

The Structure of the Gentry-Dominated Social Formation

The answer to these questions has quite a bit to do with the interrelated structures of state and class in imperial times. The term 'ruling class' probably never had more clear applicability and descriptive power than in the case of the Chinese empire. The intelligentsia, members of the state bureaucracy and landowners formed a close-knit social class known as the gentry, which exercised a strong hegemony over all important levers of economic, political and social power.

Landlords owned large amounts of land, which they rented to peasant tenants, but in whose management or supervision (much less cultivation) they played no significant part. The size of their holdings was subject to great regional variation, rendering general statistics somewhat artificial. Still, the fact that in the land reform of the late 1940s and early 1950s, 44 per cent of China's arable land was redistributed may give a rough idea of the order of magnitude (Bo, 1952, pp. 151–2, cited in Lippit, 1974, p. 3). By the second and third decades of this century, around one-third of China's peasant households were tenants, and around 85 per cent of the land they rented was owned by landlords. (The rest was rented from rich peasants and from peasants who could not work their own land, such as elderly widows or the infirm. Like so much else in China, regional variation was tremendous: tenancy rates ranged from a low of around 10 per cent of households in Shandong and Hebei to around half in Sichuan and Guangdong.) (Esherick, 1981, p. 395.) Landlords also controlled rural credit; it was to them that most peasants turned for loans, often in the form of rent deferrals (with interest), when times were bad. Finally, they were in command of local politics. Because state government was not formally organized below the county (*xian*) level, it fell to landlords to discharge the tasks of local government, such as tax collection and maintenance of order. This they did through control of lineage organizations and organization of local militias. And of course when they carried out government service such as tax collection, they made sure to retain a share for themselves by charging the peasants more than was owed to the state.

Nevertheless, landlords needed the power of the state and the support of state officials. Most generally, the threat of the coercive power of the state underpinned the exploitative tenancy system, and imperial armies were used to put down peasant revolts throughout Chinese history. Landlords also needed the state to construct and maintain the large water-control systems on which cultivation of their land depended. More routinely, they needed political influence so they would not become vulnerable to various kinds of economic squeeze and harassment by state officials. Perhaps most important, state power was, even more than land, a major source of wealth. Official salaries—between 33 and 180 taels annually for various civil service ranks in the late nineteenth century—were a mere pittance compared to the income from expense accounts, perquisites of office, and open corruption, which brought in 30,000–180,000 taels (Chang, 1962, pp. 36, 40). (By contrast, the average peasant earned in the neighbourhood of ten taels.) The average state official earned far more than the average landlord, then; and in aggregate terms, the gentry class derived around half of its income from governmental services and the like, but only around one-third from rent (Chang, 1962, p. 329).

In order to secure influence with the state and to partake of the riches that could be garnered there, landlords sought to have a member of their family join the state bureaucracy. Officeholders were recruited through the examination system, in which candidates were tested on their mastery of the Confucian classics. This is where the intelligentsia entered the picture. Land-lords needed them to train sons, nephews or sometimes even adoptees for the rigours of the examinations. (The scholars in turn either needed the landlords to employ them, or were themselves landowners or former state officials.) This required wealth—to pay the scholar-tutor and to forgo the income which the candidate could produce during years of training. Thus the children of ordinary peasants—even relatively well-off ones—were effectively barred from entering the state bureaucracy (unless they were adopted by a wealthy landlord who would sponsor their education, in return, of course, for expected loyalty and service in the future).

If a child or adoptee of a landlord managed to pass the examination and enter the state bureaucracy, his links with the landlord sub-class were only strengthened. He usually used his high income to purchase land or enlarge existing holdings. Though state officials were forbidden to hold posts in their home areas (a rule imposed by the central state to enhance its power), they could be called upon to intervene informally on behalf of their relatives with the official in their home area. And in structural terms, state officials needed the cooperation of landowners in the areas where they did serve to carry out the functions of local government at the grassroots.

Thus the landlords, state officials and scholars were bound together in a complex web of mutually reinforcing self-interest. They controlled land, wealth, political power and officially defined knowledge. They also controlled social status through the reproduction of Confucian culture (which exalted them over the peasantry), control over kinship organizations (which bound peasants of the same lineage to them, in a subordinate position, of course), and manipulation of a myriad of local cultural symbols. Their domination over the peasantry was total.

They also managed to keep the merchant class small and weak by restricting and pre-empting its development, devaluing it in social and cultural terms, and coopting it into the structure of gentry power. The state claimed for itself exclusive monopolies over the most profitable non-agrarian sectors of the economy, of which salt and foreign trade were the most important examples. It also imposed all manner of taxes and levies on trade. Confucian morality ranked mercantile pursuits lower than the cultivation of land. And the nexus of gentry power was so prepossessing that businessmen who could afford to do so often bought land themselves and tried to join the economically more idle gentry. This is one important element in China's historic failure to develop a bourgeoisie, unlike the initially much more economically and commercially backward Europe.

Another is the nature of the state and its relationship to urban space. In Europe, feudal states were weak, having dispersed land and much political power to a warrior nobility. In the interstices of the royal domains, there developed towns and townspeople (the literal meaning of the word 'bourgeoisie') who undertook trade and manufacture beyond the reach of the central state or the local nobility on their estates. Thus there was physical and political space for bourgeois development within European feudalism. But in China the central state occupied the towns itself, establishing local government offices there and keeping a watchful eye on the rise of alternative sources of economic or political power among town dwellers.

The Failure and Collapse of the Gentry-Dominated Social Formation

Marx's concept of a backward, unchanging 'Asiatic mode of production' is a caricature of the Chinese state, which is to say that it both reveals and distorts. The society which the gentry ruled had reached the highest levels of economic, political, scientific and cultural development on the planet. It had also undergone fierce dynastic and political battles. In this sense the picture of a social formation in static equilibrium, simply reproducing itself, is not appropriate. But for all its sophistication and power, which were still intact as late as the eighteenth century, China was unable on its own to make the economic and political breakthroughs that were achieved in Europe over the last few centuries. Its level of scientific and technological achievement should have prepared it to be the first to invent modern industry; yet it issued forth no Newtons or Edisons. While the nation-state was rising in Europe, destroying feudalism and nurturing rapid economic development, the Chinese nation-state, which had already been in existence for two thousand years, was disintegrating, leading to a full century of political crisis, national dismemberment and economic decline. In a sense, then, Marx's discussion of the Asiatic mode of production pointed to a basic truth: the social formation dominated by the Chinese gentry indeed proved unable on its own to produce the social, political and economic forces that could transform it into one which could survive in the conditions of the world of the nineteenth and twentieth centuries.

Let us take these two great social forces—the Chinese imperial, gentry-dominated social formation and Western imperialism—in turn. The Qing dynasty had begun to run into difficulties by the latter half of the eighteenth century, due to rising population pressure, a growing imbalance in financial and political power away from the central government in favour of the regionally and locally based gentry, and peasant-based rebellions (Moore, 1966, pp. 181-7; Skocpol, 1979, pp. 73-7). Though we can never be sure, these problems seem to be of the sort which could threaten a dynasty, but from the perspective of Chinese history there appears nothing so new in them to threaten the very structure of the social formation itself. But a new ingredient was soon to make itself felt: China's first defeat by the West in the Opium War of 1839-42.

Because Western imperialism in China coincided with the period of imperial decline, it is tempting to presume that imperialism and the economic exploitation that usually goes with it were the main cause of that decline. In fact the situation was much more complex than that. To be sure, Westerners made large fortunes in China. They also did great social damage by introducing opium on a wide scale (despite strenuous efforts by the empire to resist it). But the Chinese economy was so vast and so deeply structured historically that Western imperialism was not sufficient to undermine or reorganize it. Imperial efforts were restricted mainly to trade; foreign firms did not begin to build factories in China on a significant scale until after the Sino-Japanese War, by which time the empire was already in severe decline. And this trade did not drastically transform the structure of the Chinese economy, the way, for example, that Spanish imperialism did in introducing *latifundia* to Latin America, or that British imperialism did in

India by destroying important rural sidelines such as spinning. To be sure, sidelines were a very important part of the rural economy; in particular, they were often crucial in helping the poor survive from year to year, especially during the not infrequent crop failures (Fei, 1953, Ch. 6). But like so many generalizations about China, Fei's argument that imperialism damaged the Chinese rural economy and immiserated the peasantry has only localized applicability (though for affected localities the impact could be devastating). Even by the 1930s, the volume of imported goods (other than textiles) that could compete with rural handicrafts was less than 5 per cent of the volume of handicraft production (Perkins, 1975, p. 121, cited in Lippit, 1978, p. 279).

The major impact of Western imperialism on the Chinese empire was to weaken it politically, by creating challenges which heightened its internal political and social contradictions and forced it to attempt changes that made those contradictions manifest. Specifically, imperialism posed for the imperial state the problem of political and economic reform, a project on which it and its gentry supporters would prove decidedly ambivalent. It also created new social forces (such as a nascent bourgeoisie) and mobilized others (such as provincially and locally based gentry and rebellious peasant-based mass movements) which gradually came to undermine the state.

The first concerted response to the West—specifically to the British victory in the Opium War—was the 'self-strengthening' movement of the 1860s. It was centred on the construction of a domestic armaments industry by the state. But this resulted only in increased dependence on Western armament manufacturers for advice and equipment, and in debt to the West for loans to finance the project. The rise of a Chinese armaments industry did not spur a wider industrialization which could have provided resources to pay off the debt later.

The loss of the Sino-Japanese War of 1894–5 revealed China's weakness in a particularly humiliating way. In 1898 a movement to modernize education and government administration was later dubbed the 'Hundred Days' because it was nipped in the bud by the arrest of its leaders by the Empress Dowager Cixi, who was supported by conservative-minded gentry and officials. By 1901, reformers had the upper hand again, and a major effort at conservative modernization heavily influenced by the Japanese model to make over China's governmental, military, educational and financial systems was undertaken by the state, with the cooperation of some gentry and a small but growing Chinese bourgeoisie linked closely to the state and encouraged in its development by the effects of Western imperialism.

In Western Europe the bourgeoisie and the state provided the impetus for economic modernization. We have seen how the nexus of gentry–state relations made it difficult for China to undertake state-sponsored modernization. But China was not the first country with a strong conservative coalition between landed elites and the crown. England and France had such alliances too. But in both bourgeois forces paved the way for development of modern industrial capitalist economies.[1] In China these forces proved too weak to overcome even the declining imperial state and its gentry base.

To be sure, a Chinese bourgeoisie did begin to develop in the second half of the nineteenth century. Its early leaders were men who had managed some of the early state-sponsored industries.[2] They struck out on their own, but also maintained their ties with the state, creating a close connection between the leading strata of the bourgeoisie and the state that would continue until 1949. The developing Chinese bourgeoisie also recruited Chinese merchants, bankers, manufacturers and compradors who had served as intermediaries with foreign business. Interestingly, many gentry—particularly those who lived in the environs of the coastal entrepôts—joined the fray, contributing capital and sometimes even becoming entrepreneurs themselves. The Chinese bourgeoisie both collaborated with its Western counterpart—a common phenomenon in late-developing Third World countries subject to economic imperialism—but also gave Western business interests very stiff competition. In 1933, Chinese-owned factories outnumbered foreign-owned ones by a factor of ten, employed nearly three-quarters of the industrial proletariat, and produced two-thirds of China's industrial output (Lippit, 1978, p. 264).

But this bourgeoisie was unable to exert political hegemony to take a leading role in modernizing the Chinese economy and state. It was too little, too local, too late and too landed. First in the vastness of predominantly rural China the bourgeoisie was too small to be able to generate the financial resources that were needed to transform the Chinese economy. A strong, centralized state—along the lines of Bismarckian Germany or Napoleonic and post-Napoleonic France—was therefore required.[3] But in China the power of the regionally and locally rooted gentry to block the formation of such a state or state policies proved too formidable for the small Chinese bourgeoisie to overcome.

Second, the Chinese bourgeoisie was organized locally, in financial, kinship and home-place networks, around individual cities. They were unable to formulate a significant national political leadership or organizational presence.

Third, the fact that Western imperialism had already entrenched itself—to use the Gramscian metaphor—in China's economic and political structures posed some very basic difficulties for the Chinese bourgeoisie. Western firms occupied many of the commanding and most profitable heights of the economy, such as railways, mining and shipping, and drained off much of the 'surplus' available for reproduction and development. Western governments guaranteed special monopoly rights for their bourgeoisies, and extracted still more surplus through their control over customs duties. In addition, the distinctive pattern of Western imperialism in China—under which several Western countries established geographic spheres of influence—only reinforced the localist orientations of the Chinese bourgeoisie (as well as other social or political forces).

Finally, the Chinese bourgeoisie never fully separated itself from the gentry-ruled state or from the land. Indeed, its development was based heavily on both of these. If some of its capital came from land rent, some of its profits also returned to the land, as businessmen bought or enlarged estates as a hedge against the political and economic uncertainties of the day and in accordance with Confucian values emphasizing the virtues emanating from land. And since some of the bourgeoisie's leading lights came from people with close ties to the imperial state—or to families with such ties—as a whole it was unable to mount a unified opposition to the state. To be sure, some bourgeois Chinese did, but many did not, continuing to ally themselves with the imperial state by buying offices, for example. For all these reasons, the Chinese bourgeoisie did not fully separate itself from, and therefore could not break through, the conservative nexus of gentry-state power, which was a prerequisite for China's economic modernization.

But what about popular movements? There was certainly no shortage of them in the nineteenth century. Peasant rebellions accompanied the rise of the Taiping 'Heavenly Kingdom', a counter-state which actually ruled vast parts of central China (and received foreign ambassadors) in the 1850s and 1860s. Around the same time, the Nian Rebellion, which took its name from a secret society that provided its leadership and organizational core, gained wide popularity for its Robin Hood-style appropriations and redistributions of government and landlord property. Ethnic minorities such as the Hui (Moslems) and the Miao also participated in rebellions, as did followers of various other secret societies. In the wake of the imperialist expansion that followed the loss of the Sino-Japanese War, the 'Boxer Rebellion'—a popular movement made up largely of peasants, controlled major parts of Hebei, besieged the capital of Beijing, and killed numerous foreigners—missionaries and business people alike—from 1898 to 1900. Ultimately, a joint expedition of armies of the Western powers was organized to put down the Boxers. They went on to massacre thousands of Chinese and to demand from the imperial government the payment of a massive indemnity of 450 million taels, a burden which, on top of the 250 million paid to Japan after the Sino-Japanese War, further weakened the already shaky imperial finances.

During the latter half of the nineteenth century, then, popular movements based in the active participation of tens of millions of peasants provided a very serious threat to the empire. In the end, though, their lack of central coordination, their mutual disagreements and inconsistencies, and their inability to challenge the basic structure of gentry power within the villages prevented them from overthrowing the empire. None of the rebellions involved systematic attacks on the landlord class. Ideologically, they were orientated to millenarian or quasi-religious, syncretic themes, not to class conflict. Politically, local elites were often the leaders of the rebel forces, recruiting peasants into rebel armies on the basis of lineage or secret society organizations that they dominated. When the imperial forces—often with the help of imperialist forces—were able to defeat the rebel armies, local gentry were easily able to restore the pre-existing relations of class domination that had provided the bedrock of the state. Still, the series of mass uprisings seriously weakened the imperial state by draining it of resources needed to quell the rebellions, by making manifest its inability to command broad support, and by providing opportunities for Western imperialism to strengthen its position in China.

The Failure of the Chinese Republic

The 1911 Revolution, which marked the end of the Qing Dynasty but, more significantly, also the end of all imperial dynasties in China, was less a coordinated movement to create a new government or society than a snow-balling series of regional revolts. It began with a mutiny of troops of the anti-Manchu Hubei New Army in Wuchang (now part of metropolitan Wuhan) on 10 October 1911, a date now considered to mark the beginning of the post-imperial era. By November uprisings led by several different groups had occurred in eleven provinces from Yunnan in the south to Shandong in the north. Meetings in December among leaders of the various groups that had staged uprisings ended in disagreement on a nominee for President of a new Republic. Finally, Sun Yatsen, who in the interim returned from a trip to Europe and the United States, was chosen, and inaugurated as China's first President on 1 January 1912.

From the point of view of class relations, three points are significant about this juncture of Chinese history. First, because the gentry's power was doubly rooted in the centralized bureaucratic imperial state above and the localities below, many of its constituent elements—particularly the local landowners and the provincial leaderships they supported—could survive the collapse of the state, at least for a time. Indeed, sections of the gentry could prosper in the short run from the dissolution of the centre, as they were then relieved of state exactions, regulation and harassment. That is part of the reason they helped undertake to bring it down. The active role of the gentry in the 1911 Revolution lent a conservative character to any regime that would replace the Qing.

Second, the bourgeoisie, much of which was still gentrified, could only join the gentry in bringing down the Qing; they could not undertake the task themselves or provide the main leadership. Their presence in the revolutionary coalition was enough to make it impossible to re-establish an imperial government (though an abortive attempt was made by Yuan Shikai). But their economic and political power was not strong enough to establish a bourgeois state in its place. From 1911 to 1949, the structurally induced accommodation of a dying conservative, landed elite and a sickly bourgeois infant—foetus would be a better metaphor, since it had not separated itself clearly from its parentage—produced a sustained political crisis characterized by a devastating and in some ways paradoxical combination of, on the one hand, anarchy and then extreme weakness at the national level, warlordism, political and policy ineffectiveness, and, on the other, proto-fascist authoritarianism and militarism.

Third, the lower classes were not really represented in the leadership or political programme of the 1911 revolution. Their support was mobilized around anti-Manchu[4] and anti-foreign slogans by the gentry and bourgeois elites who led the revolt. But workers and peasants were not part of that leadership, and their interests were not seriously addressed in the revolutionary programme, such as it was. The 1911 revolution, then, could bring down the empire, but could do little to address China's most serious social, economic or political problems.

For more than a decade after 1911, no stable or legitimate national government could be formed. Beijing was the site of endless political intrigue, coups and counter-coups. In effect there was anarchy at the national level in China by the late 1910s and into the 1920s. The only coherent government was exercised by warlords over their regional satrapies. Of course, the weakness of the political centre only perpetuated China's problems both at home and abroad. Unrest continued to simmer and then began to boil over. When word reached China that the allied powers meeting at Versailles had given Germany's special rights in its Shandong sphere of influence to Japan instead of returning them to China, a historic demonstration took place in Beijing on

4 May 1919. The movement, which took its name from this date, swept rapidly and spontaneously over China, involving general strikes and demands for political reform, intellectual and cultural renewal and social change. Hundreds of political societies were formed, among them the Chinese Communist Party in 1921.

In this climate of nationalist and reformist fervour, the Guomindang (Nationalist Party), under the leadership of Sun Yatsen, emerged as a leading force. Based in Canton under the protection of a sympathetic warlord named Chen Qiongming, Sun began to build a 'national' government and an army that would unify China militarily and install that goverment in the capital of Beijing. To achieve this he made an alliance with the CCP and received assistance from the Soviet Union. At this time the Guomindang-led coalition included a very broad range of political forces, from conservative, locally based but nationalistic warlords and gentry, to liberal-minded elements of the bourgeoisie, to radical political activists, intellectuals, peasants and workers.

Of course, this coalition could not have lasted very long. Sun died before the military unification campaign could get under way, and the politically conservative and militarily minded Jiang Kaishek emerged at the top of the leadership scuffle that followed. The 'Northern Expedition', a military campaign for political unification, began in 1926. Along the way, the left and right in the Guomindang split, and Jiang moved to eradicate the left in a bloody purge that left thousands of radical workers and liberal and radical intellectuals and political leaders dead. The Guomindang was then in the hands of its conservative wing of military and political leaders, warlords, and their various gentry and bourgeois supporters.

It moved on to Beijing, where it established a national government on 10 October 1928—a date still celebrated as national day by the Nationalist government in Taiwan. But this was a weak government, which had to ally itself with extant warlords in several provinces and delegate considerable autonomy to them. More a loose confederation of regional satrapies than a national government that could command legitimacy and authority from all or most of its citizens and political leaders, it was unable to carry out even the most basic functions of government. Five military offensives were required against the main communist base area in Jiangxi, and even the last was not successful in destroying its former ally. It also proved incapable of defending the country against invasion and occupation by Japan in 1937. No significant central government or development administration could be undertaken in the countryside, where the state could not even collect taxes. Plagued with administrative and political problems, the government and the military became increasingly corrupt, inept and reactionary. The Guomindang presided over one of the worst hyperinflations in history, a product of its inability to raise the funds it needed to finance the war effort and simultaneously line the pockets of so many' of its functionaries. A political rhetoric and form of popular organization with a strong resemblance to fascism developed. For example, the Guomindang undertook mass campaigns to promote discipline and cleanliness among its citizens, and organized gangs of 'Blue Shirts' to keep opposition in line. Ultimately, it could be only a junior partner in the defeat of Japan, a feat which owed much more to the military exertions of the Communists and the United States. Following the defeat of Japan, the Guomindang military waged an unsuccessful civil war against the Communists, which it promptly lost by 1949, rather sooner than either side expected. Its leadership managed to escape to the island province of Taiwan where, initially under American protection, it was able to consolidate what to this day it claims to be China's only legitimate national government.

This débâcle was the natural product of the class basis of the Guomindang government—specifically, its attempt to rule with the support of the landlords in the countryside and the bourgeoisie in the cities (and, therefore, without the support of peasants and workers). The landlords, of course, wanted maintenance of the rural status quo in terms of class relations and a definite autonomy from the central government. They were hostile to any plans for national economic reform which might threaten their dominant economic position by, for example, taxing away part of the surplus they appropriated from the peasants or building industries which might entice them to leave the land.

The bourgeoisie had a more complex and contradictory set of interests. It needed a strong national government to help create the conditions for and even promote economic modernization. This meant, at least, national unification and peace (to stabilize markets, currency, transport, etc.) and authoritative government (to ensure labour peace, guarantee contracts, appropriate revenue from the countryside as well as the cities, etc.). It could also mean a positive state role in fostering economic development, by building or financing needed transportation and energy infrastructure, technological development and so forth.

This programme required putting vast financial resources under central administration. Because of the landlords' combination of hostility to and desire for local autonomy from the Guomindang government, these resources could not be raised from the countryside. Therefore they could only be supplied by the cities, which meant putting pressure on the working class but also on the bourgeoisie. This the Guomindang did, both in order to govern and also to enrich itself, in the process driving many members of the bourgeoisie out of business and in other ways alienating many others. Thus, the Guomindang faced a double contradiction in its relations with its class constituency: it was hamstrung by the opposition between the bourgeoisie and the landlords, a dilemma which in turn only exacerbated its conflicts with the former.

In this situation, its authoritarian and militarist character is easily explained. Historical situations in which a bourgeoisie and conservative landed class must find political accommodation have routinely produced authoritarian governments, for example in Franco's Spain, Salazar's Portugal, Fascist Italy and Nazi Germany.[5] The Guomindang had few resources besides military and coercive force at its disposal. Perhaps if it had been able to mount a more effective army capable of subduing the warlords and the communists and keeping the Japanese at bay, it could have then settled down to preside over a conservative programme of economic modernization that would have accommodated the landed class. But the multiple crises facing the Guomindang—warlordism, landed class opposition to strong central government, an ambivalent bourgeoisie, rising peasant discontent, civil war, Japanese invasion, and a very weak economy (especially in industry)—posed insuperable obstacles to the construction of a strong, effective military.

From this theoretical perspective, the frequent argument that the Guomindang failed because it was too militarist and authoritarian appears misplaced, in two senses. First, militarism and authoritarianism were as much the effects as the causes of the Guomindang's problems. Second, it was not militarism and authoritarianism *per se*, but the ineffectiveness with which they were undertaken, that spelled trouble for the Guomindang in the long run. More capable, honest and committed leadership could only have helped. Still, even then the obstacles to the Guomindang were formidable.

The analytical problem of the Guomindang is thrown into relief by comparison with the Communist-led movement, which faced many of the same difficulties (such as civil war, depredations of Japanese invaders, and economic crisis). Armed with better leadership, more appropriate military strategy, and, perhaps most important, a class basis more suited to the goal of building a strong state that could begin to tackle China's many-faceted crisis, the Communist Party succeeded where the Guomindang failed. In some ways, its success was a dialectical product of Guomindang failure, as the communists took advantage of Guomindang blunders. To this remarkable story we turn next.

The Rise and Triumph of the Communist-Led Revolution

The Failure of Proletarian Revolution and Its Implications

The Chinese Communist Party, founded in 1921, began its quest for revolution mainly among China's proletariat. This was the terrain prescribed by Marx's own work, and its revolutionary potential had been stunningly confirmed by the Bolshevik revolution in Russia just a few years before. Because of a combination of its own newness, the formidability of the fluid and confusing political situation in China at the time, and advice from the Soviet Union, the party entered into a 'united front' with the Guomindang, which in the early 1920s had not yet made its rightward turn and was the leading revolutionary force in the country. This obviated the need for the CCP to expend its energies on forming its own military organization. Instead, many of its members joined the Guomindang army, often as political commissars. The alliance also allowed it to concentrate its early efforts on organizing unions and strikes.

The united front strategy was sensible for the new party so long as the Guomindang leadership remained pluralistic and reliable (and Soviet aid helped guarantee the CCP's safety). But it left the communists defenceless when the Guomindang moved decisively and ruthlessly rightward. In April 1927, Jiang Kaishek in a surprise move broke the alliance with the CCP by slaughtering communist activists in Shanghai and, over the next several years, anywhere else in China that he could find them. The dead numbered in the hundreds of thousands. The 'white terror' of April 1927 taught the CCP a lesson which decisively influenced its future: that it needed its own armed forces.[6]

Some Communist Party leaders also learned from the April events the impossibility of making a proletarian-based revolution in the conditions prevailing in China at the time. But it took the party Central Committee as a whole quite a while to reach this conclusion. In fact, the party continued to lead urban uprisings through the rest of 1927. The reasons were several: the continuing importance of Marxian and Leninist theories; a still extant organizational base in other Chinese cities; the hope that the non-communist left of the Guomindang might yet triumph over the Jiang Kaishek-led right; and a steady stream of advice from Moscow not to abandon the cities or the Guomindang. Thus the centre of gravity of the decimated CCP did not shift away from the cities until 1931, when the Central Committee moved its headquarters out of hiding in Shanghai and into the Jiangxi countryside. Orthodoxies die hard, sometimes harder than the people who carry them.

The CCP in the Countryside: 1927-34

Mao Zedong and a few like-minded comrades were able to liberate themselves from the failed orthodoxy sooner than others. Though not the first Chinese communist to promote a rural strategy—Peng Pai had been organizing peasant unions in eastern Guangdong since 1925—Mao had urged the party to pay attention to the peasants by March 1926, sharpening his position with the publication of a report on his rural investigation in Hunan in March 1927 (Mao, 1967, Vol. I, pp. 13-59). Thus the party put him in charge of the Autumn Harvest Uprising there in the autumn of that year. When the revolt was crushed by the Guomindang, Mao and his small armed band retreated to the remote mountainous region of Jinggangshan, on the Hunan-Jiangxi border. He was joined there soon after by Zhu De and his armies, also on the run from defeats by the Guomindang.

In their early months in Jinggangshan, Mao and Zhu sought their first base of support in alliances with local outlaws, bandit gangs and secret societies that operated in the area.[7] Initially these alliances had as much or more to do with the need to survive in a hostile area than with revolutionary strategy. Nevertheless, three points are significant about this decision for understanding the Communist Party as it would operate under Mao's leadership in later years. First, it demonstrated a supreme pragmatism which Mao would subsequently emphasize in word and deed.[8] It is worth emphasizing this now that Mao has been recast as a wild-eyed idealist and utopian by many Chinese and Western writers and observers more sympathetic to the present 'pragmatist' Deng Xiaoping. Second, it shows Mao's flexibility on questions of the class basis of the revolution. Already by this time Mao had evinced this flexibility (or heterodoxy, depending on one's perspective!) when he had called the party's attention to the peasantry. Now he was allying with the rural counterpart of the lumpenproletariat. Later he would seek the support of middle and rich peasants, and even patriotic landlords.

Third, Mao's alliance with the Jinggangshan bandits reveals a basic difficulty posed by the agrarian structure of Chinese society for rural revolution in China. The Chinese peasantry was at once under the organizational and political control of local landlords and lacking in bonds of solidarity with each other. Kinship ties (made concrete in formal clan associations in the villages), clientelism linkages, and tenants' need to cultivate the favour of the landowner to ensure that they would have land to rent, all bound peasants to landowners in a pattern of authority which was reinforced and legitimated or at least justified by Confucian morality. These vertical ties, combined with the relative openness of the Chinese village in a rural structure in which the multi-village marketing area was the basic unit of commercial and social life, also served to weaken the solidarity of the peasants of a given village (Moore, 1966, pp. 201–27; Skocpol, 1979, pp. 147–54). In short, Chinese agrarian structure posed serious obstacles to any communist efforts to organize peasants in their villages. The party would eventually solve this problem, but only with patient effort and much experience. In the interim, Mao and Zhu could find their early allies only among marginal groups like bandits, who lived outside the landlord-dominated agrarian structure.

Gradually, the communist movement in Jinggangshan began to broaden its support, as it was joined by communist cadres who had survived Guomindang attacks in 1927, and as it recruited some local miners and railwaymen, peasants and soldiers from other Northern Expeditionary armies. A very radical land policy was adopted, under which all land was to be confiscated and redistributed. This frightened off many rich and middle peasants, who were the mainstays of production in this very poor section of the countryside. Mao favoured a more moderate policy under which only landlords would be expropriated and others with surplus land would be permitted to sell it. Implementation of the radical policy went slowly, and was not completed before the Jinggangshan base had to be abandoned in early 1929 under the pressure of a Guomindang blockade which helped create serious food shortages. The Jinggangshan communists moved eastward to a new base area straddling the border between Jiangxi and Fujian Provinces, establishing their headquarters at Ruijin.

In the meantime, the party centre still held firm to its proletarian strategy for the Chinese revolution. At the Sixth Party Congress—held in Moscow (for security reasons) concurrent with the Sixth Congress of the Moscow-dominated Communist International (Comintern)—the CCP stated that the working class was the most revolutionary force in China, and that the rural-based guerrilla armies were to help nurture a national revolutionary army that could attack and hold China's cities. The party continued clandestine organizing in urban areas, particularly Shanghai, trying (with little success) to build 'red' unions (to counter the Guomindang-run 'yellow' ones). A wave of strikes after 1928, which accelerated after 1930, did help to underpin the case of those communists arguing for proletarian revolution; but in fact most of these strikes were spontaneous affairs and had a predominantly economic rather than political character. The party planned a military offensive by the rural-based armies on the cities of Changsha, Wuhan and Nanchang in 1930. But when the first, at Changsha was routed, Mao and Zhu refused to carry out the assault on Nanchang with which they had been charged. In the wake of this defeat, and under continuing pressure from the Guomindang police in

Shanghai, the Central Committee of the party moved its headquarters to Ruijin.

The Jiangxi Soviet undertook a series of agrarian reforms that was variable but on the whole quite radical. The 1930 policy, set by Mao and his comrades, was less extreme than that of the Jinggangshan years. All land was to be confiscated from the landlords and rich peasants, but rich peasants, their dependents and even some landlords were allotted shares of redistributed land equal to those received by the 'masses'. This principle of protecting the interests of rich peasants in order to help assure their continuing contribution to production was to be upheld by Mao until and beyond liberation. At this time, though, it was controversial within the CCP. These policies were reversed by the 1931 land law, drafted by a group of Moscow-trained CCP leaders known as the '28 Bolsheviks', who were influenced by Stalin's stringent anti-kulak policy. It provided for the redistribution of only the poorest land to the rich peasants, and none at all to the landlords, who were also subject to being drafted for forced labour.

The radicalism of agrarian policy in the Jiangxi Soviet was coupled with certain difficulties in its implementation. Instructions were sent down from higher- to lower-level organs, with little room for those below to send information and views back upward. Sometimes this resulted in problems in carrying out the movement, including excessive *and* restrained mass radicalism. For example, in the heat of mass meetings, middle peasants—whose interests were to be protected in official policy—were misrepresented by poor peasants as being rich so that their property would become available for redistribution to the poor. Some landlords and rich peasants were also killed. There were other mistakes which resulted from too little, rather than too much, mass involvement. For example, the size of landlord and rich peasant holdings was sometimes ascertained simply by asking them to testify about themselves and their fellow exploiters. In the Jiangxi Soviet period, then, the CCP first began to recognize the complexity and difficulty of mixing leadership and mass participation in order to carry out agrarian reform effectively. It was a problem with which the party would continue to struggle for many years, and the experience garnered in Jiangxi would prove invaluable in refining and defining its distinctive style of mass work during the Yan'an period.

The End of the Jiangxi Soviet and the Long March

The CCP also faced growing pressure from the Guomindang throughout the Jiangxi years. In late 1930, Jiang Kaishek launched a military 'extermination' campaign. This and three more, each successively more massive and sophisticated, were repelled by the communists. But finally a fifth campaign launched in late 1933 managed to blockade the Jiangxi base effectively and choke it economically and militarily.

The radical approach to the rich peasants had undercut the economic base of the region's economy by attacking its most productive class. It has been argued, especially in the light of the subsequent Yan'an period's greater moderation and success, that a less radical or more effectively implemented policy would have helped garner more peasant support in dealing with the blockade. But the causality could also run in the other direction: one lesson which the CCP would learn from its failure in Jiangxi was that the peasantry would participate much more willingly in an agrarian reform if the military security of the area could be assured, so that the peasants would not have to worry about retribution by a returning pro-landlord government. (This is the actual meaning of Mao's widely misinterpreted statement that 'political power grows out of the barrel of a gun'.) The relationship between success in garnering support for agrarian reform and for armed defence was reciprocal.

In any event, the Guomindang succeeded in driving the CCP out of its Jiangxi–Fujian base area, though it failed in its goal of 'exterminating' the communists. It came close to realizing this grizzly objective during the next two years, when the CCP undertook its famous 'Long March'. To say that the party and its armed forces were decimated would understate the damage. Of the 100,000 or so who left the Jiangxi base, only 8,000 arrived in Shaanxi Province in late 1935. It was something of a miracle that the Communist movement survived at all. Even today, the Long March, filled with so much heroism and so much death, has almost a sacred character in Chinese historical consciousness. There is something special and magical about those who survived it, and it stands as symbol of the indefatigability of the Chinese revolution.[9]

More concretely, the Long March proved to be a double climacteric for the party. First, the conventional military strategy of positional warfare, which had been used in the defence against the fifth Guomindang campaign, and against which Mao and others had been arguing for several years, was renounced. Mobile guerrilla tactics were adopted and perfected in the many battles against the pursuing Guomindang armies that punctuated the Long March. Second, the '28 Bolsheviks', who had led the Jiangxi Soviet and were now blamed for its military mistakes as well as its errors in agrarian policy, were replaced by a new leadership group headed by Mao. He retained the top party post until his death forty-one years later.

The Yan'an Period

The United Front

After the Long March, the major focus and direction of the Chinese revolution underwent two major shifts. The first was the formation of a united front with the Guomindang against Japan. In 1931, Japan had invaded Manchuria, occupied it with no resistance from the Guomindang or its warlord allies, and established a puppet government. On the first day of 1933, it moved into the North China Plain, occupying large parts of present-day Hebei, Jilin and Inner Mongolia. A rising tide of anti-Japanese protests and sentiments in 1935 and 1936 produced widespread demands for cooperation among Chinese of all political persuasions to resist and expel the Japanese.

The CCP had issued such a call in 1935. In December 1936, Jiang Kaishek was placed under house arrest by General Zhang Xueliang, who threatened to kill Jiang in order to forge a national anti-Japanese united front more easily. In a brilliant display of statesmanship and political acumen, the CCP persuaded Zhang to release Jiang—the party's old arch-enemy who had betrayed it in the bloodbath of the 'White Terror' a decade before and who again had nearly 'exterminated' it just two years earlier. With this spectacular demonstration of the CCP's commitment to the anti-Japanese struggle, and with popular patriotism at fever pitch, Jiang was hard put not to sign a second united front pact with his greatest nemesis, the 'communist bandits'. An agreement was signed in July 1937, one day after the new Japanese invasion. The CCP armies were to be left intact and incorporated formally into the troops of the Nationalist government. In other words, the Guomindang and communist armies were no longer to fight each other, and were to cooperate in fighting the Japanese.

The Yan'an Way

Class Policy

The second major shift of the Yan'an period was the development of a new class constituency, agrarian policy, set of political institutions and form of leader–mass relations that came to be known as the 'Yan'an way', after the rural Shaanxi town at which the CCP established its headquarters. The party's class policy in the Jiangxi Soviet was now seen as excessively radical, having failed to promote the broad mass support and level of economic production needed to sustain the revolutionary base. Moreover, such a policy was no longer consistent with the CCP's shift toward the anti-Japanese struggle, for which it had called upon all patriotic groups in Chinese society—including the Guomindang—to unify with it. Now CCP policy called for the support not only of the poor and middle peasantry and the working class, but also of rich peasants, the petty bourgeoisie, intellectuals, national capitalists, and even a newly created class category called 'enlightened landlords' who would not collaborate with the Japanese occupation forces or their puppet governments.[10] Of course, there were not many members of the national bourgeoisie who actually participated in the CCP movement, since its base areas were primarily rural. Likewise, few landlords fitted the 'enlightened' category: most allied themselves with the Japanese or pro-Japanese political forces. But the CCP did garner support from many non-communist intellectuals, many of whom left their homes in the major coastal cities that had come under Japanese occupation and headed for Yan'an because they felt that the CCP was the leading patriotic force in the country.

Agrarian Policy

The changes in the party's class policy and actual constituency required concomitant changes in its agrarian policy. No longer was the hard line taken in Jiangxi against rich peasants and landlords appropriate. Private property—a principle dear to the petty and national bourgeoisie, many liberal intellectuals, and even (and perhaps most important) middle peasants—was now to be scrupulously respected. Thus summary expropriations and redistributions of land and property were now replaced by campaigns for rent reduction and usury control. Landlords were now to be subject to taxation, sometimes heavy or retroactive, but they kept their land. Rich creditors of poor peasants were often penalized by repayment moratoriums, but the debts were not cancelled.

Political Organization and Leader–Mass Relations: the Mass Line

The greatest innovations and most decisive break with past practice came in the area of political organization and leader–mass relations. The 'mass line' developed in Yan'an was a radically new approach which involved closer and more democratic leader–mass relations and serious attempts to reduce the underlying distinctions between party, state and army on the one hand and citizens on the other—that is, between state and society. This effort has become a lasting feature of Chinese socialist policies, and one which distinguishes them sharply from state socialist policies in the Soviet Union and

Eastern Europe, but which have been influential in Third World socialist countries such as Cuba, Mozambique, South Yemen and Vietnam (though the influence is not always admitted). The most concise statement of the mass line was made by Mao in 1943:

... Communits must ... combine the leadership with the masses ... all correct leadership is necessarily 'from the masses, to the masses'. This means: take the ideas of the masses (scattered and unsystematic ideas) and concentrate them (through study turn them into concentrated and systematic ideas), then go to the masses and propagate and explain these ideas until the masses embrace them as their own. (Mao, 1967, Vol. I, pp. 117–19.)

In Yan'an the mass line took several concrete forms. First was the reduction and streamlining of government administrative apparatuses, and the decentralization of political authority. The Chinese Communist Party, heir both to millenniums of imperial centralized bureaucracy and the newer Leninist (and especially Stalinist) form of (not too) democratic centralism, had by and large organized itself and its movement along lines of vertical political organization and power. Lower-level units were primarily, if not exclusively, responsible to higher-level ones. This preoccupied local officials with carrying out instructions they received from above, often with little regard for their suitability to local conditions or their palatability and popularity with local people. In terms of the language and concerns of policy studies, this had resulted in differences in receiving timely 'feedback' on 'performance'. In terms of politics, it had hampered democratic expression and influence. Now county-level and grassroots leaders were given expanded latitude and coordinative power in carrying out higher-level instructions in accordance with local needs, conditions and opinions. They were to 'oppose book worship'—a phrase Mao used as the title of one of his most acerbic and well-known essays—and to start thinking for themselves.

[T]he person with overall responsibility in the locality must take into account the history and circumstances of the struggle there ...; he should not act upon each instruction as it comes down from the higher organization without any planning of his own ... it is hoped that comrades will themselves do some hard thinking and give full play to their own creativeness ... (Mao, 1967, Vol. I, pp. 121–2.)

Higher-level organs were reduced in size and complexity, and told to limit their instructions to their subordinates.

Nor should a higher organization simultaneously assign many tasks to a lower organization without indicating their relative importance and urgency or without specifying which is central, for that will lead to confusion in the steps taken by the lower organizations ... (Mao, 1967, Vol. I, p. 121.)

Party officials were, in another phrase Mao used for an essay title, to stop writing 'eight-legged essays [a strict template used in Confucian commentary writing] in the Party' and instead make shorter, more direct reports to reduce red tape. The combination of streamlined, centralized leadership and local discretion and coordination known as 'dual rule' and first implemented in Yan'an would return to China in 1958. It has produced its own characteristic political tensions, some of which are explored in later chapters. But for this price Chinese socialism has managed to avoid some of the problems of one-sided authoritarianism and bureaucratism which have been the bane of state socialisms in the Soviet Union and Eastern Europe.

A second form of the mass line was the campaign to send cadres 'to the villages'. Many of the middle- and higher-level officials whose positions were abolished in the administrative simplification, along with many of the intellectuals who had flocked to Yan'an, were assigned to posts at the grassroots. They were to help strengthen local governments and the political capacities of indigenous local leaders and peasants. To ensure that these cadres would not simply take over local affairs (which could have the opposite effect of decentralization), and because of Mao's belief that leaders could lead best when the existential distance between them and the masses was reduced, these cadres were expected to participate regularly in production alongside the peasants, live in similar circumstances with them, and in general share their experiences. The cadres were supposed to learn directly about rural life from the peasants in order to be able to lead them more effectively in carrying out the party's policies of rent reduction and usury control, building up local governments and the peasants' political capacities (e.g., through literacy campaigns, newspaper-reading groups, political discussions), and resisting and driving back the Japanese.

Third was the effort to enhance the democratic and representative character of local governments by separating them clearly from the party and ensuring definite and significant representation of non-party people in them. Secret ballot elections were held regularly at village, township, county and regional levels, with universal suffrage for all men and women over 18 years of age. The only restriction was the 'three-thirds' principle, according to which one-third of offices were to be filled by CCP members, one-third by non-CCP leftists, and one-third by liberals who were not required to be particularly leftist in their political orientations. Even Guomindang members, members of the bourgeoisie and landlords were eligible for the latter category of posts. In the Yan'an base, only one-quarter of those elected in 1941 to representative positions at all levels were CCP members. Of course, the CCP did have greater representation in the higher levels of government: 57 per cent of the members of the regional congress (covering all of the Yan'an bases) were communists. But compared with the previous governmental monopoly held by the party, and in light of the decentalization of much power downward to lower levels where CCP members occupied proportionally fewer posts, the Yan'an electoral system was very significant in promoting democracy and in reflecting and reinforcing the new breadth of the political base there.

Fourth, the forms of popular political expression and the range of issues on which such expression could take place were also broadened. Village mutual aid teams and nascent urban cooperatives were run on a participatory basis. In Yan'an the 'big character poster' (*dizibao* —sometimes called 'wall poster' in English), in which citizens could write their views on any subject and post them up in a public place for all to see, first came into serious use. This form of citizen expression, distinctive to Chinese socialism, would go on to become extremely important in the Cultural Revolution decades later.

Fifth, in a continuation of practices developed during the Jiangxi Soviet, the armed forces were to play an important role in civilian affairs, in a way which subordinated them to civil authority. They were mobilized into production drives, and continued to abide by the 'three rules for attention' and 'eight points of discipline', according to which, for example, soldiers were to take nothing from the people ('not even a needle and thread'), return all borrowed items, speak courteously, pay fair prices for all purchases, and not abuse women (which meant, among other things, not bathing in their sight!).

The mass line placed tremendous demands on cadres which they could not always fulfil. Reared in the authoritarianism of Chinese traditional political culture, brought to political maturity in a Leninist-style Communist Party, and thrust into the exigencies and unfamiliar circumstances of rural life and revolution, it was easy for them to act in ways inconsistent with the goals of the mass line. A whole series of 'deviations' occurred, including 'commandism' (seeking compliance by issuing orders rather than persuasion, which could easily occur in the heat of battle or other emergency situations); 'tailism', its opposite (merely following the immediate wishes of the masses without engaging them in analysis of their views); 'subjectivism' (making decisions or formulating opinions without full investigation or consultation); 'elitism' (acting as if one were superior to others); 'bureaucratism' (merely carrying out orders and sticking to cumbersome official procedures); and 'localism', its opposite (acting in disregard of central directives and the wider political situation).

To deal with these problems and help cadres perfect their mass-line leadership styles, the CCP launched a 'rectification' movement in 1942. It was not a purge—there were no show trials and summary expulsions. The orientation was constructive—Mao used the metaphor of curing the sick—rather than punitive. At the centre of the rectification was 'criticism and self-criticism', in which each cadre—not just pre-selected targets—would analyse his/her own actions, receive public criticism from other members of the work unit, and then make a public self-criticism before the unit. In this process, then, the standards of mass-line leadership were specified by one's own colleagues in a group process. They were developed successively by dealing with a person's specific case, and then applied through public deliberation and evaluation. This was direct mass democracy in action, though always in the context of guidelines from the party centre—in particular from Mao himself. The result of the rectification was the reinforcement, not diminution, of most cadres' attachment to the party and the revolution. It also helped improve cadres' leadership skills. It elevated Mao himself as a model leader in a way that had not been done before. Finally, it firmly established the principle of constructive criticism and self-criticism, which was to become a hallmark of CCP politics and, like so many other innovations of the Yan'an years, one that would distinguish Chinese socialism from its counterparts in the Soviet Union and Eastern Europe.

Military Struggle in the Anti-Japanese War

The CCP's popularity during the Yan'an period stemmed in part from its innovative and flexible strategies on class relations, agrarian policy, political organization and leader-mass relations. Its stature was also enhanced by the leading role it took in the anti-Japanese war. The Guomindang's contribution to the nationalist resistance was flaccid and duplicitous by comparison. It used the 1937 united front agreement with the CCP more to strengthen its position *vis-à-vis* the communists than to join with them to fight the Japanese. For example, Jiang Kaishek assigned his best armies to blockade the Yan'an base. Goumindang forces often avoided engaging the Japanese, preferring massive retreats that left much of China under Japanese occupation by 1941. The Guomindang capital had to be moved far inland to Chongqing, in Sichuan. While this way of (not) waging the war involved goodly measures of cowardice and betrayal (to save energy to fight the CCP, while allowing it to bear the brunt of the anti-Japanese War), objectively speaking it had a material basis, too. The Guomindang armies were corrupt and incompetent, and their command and coordinative structures unworkable. Many of the rank-and-file soldiers were impressed into service by force and treated horribly—fed and housed minimally, and put on lengthy forced marches on which many died before the enemy was ever engaged. Thus morale and commitment were low, to say the least. The officers were generally no better than the soldiers. Many sold arms to the communists to line their own pockets. Generals were known to lose battles on purpose so as to make a financial (as well as human) killing by driving down the value of government bonds which they had sold short on the Shanghai exchanges. They also inflated figures on the number of troops under their command so they could enrich themselves with larger budgetary allotments from the Chinese government and its foreign allies, especially the United States. The centrifugal forces which had plagued the Guomindang from the outset—in particular, the need to rely on alliances with semi-autonomous warlords—made unified command and military coordination difficult. It became self-evident to most Chinese that the Guomindang could not and would not prosecute the anti-Japanese War effectively.

By contrast, the CCP armies concentrated their military energies on fighting the Japanese. They used the mobile guerrilla tactics they had developed during the Long March to wage coordinated offensives (such as the famous Hundred Regiments Offensive of 1941), while also engaging in sustained harassment behind Japanese lines. Though the CCP could not really damage the powerful Japanese war machine until the latter had been weakened by a declining position in the Pacific War, its efforts did help to keep Japanese armies at bay in many base areas. More important than their military effect was their political one: they established the Communists as the leading anti-Japanese force in China.

Nationalism and Revolution

There is a controversy among analysts of the CCP over the reasons for its rapid growth in power and popularity from 1937 to 1945. Some have argued that the Communists owe their popularity to their nationalism, not to their programmes of agrarian and political change—in other words, patriotism, not revolution, had popular appeal (Johnson, 1962). This argument is founded on the premise that a clear distinction can be drawn between the national and revolutionary struggles. It cannot. The Japanese invasion exacerbated aspects of the class struggle, and in turn the class struggle against landlords was also a patriotic struggle against collaborators. Many landlords collaborated with the Japanese and thus became associated with their hideous depredations (such as the scorched-earth policies of 'kill, burn and destroy everything') against civilian populations. The CCP-led production drives and the political reforms were the major source of relief from the Japanese blockade of the base areas. The effectiveness of the CCP's guerrilla struggles against Japanese forces was based upon its revolutionary mass-line policies. In short, the class and national struggles were so tightly intertwined as to render untenable the argument that patriotism but not revolution was the basis of the CCP's appeal and success.

Civil War and the Triumph of the CCP: 1945–49

At the end of the Second World War, the CCP had a large reservoir of popular sympathy, but it still controlled only its inland base areas, many of which were poor to begin with and had become more completely immiserated during the war. The Guomindang regained control of China's industrial and financial centres, as well as its richest farmlands, in the coastal areas and in the north-east. It also had the support of the United States, the most economically powerful country in the world after the war. Looking at this strategic balance, the CCP did not anticipate a revolutionary victory just yet. It hoped, rather, for the formation of a coalition government with the Guomindang, to give it breathing space to marshal its forces. In the United States many leaders were growing aware from the war of the structural weaknesses and practical incapabilities of the Guomindang; and the general rise of US–Soviet rivalry fuelled concerns about Soviet aspirations in the Far East. So the United States too, sought to forge such a CCP–Guomindang coalition. But Jiang Kaishek, as always ideologically fanatical and inflexible in his anti-communism, and confident of his ability to command American support even if he resisted the coalition, was intransigent.

In 1946–47, his armies undertook a major offensive against the communists, driving them out of many of their wartime bases, including Yan'an. But this was not a serious defeat for the CCP. Yan'an, a remote rural area, was important only symbolically, and the Guomindang advances were partly the result of the CCP's now perfected strategy of shunning positional warfare and fixed defence of territory in favour of mobile warfare. The CCP took up a new base in far more prosperous Shanxi, from which it launched a counter-offensive that by late 1947 had enabled it to control most of Shanxi, Hebei and Shandong Provinces, including Shijiazhuang, the Hebei capital and the first major city taken by the CCP.

Meanwhile, the Guomindang's domestic base began to crumble rapidly. Unable to finance its military exertions, its corruption and its normal governmental operations on a tax base which included neither the landowners nor the largest capitalists, it resorted to printing worthless currency. Prices rose to more than six thousand (!) times the 1937 level. Workers joined shopkeepers in staging riots and strikes in Shanghai in protest at the rising cost of food and declining standard of living. Peasant unrest grew even in areas under Guomindang control. Jiang responded with a wave of repression that shocked and alienated even many anti-communists. Key liberal leaders, including Song Qingling, Sun Yatsen's wife, began to withdraw their political support.

In the expanding communist base areas, the class struggle heated up. Late 1945 saw a renewal of the rent- and interest-reduction campaigns. 'Anti-traitor' campaigns attacked landlords who had collaborated with the Japanese, confiscating and redistributing their property and cancelling debts owed to them. This was the first land reform since Jiangxi. In the older liberated areas under secure CCP military control, land reform was gradually extended, based on mass mobilizations using the mass-line methods developed in the Yan'an period. But ever flexible (since Jiangxi days) on class relations, the CCP adopted a much more moderate line in the newly liberated zones, which were more urbanized than the older base areas. It sought the support of the middle classes, capitalizing on their disillusionment with the Guomindang. By late 1948, the CCP succeeded in signing an agreement with centrist anti-Guomindang political parties to establish a national Political Consultative Conference. On the military front, it began to occupy major industrial centres in Manchuria. Through 1949, the communist armies occupied all the major urban centres in east and north China. With the tide turning, many Guomindang generals switched allegiance to the CCP. Those remaining loyal to Jiang Kaishek followed him to Taiwan, where they have remained ever since, still laying *de jure* claim to be the government of all of China. Formally China is still in a state of civil war between rival governments. But in reality the CCP victory was complete. On 1 October 1949, the People's Republic of China was proclaimed.

Conclusion

The questions posed at the outset of this chapter can now be addressed. First, why did the Chinese empire, which had lasted for two thousand years and had achieved the greatest political, cultural and economic development in the world for many centuries, collapse? Second, why did it collapse the way it did: in utter political and economic crisis in which no government capable of ruling the country in a unified way could coalesce for nearly forty years, during which time the country was wracked by civil war, foreign conquest and revolution? Third, why did capitalism not take hold as a robust mode of production on which a politically viable state could be founded? Fourth, why did the Chinese Communist Party succeed, where the landlord class and the bourgeoisie had failed, in creating a new state with political coherence and power? Fifth, why did the revolution led by the CCP find its base in the countryside rather than the cities, and its form in a popular and participatory rather than an elitist and Leninist-style movement? Sixth, what implications does this long and complex past have for Chinese socialism under the CCP? And finally, what implications does it have for our theoretical understanding of the preconditions for socialist revolution?

The Collapse of Gentry Society

Our explanation of the first problem—the fall of the gentry-dominated social formation after thousands of years' dominance—revolves around the structure of gentry hegemony in imperial China and its dialectical transformation under new conditions in the nineteenth and twentieth centuries. The gentry's command of economic, social, political and cultural levers of power was so strong and complete that it could hold the Chinese social formation together for two thousand years. It effectively undercut the development of any social, economic and political forces that rivalled the social formation which was its structure of power. In particular, through a combination of pre-emption, cooptation and economic regulation, it was able to prevent the rise of an independent bourgeoisie from among China's mercantile strata.

In the nineteenth century, the European powers posed a threat to China's sovereignty and territorial integrity which could only be fended off by industrialization. But under gentry hegemony China was incapable of a timely response, i.e. it could not industrialize sufficiently before the state had been undermined and the economy opened to Western imperialism. Industrialization has everywhere required a strong bourgeoisie and/or leadership from a modernizing state. Gentry hegemony had prevented China from generating a bourgeoisie, as we have seen. It also prevented the state from taking the lead in fostering industrial modernization in several ways. The gentry used its political leverage to block reforms. It clung to and continued to reproduce an anti-modern Confucianism. Structurally, its local bases of political power were a powerful obstacle to the political and financial centralization which state-sponsored industrialization would require. In short, the strength of gentry hegemony which had produced a social formation that could last for two thousand years, reaching great heights along the way, was also, dialectically, the root of its inability to respond to the new challenges of industrialization of the nineteenth and twentieth centuries. This incapacity led to its demise.

We can now turn to our second problem: why did the gentry-dominated social formation fall as it did? Specifically, why was no smooth transition to a next stage possible? Why, instead, did China become a virtual political centrifuge, breaking up into rival satrapies for forty years? Again our explanation begins with the structure of the gentry-dominated social formation, which had unified China longer than any other country but which, dialectically, contained the seeds of its own destruction. In China's vastness and variegation, the gentry had ruled by developing locally and centrally based levers of power. When, for reasons we have discussed above, the centre fell, the gentry did not have to fall with it. The support among many gentry for the 1911 Revolution indicates that they sensed this clearly. Thus the gentry-dominated social formation could collapse slowly, piece by piece: first the imperial state, and then the rural mode of production, class structure and ideology. This helps explain the protracted nature of the fall of gentry hegemony (and therefore of the Chinese revolution). It also explains the centrifugal character of its collapse: when the gentry's central base of political power evaporated, but landlordism did not, the only place from which it could continue to exercise power was its local and regional bases.

Finally, the survival of the rural elite into the post-imperial period also contributed to the political and social tendentiousness and persistent conservatism of the transition. After 1911, the political field contained organizations not only of the bourgeoisie, working class and peasantry, but also of the gentry. Their presence only complicated and exacerbated what would even without them have been an explosive struggle, in at least three ways. First, unrestrained by the moderating influence of the imperial state, and in the context of the need to build and defend local satrapies against each other and would-be state builders at the centre, the landlords stepped up their exploitation of the peasantry, whose capacity to endure it was reduced by the depredations of the civil and anti-Japanese wars. So the survival of the gentry only sharpened the objective bases of rural class struggle.

Second, the landlords' continued presence weakened and conservatized the bourgeoisie and exacerbated its political crisis. We have seen how it blocked construction of a modern and modernizing state by the bourgeoisie or on their behalf. This political failure only deepened the transitional crisis by undercutting the development of China's industry. It also reproduced the centrifugal nature of the polity in two respects: it weakened the bourgeoisie so much that they could not form a coherent national base of power; and it tied them to the land, thus reinforcing their localism. Third, by forcing the

Guomindang to balance the bourgeoisie against the landlords, the survival of the latter contributed to the authoritarian and proto-fascist character of the aspiring transitional state and undermined the possibility, however remote, of development of stable popular legitimacy or acquiescence behind it.

The Failure of Capitalism

In discussing the structural factors which caused China to fracture after the fall of the empire, we have already touched upon the third question: why did capitalism fail in China? The Chinese bourgeoisie faced formidable structural obstacles to the construction of a robust capitalism. First, its development had been hampered by an age-old gentry hegemony. Second, when it finally began to develop it maintained close ties with the landed elite: it was infiltrated by their investments, and in turn infiltrated them by purchasing land and imperial office. It had great difficulty erecting the minimal political preconditions for a functioning, integrated capitalism, such as national government to provide unified currency, legal guarantees for contracts, and civil peace. The presence in China of a more industrially advanced West only made prospects for a *bourgeoisie-led capitalism* dimmer, in two ways: by providing stiff competition, and by further weakening and even dismembering the Chinese polity. These same factors, combined with the continued political power of a largely conservative and anti-modern landed elite, undercut the alternative possibility of a *state-sponsored capitalism* in China.

The Nature and Success of the Chinese Revolution under the CCP

The fourth question concerns the reasons why the CCP could succeed where the Guomindang had failed in establishing and consolidating state power. This is all the more puzzling since many of the structural conditions within which the CCP had to work were notably unfavourable to its revolutionary project.[11] The working class, though capable of considerable radicalism, was small in the national scheme of things. The peasantry was enmeshed in landlord-dominated vertical structures—tenancy relationships, kinship associations, patron–client networks, secret societies and so forth—which made it very difficult for it to attain class consciousness or organizational unity (Skocpol, 1979, pp. 148–50). Peasant support did not drop into the lap of the CCP like a ripe fruit. Quite the contrary, it had to be worked for with immense effort against considerable odds, and, as we have seen, it took quite some time and many mistakes before the 'mass line' as a way of attracting and mobilizing peasant support could be made effective in garnering the active popular following that was required for successful revolution in China. But in the end the substantive reforms, which produced genuine material gains for the majority of rural people in the wartime bases, and the mass line process that went along with them, proved very popular with a broad range of classes and groups. They in turn provided an important bedrock of support for the CCP through 1949 and beyond (Selden, 1971).

There were also some structural features of the transitional Chinese social formation that were conducive to its revolutionary aspirations. First, the peasantry was increasingly exploited after 1911. Structurally, this was occasioned by the fall of the empire, which had restrained the landlords somewhat and whose absence opened up a competitive politics that fuelled their avarice. Second, this hyperexploitation took place within an essentially unchanged agrarian structure. Unlike England, for example, where the eviction of peasants from the land and the commercialization of agriculture alleviated their radicalism by thrusting them into new occupational and residential situations, in China the peasants remained together on the land, in a pre-commercialized, pre-modernized agriculture, to suffer under the landlords. Peasants are likely to be more radical when their pre-existing way of living and making a living is preserved but strained than when that way of life is uprooted (Moore, 1966, Ch. 9).

Third, there was a structural weakness at the bottom of the landlord-peasant relationship that made China more prone than many other agrarian societies to peasant rebellions. While Chinese peasants were, to be sure, under the pervasive dominance of the landlords, this domination was more broad than deep. The landlords did not take part in or make a meaningful contribution to peasant production or consumption.[12] When push became shove, the Chinese peasants did not need their landlords, and so were structurally predisposed to rebellion when things got bad enough, as they did in the first half of this century. Of course it is a long way from rebellion to revolution, but peasant rebelliousness could provide a starting-point for revolution (Thaxton, 1983).

Fourth, the centrifugal character of the Chinese polity in these years was a great boon to the CCP, affording it the opportunity to establish base areas in remote regions in which it could test out its policies and nurture its resources. It is no accident that these base areas were often founded in border regions, so that the mobile political and armed forces of the CCP could more easily elude provincial leaderships who lacked coordination by central state authorities.

Fifth, the protractedness of the post-imperial transition, which we have traced to its structural contradictions, gave the CCP badly needed time to overcome some of the structural obstacles it faced, to learn from its mistakes, and to develop experience in government administration, movement organization and political mobilization.

The CCP victory was also a dialectical product of the failures of the Guomindang. It profited from the influx of a large number of patriotic but previously non-communist intellectuals and students as they became disillusioned with the Guomindang's inability to defend China against Japan, its gross corruption, and its inability to lead China forward toward modern economic development. The CCP took cunning advantage of the military blunders and inappropriate strategies of the Guomindang armies. It could turn the misery caused by the economic policies (and non-policies) of the Guomindang, such as the hyperinflation and utter lack of developmental action, against not only the government but also against the landlords associated with it.

When all the favourable and unfavourable structural facts are added up, though, it still remained for a skilful and committed leadership with some fortuitous historical contingencies to overcome the obstacles and take advantage of the opportunities with which the Chinese social formation presented the Communist Party. Without the Japanese invasion, Jiang Kaishek might well have been able to concentrate his military resources on the communists and reach his most treasured goal of 'exterminating' them; after all, he almost did it even with the Japanese on the scene. The Japanese invasion also provided the impetus for the major shifts in CCP class and agrarian policies and political methods that proved successful where previous ones had failed. This brings us to the political brilliance of Mao Zedong and his like-minded comrades in formulating those innovative policies and leadership methods, and the extraordinary commitment of thousands of CCP cadres in carrying them out under the most difficult circumstances. The Chinese revolution was partly a triumph of historical and class forces, but it was also a triumph of human will against such forces.

The fifth question, concerning the rural base and popular participatory character of the CCP movement, has already been touched upon. Neither of these features of the party's revolutionary strategy came easily to it. Indeed, it took fifteen years of failure with an urban and more Leninist approach before the CCP officially replaced it. One could argue that the rural and popular character of the revolution was structurally determined: the working class was too small and weak to be the main base of the revolution, the Guomindang was bound to turn on it, and the peasantry could only be won over with something like the mass line.[13] But there is something a bit too deterministic about this. The Chinese working class might have been able to grow into a more formidable revolutionary force if it had not encountered an enemy ruthless and shrewd enough (at least in the short run) to destroy its radicalism early. And there was nothing that compelled the Guomindang to act as it did toward the urban left, which was actively supporting the Guomindang's Northern Expedition at the time. The April 1927 coup was very much the work of Jiang Kaishek, and it did not have the support of many, more liberal-minded Guomindang leaders of the day. So one could argue that it was as much Jiang Kaishek and his right-wing allies in the Guomindang as it was the inexorable forces of history that undercut the CCP's proletarian base and drove it—very hesitantly and reluctantly at first—into the arms of the peasantry.

It is also circular and functionalist to argue that the mass line was formulated and implemented successfully because it was the only way the rural revolution could be consummated.[14] After all, the revolution need not have succeeded! Or it could have attracted much less active support than it did and still have won by default. The failures of the Jinggangshan and Jiangxi days were eventualities of this sort. One can conclude from those failures and from the successes of Yan'an that rural revolution required strong popular participation to succeed fully. But it took creative leadership and committed supporters to make this discovery in the crucible of China's revolutionary praxis. Mao and his comrades were not mere products of history; they also made history.

History, Revolution and Socialism

But how did the past history affect the way the CCP made future history? This is our sixth question: what implications did China's complex past have for its distinctive brand of socialism?

First, China's vastness and variegation, which have expressed themselves in different ways throughout China's history—such as the reliance on locally based elites in imperial days and the centrifugal forces of the transitional period—have also been manifest in its revolution and, as we shall see, in the structure of its socialist political economy. A Communist Party operating in nearly twenty base areas spread over all of China could not have sustained the highly centralized structure of command and discipline associated with Leninism. That the CCP and its revolution were so dispersed was a function of the difficulty which weak and hostile political forces had reintegrating the vast Chinese polity. The relatively decentralized nature of the CCP, at least in revolutionary days, is, therefore, partly attributable to China's size. In addition, the structure and character of local politics in China since 1949, in which grassroots organs, their officials, and even citizens have a certain political manœuvrability, and in which local cadres with political bases in their constituencies below and the state above have been important in mediating between state and society, resonate to the political structure of imperial days. China's size and complexity have set real limits to state domination of society in the manner of the totalitarian model. Finally, China's size and complexity have also put constraints on market-orientated reform of economic planning. Though many Chinese economists and economic planners are attracted to the Hungarian model of controlled market reform, they say that the model may not work in their country because its vastness poses too many difficulties regulating the market forces they wish to utilize.

A second heritage from China's past is the populism and voluntarism that have characterized the Maoist approach to socialism and development. The mass line forged in Yan'an days would find expression in the political campaigns, periodic party rectifications, and egalitarian commitment to 'serve the people' that are hallmarks of Chinese socialism. The miracle of the party's survival after April 1927, the unstinting exertions of the Jinggangshan, Jiangxi and Yan'an periods, the heroism of the Long March, and in the end the surprising triumph of the poorly equipped and ragtag communist forces against the US-backed Guomindang, all lent to Chinese socialism a potent voluntarism—a belief that nearly anything was possible with enough hard work and commitment. This found expression in Mao's very popular (or at least highly popularized!) essay on 'The Foolish Old Man Who Moved the Mountain', in which he drew an analogy between the CCP and a fabled man who singlehandedly tried to move Mounts Taihang and Wangwu, which were obstructing his doorway (and for his efforts was given God's help in clearing them):

We must persevere and work unceasingly, and we, too, will touch God's heart. Our God is none other than the masses of the Chinese people. If they stand up and work together with us, why can't these two mountains [imperialism and feudalism] be cleared away? (Mao, 1967, Vol. III, p. 322.)

This faith in the power of the organized and committed people would inform many of the key developments of Chinese socialism, such as the Great Leap Forward and the Cultural Revolution.

But juxtaposed with this popular impulse was a third, contrary inheritance: the elitist character of traditional political culture and the absence during the transition of the development of any serious liberal impulse. To its credit, the CCP did develop its own form of mass-line democracy, but this grew in the absence of any concept of individual rights and in the double presence of elitism and authoritarianism characteristic of both imperial and Leninist politics. As a result, the mass line could not grow into a democratic politics that managed to protect individual rights and interests while also forging and articulating class, group and mass ones. Moreover, mass-line politics have repeatedly encountered resistance from more bureaucratic and authoritarian political styles and practices, as we shall see. Even Mao could take the most extreme positions in favour of mass democracy—announcing during the Cultural Revolution that 'rebellion is justified'—but soon after call in the army to quell the fighting. At the symbolic level, too, the persona of Mao Zedong as a man respected like an emperor, but revered for his faith in and commitment to populism and egalitarianism, manifests this contradiction of Chinese socialism. Even in death this remains so. Mao's tomb, built in the centre of Tiananmen Square, which is the centre of Beijing (and which in turn is the centre of China, which is the centre of the world to Chinese), is no less prepossessing than that built by any emperor. But there is a great difference: where the ordinary citizen was forbidden to cast eyes upon the emperor, now the depressing sight of Mao's cadaver is on display for one and all to see. The popular democratic and authoritarian elements of Chinese politics still form one of its central contradictions today.

A fourth historical legacy affecting Chinese socialism is the question of nationalism. China's history provides it with the longest and greatest national heritage in the world. But its nationhood was threatened by the failure of timely industrialization. Neither capitalism nor socialism could take hold in China unless they could re-establish and defend China's national sovereignty, and that required building up the country's industry. This imperative has posed deep structural problems for Chinese socialism, which has also been committed to raising living standards and to serving the interests of the peasantry that comprises the vast majority of the Chinese people and was the primary basis of the revolution.

A fifth and related problem inherited from the past is the failure of agricultural commercialization. Rural agrarian society underwent little structural change until the land reform. The CCP liberated a country of peasants still living in their traditional villages, with strong ties to land, village and kin. This affected the way in which rural development and change could proceed. With the brief (and disastrous) exception of the Great Leap Forward, the party would choose to develop the countryside basically within the old social structure: as we shall see, peasants were not uprooted from their homes, collectives were formed along boundaries conforming to pre-existing residential contours, and the traditional family was preserved and put at the service of collective production, to name just a few instances. In other words, there was something distinctly traditional about China's rural transformation. Its reformist leadership is now arguing that the preservation of this agrarian structure is setting real limits to its efforts to modernize China: for example it is difficult to replace old village leaders, whose power may be based on kinship or patron–client networks or good social skills, with technocratically capable ones; or it is hard to get peasants to give up the mentality of economic self-provision and to join the wider commodity economy completely. Yet even the reforms intended to commercialize Chinese agriculture fully have been based upon the household, which is the most basic unit of China's traditional agrarian structure.

Implications for Theory of Revolution

China's was the first socialist revolution to draw its main social base from the countryside, thereby refuting the orthodox Marxist emphasis on the revolutionary primacy of the proletariat. The condescension with which Marx and many Marxists regarded the peasantry, and their attribution of reactionary tendencies to it, have had to be completely rethought. That these statements seem commonplace today testifies partly to the power which the Chinese revolution had in inspiring rural-based socialist revolutions in other countries.

The Chinese revolution has much to teach us about the role of peasants in revolution. First, and contrary to the view that China's was a 'peasant revolution', it is yet another case of the inability of the peasantry to make revolution on its own. Chinese history is full of peasant rebellions, but the attempt to make a revolution—a 'basic transformation of a society's state and class structures'[15]—requires a leadership with an analysis of the past, a vision of the future, and a political strategy and organization to lead society in transforming the former into the latter. The Chinese case puts particular emphasis on the importance of creative, insightful and committed leadership, which could forge a revolutionary base even in an agrarian social structure that was decidedly unsuitable to the peasant solidarity and autonomy which are key factors of revolutionary conduciveness.

But in China even a peasantry inclined toward or capable of revolution and a revolutionary leadership were not enough. The CCP success was in part a product of the multifaceted Guomindang failure. The CCP did not bring the Guomindang down alone. In that feat it received much help from Japan and from the Guomindang itself. With better leadership and without the Japanese invasion it is conceivable, though structurally unlikely, that the Guomindang could have stabilized its rule and coopted or 'exterminated' the

CCP. Skocpol's argument that successful revolutions depend very heavily on a serious state crisis is quite apposite in the Chinese case (Skocpol, 1979, Ch. 2, Conclusion and *passim*).

The Chinese revolution also indicates how important it is for rural revolutionaries to establish their own armed forces and to use them to set up secure base areas within which peasant support can be built, experience gained, and revolutionary resources nurtured. This lesson may seem self-evident today, in the light of China's own history and that of almost every other successful revolution (and many unsuccessful ones, too) of the last fifty years. But before the CCP learned it, it nearly paid for its ignorance with its life—as the vast majority of its members and so many sympathizers and activists did.[16]

The Chinese revolution also suggests the importance of a flexible and graduated policy on class relations and struggle. The CCP's radical attacks on landlords and rich peasants in Jinggangshan and Jiangxi did not advance, and may even have set back, the revolution. Its policy of broad class coalition— 'uniting the many to oppose the few'—in Yan'an days proved much more salutary. The land reform, which attacked the landlord class and finally wiped this remaining stratum of the gentry off the stage of history, came at the very end of the revolution.

This suggests a larger methodological point: the need for a distinction between the importance of class struggle in the grand dialectics of revolutionary analysis and in actual revolutionary praxis. Our class-structured analysis of the fall of gentry hegemony and the failure of the bourgeoisie suggests the importance of class relations and struggle at the foundation of the Chinese revolutionary dynamic. But in our analysis of the actual course of the CCP-led movement, class struggle took a seat alongside the quality of leadership and historical contingency in explaining revolutionary success. The Chinese revolution teaches revolutionaries everywhere that there need be no contradiction between class conflict and class compromise—and, more positively, that class compromise can often be the most effective way of leading and prosecuting the class struggle.

2 Chinese Socialist Development, 1949–85

1949-52: Recovery and Consolidation

The euphoria of 1 October 1949 went hand in hand with very difficult problems facing China and its new leaders, and with rapidly shifting currents within which those problems would have to be confronted. The civil war was still raging. Land reform was incomplete in many places, and had not yet begun in others. The CCP had little experience in urban administration and leadership, and none in national government, while its relations with the proletariat were weak. At the end of almost forty years of revolutionary, civil and foreign war and political incapacity, and a century of imperialism, the economy was in disastrous shape. Unemployment, inflation and starvation demanded urgent solutions, and deeper structural problems of underinvestment, shortage of skilled personnel, and multiple imbalances would also have to be tackled. Society, too, was in deep crisis: disease, prostitution, drug addiction, illiteracy, corruption and gangsterism were epidemic, and social services non-existent or in utter disarray. To compound the difficulties, China would soon find itself embroiled in the Korean War, which brought China face to face with the military might of the United States and prolonged the civil war by strengthening the United States' resolve to defend and support the Guomindang.

The proportions and nature of the crisis are similar in some ways to that facing the Bolsheviks after November 1917, when they, too, faced economic and social breakdown, and continued civil and foreign war. But the CCP responded quite differently. Where the Bolsheviks initiated a period of radical transformation, including rapid, sweeping nationalizations, tight central control of the economy, and summary and sometimes forced appropriation of food from the peasantry, the CCP moved much more cautiously and moderately. It continued its practice of forging broad class coalitions and limiting class struggle. Nationalization was carried out selectively, and centralization of levers of economic power proceeded gradually. Just as the Chinese revolution had proceeded very differently from the Russian, so now in power Chinese socialism took its first steps on what would continue to prove to be a very different trajectory of development, one no less pathbreaking and, history seems to be showing, perhaps somewhat more influential for other countries than its predecessor.

Rural Transformation: the Land Reform

The Chinese land reform is perhaps the most sweeping and successful rural transformation in history. In one stroke it provided poor peasants with land and relieved their exploitation by tenancy, ushered the remnants of the Chinese gentry at last from the stage of history, and galvanized a new kind of mass-based politics and government at the grassroots. Moreover, it did so without precipitating a production crisis, always a danger in land reform; to the contrary, it actually helped promote the recovery of the rural economy. Finally, it managed to avoid a bloodbath. Though violence was done to many landlords, the vast majority remained physically unhurt and survived into the socialist period as owners of small plots which they had to learn to work like the peasant cultivators they had exploited for thousands of years.

All this was accomplished in the face of several serious obstacles. One of these was structural. As we have seen in Chapter 1, the Chinese peasantry was historically bound up in a web of vertical relationships and institutions—kinship associations, patron–client ties, religious institutions, secret societies—dominated by landowners. This undercut the potential for peasant solidarity against landlords, and gave the landlords considerable leverage with which to oppose the land reform.

In this situation, matters would have been much easier if the landlord class had simply evaporated, as it had done in Korea when the Japanese, who owned much of the land, were defeated. But China was not blessed with such a conjuncture. The Chinese landlords were by and large still on the scene, and used all the levers of political and social power at their disposal to undermine the land reform. They were expert at attempting to bribe and blackmail communist cadres, for example by having their wives or daughters seduce local activists and then exposing them and undermining their credibility as allies of the poor. The landowners also attempted to enforce tenancy relations through cooptation, promising favourable treatment to those who would oppose the land reform, persuade others to do so, and continue to pay rent secretly. They attempted to conceal their holdings by burying gold and transferring formal land titles to poor relatives or 'non-profit' institutions such as religious or kinship organizations. They threatened physical violence against land-reform cadres and their peasant supporters, and hired thugs to make good on those threats. Perhaps their most potent threat was the possibility of a return to power by the Guomindang, which was by no means an impossibility, particularly in the zones liberated at an early stage. Fear of a 'change of sky' dampened the willingness of many peasants, who felt weak and feared they might again be dependent on landlords to rent them land or loan them money, to join in attacks on their exploiters. Dialectically, this fear presented the CCP land reform leadership with an equally difficult problem: once they persuaded peasants to join in the land reform, often the peasants were then inclined to commit deadly violence against their landlords to prevent any future revenge.

To ascertain the full extent of landlord holdings, build solidarity among the structurally fragmented peasantry, and overcome the peasants' difficulties in coming forward to attack the landlords, the CCP relied on the mass-line methods developed in Yan'an. In the archetypical pattern, land-reform cadres would begin by locating potential activists—people with strong anti-landlord feelings, a certain capacity to articulate them, and the social skills and stature needed to persuade others to join them. Confidential conversations with such people were used to build networks of support and eventually to prepare the ground for a mass meeting. Here the landlord would be publicly accused, his holdings exposed, and the extent of his exploitation evaluated. Then his property would be seized and, through another series of mass meetings and deliberations, redistributed.

Of course, things almost never went this smoothly in practice; archetypical was not typical. Mistakes and setbacks were frequent. Mass meetings were called prematurely, and their failure to evince serious attacks on landlords set events back to, or even short of, square one. Landlords, too, could play the game, and sometimes mobilized their supporters to defend them or to attack the activists. Then there were excesses: peasants often wanted to attack rich peasants and even middle peasants as well, so as to enlarge the stock of property to be redistributed. Then there was perhaps the most difficult moment for the mass movement: the division of the 'fruits' of the struggle. Bitter disputes ensued over thorny issues. Should activists receive more or better property as a reward or just deserts for having led the way in the movement? What about cadres who appropriated more or better property for themselves or their friends or kin? What was to be done in the event that there was not enough confiscated property to provide for the needs of all the poor, a situation which was quite common, especially in North China where tenancy was much lower than in South China? What about special individual cases, such as poor widows who were forced to rent out their land because they could not work it themselves? How was a middle peasant, who was not entitled to receive any redistribution, to be distinguished from a poor peasant, who was? And how was the party to exert leadership and provide guidance in dealing with these matters without dampening the mass initiative and power that was required to make the land reform successful in the first place?

To minimize these problems and deal effectively with them when they did arise, the land reform required a complex mix of party leadership and mass participation. Cadres armed with the latest party instructions and clarifications had to make peasants aware of the problems and persuade them to abide by the party's policies to resolve them. But they also had to listen carefully to peasants' opinions and complaints and report them to their local superiors. At other times they had to subject themselves to criticism from the peasants for mistakes they had made. Somtimes part of the land reform process had to be repeated to resolve errors made in the first go-round.[1]

In the end, the Chinese land reform was a stunning success, partly despite these difficulties and partly because of them. First, the structure of land-ownership became far more equal (though, by design, it drew up far short of complete egalitarianism, a point to which we shall soon return). Landlords, who comprised 2.6 per cent of households, saw their landholdings drop from 28.7 per cent to 2.1 per cent of China's crop land. The holdings of poor peasants and landless labourers, who comprised 57.1 per cent of the house-holds, doubled from 23.5 per cent of cultivated land to 46.8 per cent. Tools and livestock were also redistributed.

Second, the rural economy made a rapid recovery during the land reform. In general, land reforms can pose a great danger to production, as peasants and landowners unsure of their future holdings disinvest in the land (by failing to maintain it) or actually refuse to put it under crops. They may also destroy productive resources like seed or livestock and drain down reserves of food, preferring to eat them than see them expropriated. But the Chinese land reform did not precipitate an economic crisis. On the contrary, it provided the conditions for rapid recovery. Grain production grew from 113 million tons in 1949 to 164 million tons in 1952 (which exceeded the previous all-time record), cotton production tripled, and fish production nearly quadrupled, to mention just a few important indicators. Gross value of agricultural output increased nearly 50 per cent. Such a record would be impressive at any time, but it is especially remarkable in the context of a massive land reform.

To be sure, the increase was in part a result of what from a purely economic point of view could be called the 'artificially' depressed level of production in 1949, due to the civil war. With the restoration of peace for the first time in many years, the economy could easily rebound as existing but unused or underutilized capacity was brought into play. But other factors specific to the land reform were at work as well in fostering the rapid recovery. The CCP's efforts to reassure the peasantry, and its insistence on protecting the holdings of the most productive strata of rich and middle peasants, were of great help. The speed and timing of the land reform were also important. To help maximize peasant participation, the winter slack season was often used. Once prepared, the movement in a particular village was undertaken with a definite celerity so as to minimize the time that property owners would have to destroy or sell off their assets and prepare their defences. Finally, the land reform liberated the productive energies of the peasantry as well as the investment resources at their disposal. Analysis of data from 1933, one of the last years for which comprehensive and reliable statistics exist, has shown that the Chinese rural economy was producing a surplus of more than 25 per cent of national income. Much of this had gone to subsidize the high levels of leisurely living of China's landed elite, through rents and taxes. Now this surplus accrued to the peasantry, who could and did use it to invest in expanded reproduction of the agrarian economy.

Third, the landlord class was destroyed, while most landlords were not. There is a grizzly and polemical debate, based on very poor data, about precisely how many landlords died in the land reform. Somewhere in the range of half a million to a million landlord deaths is about the best one can conclude from it. Evaluation of these awful numbers involves thorny moral questions which must also take into account two facts: first, that many of those landlords killed were themselves guilty of serious crimes and that the tenancy system they supported was responsible for the deaths of untold numbers of peasants through physical exhaustion, deprivation and famine; and second, that in much of rural China land reform took place during the last years of the very bloody civil war, when many landlords were actively supporting the Nationalist cause.

To be sure, during radical periods before 1949 CCP policy did implicitly encourage peasant violence against landlords (or at least it functioned in this way). In September 1947, for example, what was deemed an excessively slow pace of land reform was blamed on landlord and rich peasant infiltration of the party, and a mass mobilization to criticize and reverse this was called for. But apparently it resulted in physical attacks against landlords, for by January 1948 Mao himself wrote:

We must insist on killing less and must strictly forbid indiscriminate killing. To advocate more and indiscriminate killing is entirely wrong; this would only cause our Party to forfeit sympathy, become alienated from the masses and fall into isolation. Trial and sentence by the people's courts ... must be carried out in earnest.

[Mao, 1969, Vol. IV, pp. 185–6; translation slightly altered to improve accuracy and readability.]

In fact, landlords were specifically to be allowed to retain small plots of land sufficient to sustain themselves and their families. Mao argued that they could be used 'as a labour force for the country', while the party could also 'save and remould them'. Perhaps he also had in mind their function as a living symbol of the reversal of the old exploitative class structure. In any event, Mao concluded: 'Our task is to abolish the feudal system, to wipe out the landlords *as a class, not as individuals*.' (Mao, 1969, Vol. IV, p. 186; emphasis added.)

This was accomplished not merely by expropriating the landlords' property, though certainly this was an important element. In Chapter 1 we have seen that the landlords' power did not rest on land alone. It also involved their *political* control of the peasantry through the vertical institutions (such as kinship associations, etc.) and through the complex of Confucian values, local customs, and traditional ways of acting and thinking that comprised a culture of gentry hegemony and peasant subordination. These levers of power operated, then, at the levels of social relations and consciousness. So that is where the CCP attacked them. The mass line process of having peasants confront their landlords personally and publicly went right to this level. Marx's third thesis on Feuerbach contains a relevant insight: 'The coincidence of the changing of circumstances and of human activity can be conceived and rationally understood only as *revolutionizing practice*' (Marx, 1959, p. 243, emphasis in original). Here Marx is noting that revolutionary action can, dialectically, change the world ('circumstances') and also the people who are changing it. In other words, revolution revolutionizes the revolutionaries—it is a verb as well as a noun. In this case, the land reform not only changed the 'circumstances' of land tenure, but also involved 'human action' which changed the way the tenants thought about their landlords and themselves. In doing so, it reached down to an important if non-material underpinning of landlord hegemony. With the land reform, the landlords— whose fall after thousands of years' domination had begun in earnest with the collapse of the imperial state four decades earlier—finally had their remaining sources of *political, social* and *cultural* as well as economic power cut out from under them at last. The class struggle against the tenacious old ruling class was completed.

In political terms, the land reform was not just a blow against the land-lords. Its fourth result was the development of new political leadership and institutions at the grassroots. New activists and local cadres were recruited during the land reform. These new local leaders as well as older ones were put through some of the most difficult tests of their leadership skills and their commitment. Many of China's corps of grassroots cadres who would preside over local affairs during the succeeding decades of collectivization and rural transformation got their start in the land reform.

In addition to these peasant leaders, the land reform also gave many urban activists their first exposure to conditions in the countryside. To help guide the movement and correct its 'deviations', the party organized 'work teams' comprised of urbanites, some of whom were party and government officials, but many of whom were simply young people from the newly liberated cities who had little or no prior involvement with the party or the revolution but were sympathetic to them. The work teams were given brief training and then dispatched to the countryside for several months or more to help the peasants carry out the land reform. Service on the work teams proved to be a real eye-opener for many urban Chinese, who had never been to the rural areas before and had no appreciation of the gravity of conditions and the nature of peasant culture. It was the first step in the Maoist attempt to bridge the gap between rural and urban forms of consciousness and life, which would prove to be one of the boldest and most distinctive themes of Chinese socialism.

The land reform also helped develop and invigorate local political institutions. Peasant associations in villages came to life. The village-wide meeting, which must have been strange and new in the fragmented and landlord-dominated society of Chinese villages, became a central forum of political action during the land reform and continued as such for the next three decades. Above the grassroots level, county (*xian*) party and government institutions, charged with overseeing the land reform, acquired a political weight, coordinative capacity, and network of linkages with grassroots political leaders and institutions which they have retained up to the present day.

A fifth result of the land reform was its legacy of class relations and inequality. Though it struck a great blow toward greater equality by expropriating and redistributing most landlord property, it stopped well short of full equalization, a manoeuvre which the party had rejected since its unsuccessful radical experiments in Jinggangshan and Jiangxi. The land reform specifically protected rich peasants. The 1950 Agrarian Reform Law targeted landlords, and stipulated that:

Land owned by rich peasants and cultivated by them or by hired labor, and their other properties, shall not be infringed upon. Small portions of land rented out by rich peasants shall also be retained by them (Hinton, 1980, Vol. I, p. 63.)

Only if they were renting out more land than they were working could the rich peasants be subject to expropriation, and even then only the rented portion was to be touched. The property of middle peasants (including 'well-to-do middle peasants') was fully protected. No industrial or commercial property was to be expropriated, even if it were owned by landlords.

As a result, post-land reform society contained certain class (not to mention spatial) inequalities carried over from the past. Rich peasants, who comprised 3.6 per cent of rural households, still held 6.4 per cent of crop land (down from 17.7 per cent before the land reform). The 35.8 per cent of households classified as middle peasants ended up with 44.8 per cent of land, while poor peasants and landless labourers—57.1 per cent of households—had 46.8 per cent. These aggregate figures do not reflect a rather more egalitarian situation in many villages—especially in North China—which had relatively fewer landlord holdings and more rich peasant ones. There and elsewhere, many poor peasants were left with very small subsistence or even sub-subsistence plots. They would soon be forced to seek additional land to farm through rentals. This set up a new area of exploitation which provided the basis for future political conflicts and, in an interesting dialectic, for the party's decision to promote mutual aid and collectivization, the next stages of socialist transformation.

Transition in the Cities: Social Reform, Nationalization and Political Consolidation

From the point of view of epoch-making changes in class relations, the changes in the cities were much less striking than those in the countryside. The sheer magnitude of crisis in the urban centres, the party's inexperience and lack of a strong political and social base there, the drain on its energies caused by the land reform and the Korean War, and its general propensity to move gradually, all combined to cause the CCP to adopt a generally cautious approach to the class conflict. This was summed up in the party's character-ization of the political nature of the period as 'new democracy' based on a coalition of the national and petty bourgeoisies as well as the peasantry and the proletariat. Nevertheless, the quality of urban life and government were vastly improved by the CCP's skill in constructing and consolidating new political institutions and by its radical—in the strict sense of root-seeking (rather than extreme or leftist)—approach to social problems.

Prostitution, gambling and opium addiction had reached epidemic proportions in many of China's large cities. The Guomindang had actually cooperated with the organized criminals who ran these operations, using them for political intelligence and repression and also collaborating with them through state corruption. Thus the CCP's attacks on these social ills were important politically, too: they struck at a core of continuing Guomindang support and sabotage, while also helping the CCP prove its effectiveness and benevolence to the urban population at large. The new government used combinations of carrot and stick, and of mass mobilization and state action, to strike swiftly and deeply at these problems. Prostitutes and drug addicts, regarded as victims of the social crisis engendered by colonialism and Guomindang reaction and incapacity, were enrolled in rehabilitation programmes. Petty pimps and drug dealers were let off with a stern warning and perhaps some local mass criticism. Major pimps and dealers were subjected to public trials and severe punishment. Meanwhile, campaigns were organized to educate the public about the evils of prostitution, gambling and drugs for the nation, the individual and the family, while the major centres of such activities in the urban neighbourhoods were raided and closed down. Within two years these major social problems were basically eradicated, and an important node of political opposition eliminated.

The new state also moved vigorously to reform family relations and strike a blow against oppression of women in both the cities and the countryside. Under the new Marriage Law, women were given the right to own property, hold employment, and divorce husbands who had maltreated or abandoned them. Concubinage and forced marriage were made illegal. The law was also designed to protect children. Infanticide and the sale and betrothal of children, which had particularly victimized girls and poor families, were forbidden, and children born out of wedlock were given equal legal protection. Mass campaigns to promote the new family relations and criticize abusive husbands and fathers were organized.[2]

Economic nationalization proceeded much more slowly. After the defeat of Japan, which had occupied China's industrial heartlands, control of heavy industry and mining had been consolidated under an amalgam of state control and private profit for the Guomindang elite families; the CCP referred to this sector as 'bureaucratic capitalism'. When most members of this stratum fled to Taiwan, leaving their productive assets behind, it was natural and easy to nationalize this sector; indeed, there was little else that could be done with it. Foreign-run firms were also nationalized, though through a process of negotiation and compensation which kept the factories running, provided training for Chinese technicians, managers and workers to run them, and even protected future business relations with the foreign firms. Thus in short order the new government found itself in control of the industrial core of the economy, which accounted for about one-third of industrial output value, more than three-quarters of fixed capital, and about 700,000 employees.

However, Chinese heavy industry was poorly developed, and the lighter sectors bulked much larger in the urban economy. (Outside of Manchuria, consumer goods production made up more than 90 per cent of industrial output.) These were under the control of what the CCP termed the 'national capitalists': private entrepreneurs who were not closely tied economically or politically to the Guomindang. They were designated as part of the CCP's class coalition during the period of 'new democracy', so their interests were scrupulously protected. The CCP leadership realized that it needed their technical, managerial, commercial and entrepreneurial expertise to effect the economic recovery which was a central goal of the period. (In the context of the sharp constriction in China's access to world markets during the Korean War, it became particularly important for the CCP to seek economic allies wherever it could.) Thus the national bourgeoisie's assets were not subject to nationalization, and they could continue to make and appropriate profit. As early as 1947, the party had actually criticized nationalizations undertaken by newly victorious cadres and armies who marched into the cities and by their radical working-class supporters, all of whom were told to get down to work in the name of national economic recovery. In return, they would be rewarded as the national capitalists now came under new forms of regulation concerning wages, working conditions and even pricing and marketing practices (over which control was also exercised through gradual nationalization of wholesale—but not retail—trade).

Despite their reduced autonomy, though, the number of private industrial firms increased sixfold to 150,000 between 1949 and 1953, and employed over two million workers—three times the number employed in the state sector. This was in addition to the plethora of *petit bourgeois* enterprises, such as self-employed artisans and service providers, which continued to operate and proliferate unencumbered. (This proliferation of private firms is evidence of the success of the CCP in promoting business and political confidence among the bourgeoisie and *petit bourgeoisie*.) Thus by 1952, China's urban economy was a mixture of state and private forms. The state sector accounted for 56 per cent of gross industrial output value, 27 per cent was produced in what was called the 'state capitalist' sector (comprising some joint state–private firms but mainly private firms operating under state contracts and instructions), and 17 per cent in purely private capitalist firms.

The urban-based industrial and commercial economy performed very well in the recovery years of 1949–52. The hyperinflation that resulted from the Guomindang government's inability to finance itself was brought quickly under control. The state budget was balanced as taxes were simplified and revenues raised from industrial profits of the state sector. Gross value of industrial output increased two and a half times, with heavy industry out-pacing light. Retail sales volume doubled. Even world trade volume increased 50 per cent, despite the US-led Western embargo. Perhaps most significant for the future, investment in capital construction increased almost fourfold, to 20 per cent of net domestic expenditure by 1953.

The CCP leadership also acted with vigour to establish and consolidate its political control in the cities. Since it had not been able during the revolution to establish its own organs of government and administration in the cities, it was forced to utilize many of those it inherited from the Guomindang period. By and large, the lower-level officials had stayed on after 1949. The new government placed these institutions and bureaucrats under its political control by subordinating them to new state ministries and assigning party members to supervise them. For example, the police were now placed under the authority of the Ministry of Public Security, and party cadres were assigned to key command posts. At the same time, the CCP leadership made a move to create new grassroots organizations. In the neighbourhoods, urban residents' committees were made responsible for public information and propaganda work, dispensation of municipal services, local dispute arbitration and judicature, and gathering intelligence and information for the state. They were quite valuable in the campaigns against prostitution, drug addiction and organized crime. Women's and students' federations and trade unions were also formed. The Women's Federation was particularly important in promulgating and enforcing the new policy on gender and family relations.

Of course, the CCP had acquired its own special appreciation of the political truism that institutions are no better than the people in them. In fact, Mao and his followers would prove downright suspicious of political institutions as breeding grounds for ideological, social and economic stagnation and even counter-revolution. The early 1950s, therefore, saw the use of political campaigns to galvanize the personnel of the new state and purge from them certain tendencies deemed unhealthy by the party leadership. A 'three-anti' (*san fan*) campaign was launched to fight corruption, waste and elitism among officials held over from the Guomindang state, new party recruits and even old party cadres. A 'five-anti' (*wu fan*) campaign against bribery, tax evasion, fraud, and theft of government property and economic secrets was directed at members of the national bourgeoisie who were not complying with the plans the state had for them. In both campaigns the familiar mass-line methods of persuasion and discreet solicitation of information along with public mass criticism were employed. These were not purges in the Stalinist sense. They were not used by top elites to eliminate political rivals.

Less than one cadre in twenty was formally censured in the *san fan*, and most of these were simply demoted or dismissed rather than imprisoned. In a similar vein, penalties under the *wu fan* —meted out to three-quarters of the businesses in the major cities—were mainly financial. This was not a frontal attack on the national bourgeoisie in the way the land reform attacked the landowners. But it did put them on notice that their position in socialist China was becoming more tenuous.

Socialist Transition, 1953–57

With the recovery complete, the consolidation of the new state well in hand, and the end of the Korean War, the conditions for the next stage of China's socialist development were in place. Industrial and agricultural output were back to levels achieved in the 1930s, which were historical records but were still quite low in absolute terms. The rapid rates of growth of the recovery years were partly statistical artifacts of the very depressed base line of 1949; they also rested upon the mobilization of existing but underutilized resources. To be sure, the CCP's policies over the period 1949–52 had been sensitive and skilful in fostering the conditions under which those resources could most effectively be brought into play. But economic growth via resuscitation could only occur once. Now new ways would have to be found to propel the Chinese economy forward on a sustained basis.

Like the revolution and the early period of CCP governance that had preceded it, this stage would also be characterized by rather different approaches in the countryside and the cities. It also held some surprises in store: the shrewdest observer looking at China in 1952 would have been hard put to predict the developments that were about to break on to the scene. Even a retrospective structuralism, which would predict the past by seeing events as necessary or pretermined outcomes of ineluctable forces and conditions, fails to provide compelling explanation of that period. Specifically, these years saw the erection of bureaucratic central planning and management in industry and commerce, and of rapid collectivization in agriculture. Moreover, for the first time agriculture began to be exploited in order to finance industry.

Industrial Centralization: the First Five Year Plan, 1953–57

Since 1927, relations between the CCP and the Soviet Union had been stormy. Stalin and the advisers he sent to China had persistent doubts about the agrarian base of the revolution. After the defeat of Japan, the Soviet Union raced the CCP and the Guomindang to receive Japanese surrenders. It even went so far as to loot industrial enterprises under Japanese control, packing up as much as possible and shipping it back to the USSR. On Mao's first visit to the Soviet Union in 1950, he was humiliated by being forced to wait for days at a time to see Stalin. The Soviet Union manœuvred China into the position of doing most of the fighting in the Korean War. In his own leadership of the Chinese revolution, Mao had already evinced practical concern with the bureaucratism, centralization and elitism that characterized the Soviet Union under Stalin, though as far as we know he would not critique the Soviet system for such ills until the late 1950s. It is therefore somewhat surprising though, as we shall soon see, not at all inexplicable, that in 1953 the CCP embarked on a programme of industrial development that explicitly aped the Soviet model.

The First Five Year Plan covered 1953 to 1957, but was not enunciated until 1955 (retroactively incorporating the 1953 and 1954 plans), perhaps indicating some ambivalence or even controversy surrounding it. It involved several elements that departed from previous Chinese practice. First, planning was to be highly centralized, in contrast to the local and regional self-reliance that had grown out of revolutionary wartime conditions when the CCP occupied isolated base areas. Second, at the macro level, the economy was to be administered by vertically organized government ministries, with almost no role for horizontal coordination by local or regional political authorities. In other words, dual rule now gave way to a more singularly vertical pattern of authority.

Third, investment priority was given to heavy industry, while agriculture was left to fend for itself. Investment capital—which would be required in large quantities for the heavy industry envisioned by the plan—was to come in small measure from the Soviet Union but primarily from the Chinese countryside. The Soviet Union provided credit and technical assistance for 156 major projects in what was perhaps the largest transfer of technology ever carried out by any country. But this was just a drop in the vast bucket of China's plans for high-speed industrialization, amounting to only about 3 per cent of total state investment. Moreover, most of this came as loans (with short-term repayment periods to boot!), not grants. So most of the cost of industrial investment during the First Five Year Plan was paid by the Chinese people, most of whom were peasants.

This does not mean that the peasants were immiserated or sacrificed to industrialization. Total tax collections from the countryside declined from 17 per cent of output in 1949 to 13.2 per cent in 1952; thereafter the agricultural tax was fixed in absolute terms at the 1952 level for each household, so that with increased production the proportion paid as tax declined (Shue, 1980, pp. 122, 126).[3] Of course taxes do not comprise all or even the most important transfers of resources from the peasantry to the state. Starting in 1953, with the policy of unified grain purchase, the state set quotas for each locality to sell grain to the state. Prices were stipulated to be prevailing market prices, and indeed the terms of trade between agriculture and industry did move in favour of the former through 1955 (Shue, 1980, p. 222). Moreover, the state did not take advantage of unified purchase to raise the level of extraction from the countryside: total grain marketings as a percentage of total output remained fairly steady through 1958 (Lardy, 1983, p. 34). Overall, living standards and rural reinvestment rose significantly during the First Five Year Plan (Lardy, 1983, p. 144; Shue, 1980, p. 212, n.). So while the First Five Year Plan did transfer considerable resources out of the countryside to finance industry, and perhaps hurt the rural sector compared with its potential performance under different investment priorities, the burden borne by the rural sector, spread over the vastness of rural China, was moderate enough to permit growth of rural accumulation and income too.

Fourth, the new heavy industry was to take the form of very large complexes concentrated in a few big cities. For example, the steel centre at Anshan attracted almost one third of the Soviet-aided projects and 35,000 new workers; by 1957 it would produce two-thirds of China's steel. Such massive concentration of production reinforced the state's capacities for central planning and control of the economy. It tended to pre-empt industrial development in medium-sized cities. The size of these enterprises was also unsuited to participatory management.

Fifth, the pace of nationalization was accelerated. By June 1952, Mao had already concluded that the national bourgeoisie ought no longer to be included in the class coalition of the socialist state. In 1953, the state began to convert many private firms to joint state–private ownership and to subject them to the same state planning and management as the state-sector plants; the only significant difference was that in the joint state–private plants the former owners were often retained as managers and were paid dividends out of part of the firms' profits. By 1956, the private sector in industry had been eliminated. Two-thirds of gross industrial output value was produced in state-run plants, and one-third in joint state–private firms. The state was fully in command of China's industry.

Sixth, factory management was consolidated in the hands of managers who were given great authority. A more participatory form of management known as the Shanghai or East China system, which had been employed selectively and experimentally since 1947, gave way to 'one-man management' along Soviet lines.[4] This was a natural result of the fact that the industrial nationalizations were carried out by administrative fiat rather than mass movement (as in the land reform). There simply was no institutional or political basis to advocate or carry out participatory management. One-man management was based upon strict hierarchical, bureaucratic command in industrial administration and management. Factory directors took orders from their superiors in the ministries, and exercised tight control over the workers in their factories. They frequently employed piece-rate and quota systems to control and motivate workers, which in other socialist countries have depoliticized workers by pitting them against each other while simultaneously intensifying work.[5] During the first two years of the plan, Chinese economists boasted of a 42 per cent rise in labour productivity as against a 7 per cent rise in workers' real incomes.

The Chinese leadership adopted this Soviet-style, and in many ways un-Chinese, plan for several reasons. It utterly lacked experience in industrial development, and the only source of advice then available was the Soviet Union. In fact the Soviet Union was a rather attractive model because of its impressive performance in a context originally quite similar to China's. Like China, the Soviet Union had embarked on industrialization in a large, poor and war-torn country which had had a very late start compared with the West and had rather little infrastructure with which to work. Like China, the Soviet Union was largely isolated from foreign sources of capital, markets and technology, and so had had to pull itself up mainly by its own bootstraps. Like China, the Soviet Union was not just isolated in the world but also severely threatened by it: both countries had found themselves under attack from Western capitalist countries soon after socialist governments had been established. The Soviet Union had achieved dazzling results in rapid industrialization, in a quarter of a century building a modern industrial economy powerful enough to enable the country to drive back Germany and emerge from the Second World War as a superpower that could contend with the United States. The prospect of equally rapid growth of industry and defence capability had strong appeal to the nationalist as well as the socialist proclivities of China's leaders, who began to talk of overtaking Great Britain economically. Finally, the prospect of Soviet aid, at a time when China was strapped for resources and no other sources of credit or grants were available, was not to be taken lightly.

The First Five Year Plan strategy produced results which were impressive enough to sustain such talk. Industrial output grew faster than the very high target of 14.7 per cent per year, even according to the newest, downgraded

Chinese statistics which peg it at 15.5 per cent, below some Western estimates.[6] Heavy industrial output nearly tripled, while light industry grew 70 per cent. Railway freight volume more than doubled. Of course, agriculture could not grow at anything like this pace. Gross output value there grew only at an average of 2.1 per cent per year, a sharp decline from the heady figure of 14.1 per cent during the recovery years of 1949–52. Output of key crops grew very slowly in 1953 and 1954, and erratically thereafter, as the Table 2.1 shows. Although agricultural production and rural economic conditions were not in deep crisis, this level of performance was a thin reed upon which to rest the grandiose plans for rapid industrialization. It would be difficult to sustain the high rate of accumulation demanded by the Soviet-style strategy—already at about 20 per cent of output—if agriculture were stagnant or growing only marginally. Markets for industrial output would also pose a problem. China's urban population and labour force had grown around 50 per cent from 1952–57, putting great stress on food supplies. In purely *economic* terms, the imbalance between agriculture and industry could threaten the success of an industrialization strategy that gave primary emphasis to industry.

Economics aside, Soviet-style industrialization posed severe *political* problems. The Soviet Union had paid a very high price for its industrial achievements: the devastation of its peasantry (including 7 to 10 million deaths), which it looted for capital, and in partial consequence the long-term stagnation of its agriculture. It was politically possible for Stalin to pay this price because the peasantry was not the leading component of the revolutionary coalition that brought the Bolsheviks to power and sustained them.

Table 2.1 Annual growth rates of grain and cotton output, 1953–57

Year	Growth of foodgrain output over previous year (%)	Growth of cotton output over previous year (%)
1953	1.6	−9.9
1954	1.3	−10.1
1955	8.9	42.5
1956	0.3	−5.7
1957	4.9	13.5

Source: Computed from Eckstein, 1980, p. 63.

The Bolsheviks also had little feeling for, understanding of, or organizational base in the peasantry. It was much more difficult for the leaders of China's rural-based revolution to exploit the peasants. The experience of the mass line also made it difficult for many Chinese leaders—particularly those in agreement with Mao—to accept the bureaucratization, hierarchy, inegalitarianism and concentration of authority that accompanied the Soviet model. Meanwhile, the decline of dual rule at the expense of vertical, technocratic authority reduced the role of the party *vis-à-vis* more apolitical government institutions and officials, many of whom were trained and had risen to their posts in the Guomindang period.

Finally, the dependence on the Soviet Union which the First Five Year Plan engendered grated on the nationalist sensibilities of the Chinese people, while difficulties in day-to-day social relations between Soviet and Chinese officials and experts caused irritation. The deep concern about Soviet influence in China was expressed perhaps most pointedly in the first purge of a top party leader since the establishment of the People's Republic. In late 1953, the party Politburo decided to expel Gao Gang, the head of the party and government in Manchuria, which has a long border with the Soviet Union (and had recently been under Japanese rule for over a decade), for establishing an 'independent kingdom' there. Gao was particularly close to the Soviet leadership, having visited the Soviet Union several times. He had gone further than any other Chinese leader in implementing Soviet-style industrialization. So the anti-Soviet overtones of his purge were clear.

In retrospect, then, it is clear that the Chinese leadership undertook the Soviet-style strategy for rapid industrialization with a definite ambivalence. The extent and contours of political controversy which the plan may have engendered remain shrouded. It has not been subjected to the sort of thoroughgoing vilification that the Maoists later visited upon the subsequent and somewhat similar period after the Great Leap Forward, or that the present leadership has heaped upon the Great Leap Forward and the Cultural Revolution.[7] But the plan was indirectly yet clearly criticized by Mao in a major 1956 speech entitled 'On the Ten Major Relationships', where he expressed concern about imbalances between, among others, inland and coast, centre and locality, and, most prominently, industry and agriculture (Mao, 1977, pp. 284–307).[8] This last question was causing serious controversy among planners and politicians, and was at the root of the unexpected decision to promote rural cooperativization.[9]

The Socialist Transformation in Agriculture, 1953–57: Mutual Aid Teams and Cooperatives

The land reform destroyed the landlord class, but left in place a definite class structure, in which poor peasants had less land and capital than middle and rich peasants. These inequalities soon began to provide the basis for new kinds of class exploitation in many places. Poor peasants whose holdings were too small to get by were forced to borrow money or rent land from rich peasants, sell their labour to them, and in some cases—for example, when loans could not be repaid—even sell their land to them.

The party viewed these developments with alarm, and took several creative steps to stop them. First, it began in the early 1950s to promote the development of mutual aid teams. These were voluntary associations of several households—generally five to ten or so—that exchanged labour and resources with each other on a temporary, seasonal or year-round basis. The mutual aid teams had several benefits. They helped raise production through shared knowledge and rationalized utilization of productive factors—for example, households with more land than they could farm efficiently could combine with those with too much labour, to the advantage of both. They provided peasants in economic straits with a way to resolve their problems without having to turn to rich peasants for 'help'. They were also a first step toward collective forms of organization which the party had in mind for the future. The formation of mutual aid teams was promoted in several ways: through mass line methods of persuasion, mobilization and emulation; by designing them in conformity with the traditional contours of civil society—i.e., along kinship or neighbourhood lines; and by offering material benefits such as preferential marketing opportunities and credit. Rich peasants and landlords were excluded in order to ensure that they would not utilize the mutual aid teams as ways of organizing exploitation of their poor neighbours. In fact, to the extent that the mutual aid teams denied rich peasants opportunities for exploitation, they constituted the first step in the gradual attack on the rich peasants as a class, which was the next phase of China's class struggle.

A second step in this attack was the institution of unified grain purchase and supply in late 1953. Peasants were required to sell specified quotas of grain to the state; surpluses could be saved, sold to the state at premium prices, sold to local supply and marketing cooperatives, sold on government-regulated markets, or exchanged in limited quantities with neighbours. To encourage production, prices were set in accordance with local market conditions, and quotas at levels well within the productive capacities of each household. Private grain merchants were closed down. All sales of grain to cities were now handled by government agencies. Unified grain purchase and supply had a double effect on the economic class relations in the countryside: it gave poor peasants a place to turn when they were short of grain, so they did not fall into the clutches of rich peasants or merchants; and it undercut the incomes and economic activities of the latter groups, who had made good money by taking advantage of the seasonal ebb and flow of grain prices.

A third measure was the establishment of rural credit cooperatives, which operated on the same principle as unified purchase and supply. By providing an alternative source of credit, it undercut one more in a shrinking repertoire of mechanisms by which richer peasants could exploit the poor. By 1954, mutual aid, unified purchase and supply, and credit cooperatives had in effect set up formidable obstacles to exploitation through rent, speculation and usury. Within the parameters set by the unequal ownership of land, it was increasingly difficult to get rich or stay rich except by working hard and producing more.

In the meantime, the question of agricultural cooperativization was beginning to present itself, though for different reasons to different leaders. There was a broad consensus that the Soviet approach—Stalin's attack on the peasantry during the Soviet collectivization and the havoc this wrought on agriculture—was to be avoided in China. But beyond that there were disagreements about the purposes and pace of cooperativization.

For some, its primary purpose was to guarantee grain supplies to the state to feed workers and finance industrialization. They advocated a gradual pace of cooperativization so as not to interfere with production or induce peasants to consume or hide the surpluses which the state needed. In line with their overriding concern for production, the advocates of this position also argued that it made little sense to form coops until such time as they could be equipped with modern agricultural inputs from industry (such as tractors, cement and chemical fertilizer), so their larger scale could be best put at the service of increased production. Liu Shaoqi was the most prominent person associated with this view; he criticized the 'premature' establishment of coops and ordered their disbandment.

For others, including most prominently Mao, the major purpose of coops was to combat rural class inequality and stratification (mainly by eliminating the rich peasant class) and to transform the rural mode of production from one based on the individualism of private smallholders to one based on cooperative forms of management and work. To head off the potential snowball of class restratification, no time could be lost in forming coops, it was argued. Moreover, coops did not need to wait for the availability of modern inputs. They could register increases in production by rationalizing the use of existing productive factors—for example, by organizing labour more efficiently and optimizing the utilization of existing scarce inputs and resources (such as oxen or tractors).

The difference between these positions could be summed up thus: some were primarily concerned with collecting from the peasants, and some with collecting them together. A consensus for the former position had formed among the top leadership of the party by mid-1955, which was reflected in Vice-Premier Li Fuchun's report to the Second Session of the First National People's Congress. Li said:

Only when agriculture . . . turn[s] gradually from individual to collective management, and on this basis equip[s itself] . . . with modern technique, can the productive forces of agriculture be greatly developed, its capacity for reproduction increased and output raised *to meet the demands of the nation's industrialization*. (Li, 1955, p. 47; emphasis added.)

Within weeks of Li's speech, Mao countered with his own, in which he replaced the previous goal of 1,000,000 coops by the end of 1957 with a new one of 1,300,000 by autumn 1956. He took on the opposition directly:

An upsurge in the new, socialist mass movement is imminent throughout the countryside. But some of our comrades, tottering along like a woman with bound feet, are complaining all the time, 'You're going too fast, much too fast.' Too much carping, unwarranted complaints, boundless anxiety and countless taboos—all this they take as the right policy to guide the socialist mass movement in the rural areas. No, this is not the right policy, it is the wrong one. (Mao, 1977, p. 184.)

To be sure, Mao spoke of the productive benefits that would accrue from cooperativization and that in turn would aid industrialization (Mao, 1977, p. 197). But he also emphasized:

As is clear to everyone, the spontaneous forces of capitalism have been steadily growing in recent years, with new rich peasants springing up everywhere and many well-to-do middle peasants striving to become rich peasants. On the other hand, many poor peasants are still living in poverty for shortage of the means of production, with some getting into debt and others selling or renting out their land. If this tendency goes unchecked, it is inevitable that polarization in the countryside will get worse day by day. Those peasants who lose their land and those who remain in poverty will complain that we are doing nothing to save them from ruin or help them out of their difficulties. (Mao, 1977, p. 202.)

Mao's bold stroke settled the issue. Cooperativization accelerated rapidly. Within six months, 1,900,000 lower-stage agricultural producers' cooperatives (LAPCs) had been organized, half again as many as Mao had called for in his upwardly revised target. The LAPCs averaged around thirty households. But this number was flexible so that, in the interests of providing a workable social base, the composition of the cooperatives could fit the traditional contours of civil society. For example, a cooperative would normally be formed around a small hamlet or a neighbourhood of a larger village. Or where there were feuding lineages whose rivalry might interfere with the smooth operation of the cooperatives, the lines could be drawn along rather than across clan lines. Towards this same end of maximizing social support for the LAPCs, they were organized in a participatory and voluntary process. The party went all out to use its time-honoured mass line methods of persuasion and mobilization, and there is no evidence that coercion or administrative fiat were employed to any serious degree.

The LAPCs differed from the mutual aid teams not only in size, but also in the fact that now productive resources were actually pooled and farming was carried out collectively. In terms of productive relations, they were 'semi-socialist', i.e., peasants owned unequal numbers of shares in accordance with the amount of property they had contributed. The net income of the cooperative was distributed partly as interest on shares, and partly as remuneration for work done. Thus the socialist principle of 'pay according to work' coexisted with the capitalist principle of 'pay according to ownership'. In order to minimize the effect of the latter—which averaged around a quarter of output—and to prevent the cooperatives from being used for economic exploitation of those with fewer shares, more prosperous and pro-pertied middle peasants were to be drawn into the cooperatives only gradu-ally, and rich peasants were to be excluded altogether.[10]

In fact, by this time many rich peasants were ready to capitulate and join cooperatives, partly because their economic opportunities had already been so circumscribed by credit and commercial policies, and partly because they saw the writing on the wall and felt they ought to join up before their property was expropriated. But the party was not yet prepared to have cooperatives accept them. In class terms, the LAPCs constituted yet another blow to the rich peasants, who were now deprived of the supply of hired labour which many of them still depended upon to work their relatively larger holdings. So their last remaining legal and practical source of wealth—their property—was also made less of an advantage (Shue, 1980, p. 299). One device used to drive this point home was for the cooperative members to help rich peasants work land which the latter could not work themselves. This helped increase production, and by not accepting any payment for this work the cooperative members were able to embarrass the rich peasants, while at the same time providing a living lesson to themselves and the rich peasants about the superiority of cooperative farming.

Now events were moving very rapidly. Mao's speech had triggered a flurry of grassroots activism among peasants and local cadres that whet appetites for still further socialist advances. Moreover, the poor peasants were unhappy with the fact that some of their wealthier neighbours who did the same amount of work in the LAPCs were receiving more income merely because they had come out of the land reform with more property. These high spirits and pressures eventuated in the nationwide movement to form higher-stage agricultural producers' cooperatives (HAPCs). By mid-1956, eighteen months sooner than the target date which the party had set in January of the same year (and which was itself advanced from earlier targets by one or two years!), 90 per cent of the peasantry had formed almost half a million HAPCs. They were much larger than LAPCs, averaging 160 households. They were also fully socialist in character: shares were abolished, and distribution was solely according to work. As before, the boundaries of the HAPCs were drawn along the contours of civil society. There is a debate about the extent to which the higher-stage cooperativization was brought about by the mass line politics of previous stages. Some Western scholars argue that the rapidity of the movement violated the step-by-step approach of the past, and could not have occurred without state coercion, threats or administrative fiat (Selden, 1982). This is also the position now taken by the Dengist leadership in China. Other Western scholars note that the tendency to 'strike while the iron is hot', returning later to 'rectify' mistakes and 'deviations', is deeply rooted in Maoist political practice (Shue, 1980, p. 323 and *passim*). For now there is simply not enough evidence from objective first-hand accounts or research to resolve this debate.

But two points can be advanced confidently about the issue of coercion. First, the movement to form HAPCs in China did not involve the use of military force, physical violence and mass deportations, as was the case in the Soviet collectivization. Nor did Chinese peasants respond with the widespread sabotage or passive resistance that their Russian colleagues did. As a result, the Chinese rural economy was not thrown into anything like the economic crisis that occurred in the Soviet Union. Although growth in grain production in 1956 was slow (partly because it was so high in the previous year), it was very good in 1957 (Table 2.1).

Second, the use of coercion, threats or administrative fiat assumes an unwillingness to join the cooperatives. No doubt some peasants felt this way: many (though, we will see, not all) rich and middle peasants stood to lose out, and no doubt some poor peasants had their doubts about the feasibility of the large new units. There is no question but that coercion, threats and administrative fiat were sometimes used to get such people into coops. But the party regularly and vociferously criticized such tactics, branding them as 'commandist' and therfore inconsistent with the mass line. The party's policy had always been that each new stage since the land reform could only be taken if the likely result were increased income for 90–95 per cent of those involved. The logic of cooperativization was, then, predicated on economic self-interest and its consonance with cooperative economic organization.

This consonance was, in the party's view, built into the cooperative form itself: this was the belief in the economic superiority of socialism. But, as with mutual aid, the party also took steps to make the cooperatives economically attractive by offering credit, tax and marketing advantages to them. In some cases, for example, rich peasants actually raised their incomes by joining the HAPCs because the heavy taxes which they had been forced to pay as individual farmers exceeded their incomes from property ownership. And while available data are incomplete, it is very likely that the poor peasant majority saw its income rise with each new socialist advance. It is not at all clear that the cooperativization was broadly unpopular (and so would require widespread coercion). On the contrary, it probably advanced the economic interests of most peasants, including even some rich peasants, at least in the short run.

At the same time, the higher-stage cooperativization dealt yet another blow to the rich peasantry by undermining the last major element in the structure of private ownership and enterprise which had operated in their long-run interest. Now the drive for cooperatives was to be complete. At the grassroots level, the cooperatives needed to incorporate the property of the rich peasants, and at the centre the party offered to convert their official class status (and that of former landlords) to that of ordinary peasants as a way of softening the blow and reducing their resistance. So the former rich peasants were now drawn into the HAPCs. By 1956, then, the goal of complete equality of ownership of productive resources within villages, which during the land reform just a few years earlier had been cherished by the poor but resisted by the party, was realized.

It is frequently argued that in general economic equality and growth are incompatible. But the Chinese cooperativization advanced both. It did not harm agricultural production in the short run. It laid the foundation for further development of agriculture. By enlarging the fields, it facilitated the use of tractors. The larger size of the production unit more generally made it possible to rationalize resource utilization. The capacity of the cooperative to coordinate large amounts of labour and resources also enabled it to undertake infrastructure projects (such as farmland reclamation and water conservancy) which were beyond the scope of individual households but were necessary for further agricultural development. The elimination of payments to property (that is, rent and interest), which even under the LAPCs had amounted to nearly one-quarter of output, freed resources to help finance such development projects. The cooperatives provided an institutional context for developing and promulgating new agricultural techniques and information. There is another dimension to this as well: while most individual households would not be willing to take the risks involved in trying a new technique, the coops could do so by allocating a small amount of resources to experimentation and reducing the risks involved by spreading them over a large number of households.

Political Conflict, 1956–57

Political conflict was building up slowly during the 1950s with the debate over cooperativization and a definite concern, at least on Mao's part, about some of the effects of the First Five Year Plan. It heated up in 1956 and 1957 and found expression in the Hundred Flowers movement and the subsequent anti-rightist campaign.

As the Second Five Year Plan for 1958–62 began to be considered, both supporters and critics of the first plan began to focus on intellectuals to advance their positions. But they did so in very different ways. Leaders who wanted the second plan to follow the basic contours of the first plan emphasized the need for the scientific and technical intelligentsia to contribute their talents and skills to make it work effectively. New inventions, better techniques, more scientific management, would all contribute to the industrialization effort. They urged the party to adopt policies to encourage these intellectuals by allowing them latitude to select and pursue their enquiry and promoting scientific debate. Other leaders who were concerned with the political implications of the first plan—such as bureaucracy, elitism and authoritarianism—saw intellectuals as a potent source of criticism of these tendencies. In this context, a movement to encourage more intellectual autonomy and freedom of expression—in Mao's phrase, to 'Let a hundred flowers bloom, a hundred schools of thought contend'—was launched in 1956. Naturally, the direction and scope of the movement were hotly contended, and China's intellectuals were caught and eventually wounded in the crossfire.

Many top party leaders, and most of the middle-level party and government officials, sought to restrict the Hundred Flowers movement. At best it threatened their growing political prerogatives by subjecting their exercise of authority in ministries and factories to scientific scrutiny: economic bureaucrats would now have to justify their actions to economists, factory managers to engineers, and so forth. At worst, the movement presented the prospect of a broad-gauged political critique of the way power was organized and wielded in an increasingly bureaucratic China, or even of socialism itself. The spectre of Hungary—where critical intellectuals had been at the heart of an uprising that was only put down with (heaven forbid, the more patriotic among them must have thought!) the 'help' of the Soviet Union—haunted many party leaders. For all these reasons they had little interest in hearing from scientists and technical specialists, much less from socially- and politically-minded critics. The Hundred Flowers movement was given formal approval at the CCP's Eighth Congress, but then conveniently set aside. It was actually suppressed in early 1957.

It was precisely this sort of bureaucratic defensiveness with which Mao was concerned. In February he went on the attack. In an important speech—to a government rather than party forum—he warned of the rise of 'contradictions' between the party leadership and the people, and began to speak of class struggle under socialism.[11] In Marxist discourse the concept of class struggle carries a definite dialectical grandeur, and is linked to nothing less than revolution. Mao was, therefore, opening a Pandora's box whose contents were utterly new and, to many in the state leadership, quite dangerous—the prospect of revolution in a socialist state, pitting the masses against their leaders. For now Mao felt that the main battleground of such conflict was ideological, so he stopped short of trying to mobilize mass uprisings (a stage to which he would elevate the struggle within a decade during the Cultural Revolution). In 1957 he contented himself with trying to draw out the ideological issues and cleavages by inviting comments and criticisms from the intellectuals.

The speech was not published immediately, and in the next few months the party bureaucracy tried to downplay it while Mao pressed the point. Mao prevailed, a party rectification campaign was launched, and a torrent of criticism from intellectuals—who at first held back, fearing the consequences and remembering that the Hundred Flowers movement had been put on hold—issued forth. *Ad hoc* organizations of students, writers and liberal political figures sprang up, public forums were held, and 'big character posters' and underground newspapers appeared, often carrying scathing attacks. The Hundred Flowers movement was revived and accelerated.

The content of many of the criticisms shocked and worried even Mao. To be sure, Mao elicited the attacks on bureaucracy, elitism and authoritarianism he had sought. But many critics went further, attacking the state for failing to live up to socialist ideals in general or, even more serious, critiquing socialism itself. By June, the party, with Mao's support, launched an 'anti-rightist' campaign. Mao's February speech was published, but in a revised version which contained criteria by which to identify permissible and impermissible criticisms. Specifically, they should help promote 'socialist transformation', 'people's democratic dictatorship', 'democratic centralism', and the party, among others. The anti-rightist campaign came down most heavily on outspoken writers who demanded that literature and art conform to concrete reality rather than socialist realism, i.e., that it reflect actual and not ideal conditions. Ding Ling, the brilliant leftist writer who had been an important party leader in cultural affairs, was expelled from the party, banished to labour reform, and had her works taken out of circulation. Others, including liberal politicians and ideologists who had joined the state and been bold enough to use the opportunity to voice deep criticisms against socialism or the state's socialist character, were 'sent down' (*xia fang*) to the countryside for re-education or subjected to mass criticism (in some cases by their own children) and self-criticism, after which they resumed not insignificant political positions within a few years. In any event, the effect of the anti-rightist campaign on the intellectuals and on the possibility of legitimate dissent in socialist China was chilling.

Some scholars have argued that Mao's reversal was supremely Machiavellian: he drew intellectual opponents into the open, used them to put a scare into the party bureaucracy and make his ideological points against them; and then eliminated them. Others feel that Mao simply failed to anticipate the depth and nature of criticism then extant in Chinese society, or that he focused too exclusively on his own critical preoccupations. Without some way of getting a deeper insight into Mao's own thinking at the time, the question cannot be resolved. In any event, this series of events indicates just how difficult it was for Chinese socialism to subject itself or be subjected to sympathetic critique—that is, criticism which proceeded from a commitment to socialist values. Partly the problem was a lack of consensus on what those values were or ought to be; partly it was the inability of the state leadership, including Mao, to accept and tolerate criticism which pushed up against or beyond what they took to be the ill-defined boundaries of socialist commitment, or to recognize that others may have drawn the boundaries differently. This problem would continue to plague Chinese politics.

The Great Leap Forward

By 1957, basic transformations in China's class structure and institutions of political economy were complete. The gentry, rich peasantry, and various bourgeois strata had been dispatched, industry and commerce nationalized or collectivized, and agriculture cooperativized. This had all been accomplished without economic crisis, and the security of the socialist state had been preserved against pronounced foreign threats. The early phases of socialist transition and consolidation could be said to be over.

Now attention had to be turned to deeper structural questions. In agriculture, there were the long-standing problems of underemployment and low labour productivity. This was partly a product of China's enormous population and its limited space—even today China must support around 22 per cent of the world's population on 8 per cent of the world's arable land. Throughout the 1950s no effort was made in China to restrict population; in fact, the warnings of some demographers were drowned out by Maoist paeans to the virtues of a large population and noisy denunciations of Malthusian theory as bourgeois ideology. Underemployment and low labour productivity also had to do with the failure of Chinese agriculture to make a breakthrough to modern technology. China's traditional agriculture was, to be sure, one of the most advanced in the pre-modern world, having achieved very high levels of land yield through the accumulation of centuries of experience and the very intensive application of labour to land. (Much Chinese farming is more aptly called gardening.) For this reason, Chinese agriculture was butting up against the limits of its traditional technological base, a phenomenon known as a 'high-level equilibrium trap' (Elvin, 1973, pp. 298–316). Without introducing modern technological inputs, Chinese agriculture could produce no more than around 185 million metric tons of grain, a level it had reached by the mid-1950s (Stavis, 1974, pp. 7–11). The reorganization effected by cooperativization had rationalized the use of existing resources, enabling more to be squeezed from them than ever before; but it had not itself introduced the new ones that were needed.

But in 1957 China was not yet ready to embrace modern agriculture and its implications. Much Western agricultural technology—which was orientated to the more extensive, less labour-intensive agrarian system of the United States and Western Europe—was inapplicable to Chinese conditions. The 'green revolution' technology in advanced seed strains and associated inputs was just beginning to be developed. Chinese industry was not geared to the production of agricultural inputs, so a simple shift in sectoral priorities toward agriculture would not have helped agriculture very much.

Industry had problems of its own, too. With agricultural growth levelling off after the post-war recovery, it was increasingly difficult to use it to finance further expansion of the industrial base, which the Second Five Year Plan envisioned as following the expensive, high accumulation, capital-intensive, heavy industrial emphasis of the first plan. Meanwhile, urban unemployment was rising, partly as a result of migration of peasants to cities, while the strategy of heavy industrialization promoted capital- rather than labour-intensive production.

The appearance of these structural problems in the economy was accompanied by conjunctural ones in politics. Relations with the Soviet Union were deteriorating after 1956, as the Chinese leadership began to distrust Khrushchev, whom they regarded as unpredictable and unreliable (because of his surprise denunciation of Stalin), and potentially dangerous (because of his invasion of Hungary). Moreover, China had actually begun to register negative balances in its economic relations with the Soviet Union after 1956 as it repaid earlier loans. So at best the Soviet Union could not be counted upon to assist China in solving its economic problems, and at worst was beginning to pose a new threat.

Another conjuncture was the sharpening political conflict in China. Through the First Five Year Plan, lines of disagreement had begun to be drawn between certain leaders associated with the party and government bureaucracies, who favoured a development strategy for China patterned broadly on the Soviet model, and others whose continuing commitment to the revolutionary values forged in Yan'an days led them to be critical of that strategy and to begin to seek something different but as yet ill-defined. As we have seen, this political conflict had come into the open in the debate over cooperativization and in the conduct of the Hundred Flowers campaign.

The structural economic problems which China was facing could have been met with an attempt to muddle through. Indeed, muddling through has proven a viable option in the post-Stalinist Soviet economy for decades now. The Second Five Year Plan proposed just such a 'solution'. But in China politics—as always—made the difference. Mao would not sit still for business as usual, and he was able to seize upon innovations forged by peasants and local cadres and to capitalize upon the strain in Sino–Soviet relations to launch China on a different and historically unprecedented path of political change and economic development known as the Great Leap Forward.

Overall, the logic of the Leap involved four basic elements, each a signifi-cant departure from that of the five year plans. First, the priority of heavy industry was to be replaced with a simultaneous emphasis on heavy industry, light industry and agriculture. But this was not just a matter of sectoral priority in a macroeconomic plan. Second, and corollary, the very distinction between industry and agriculture, and between urban and rural, was to be overcome in the economy and also in social life and consciousness. Farms were to have industries, and peasants were to work in them; urban factories were to raise food, and to help peasants harvest crops in the busy seasons. Third, the emphasis on capital intensity, which was proving difficult to sustain financially and also was not addressing China's employment problem, was now to be reversed. Economic growth was to be fuelled by mobilizing the resource with which China was most well endowed—labour. Fourth, central planning, which took the entire economy as its unit and strove to maximize efficiency and comparative advantage nationally, was to give way to a more decentralized pattern with local and regional horizons of calculation and self-reliance.

In the countryside, the Great Leap involved the creation of large units known as people's communes. It is important to emphasize that they were the product of spontaneous mass creativity as well as radical leadership. Peasants and local cadres at the grassroots had begun experimenting with amalgamations of HAPCs in early 1958, and in the context of an excellent summer harvest the movement acquired a momentum of its own over the summer. It caught the attention of Mao and his associates, who dubbed these new units 'people's communes' and put their imprimatur on them. The pace of events caught the more circumspect of China's leaders off guard, and by August an enlarged session of the Politburo had no choice but to state its approval.

The communes departed from the coops in several important respects. First, they were combined units of political, social and economic life. They incorporated township (*xiang*) governments and local units of party organization that had remained distinct from the cooperatives, while also providing an expanded array of social services and functions (such as child care, health services, education, food and in places even housing). Second, they combined agriculture and industry. They had their own factories and workshops, and integrated them with farming not only in management and finance but also planning, turning out industrial inputs for agriculture and industrial products using agricultural outputs. Third, they were much larger than cooperatives. When first formed in 1958 they averaged around 5,000 households, and after being reduced to more manageable size in 1959 they still averaged 1,600 households, ten times the HAPC average of 160.

Nevertheless, in its August document the party specified important continuities with the cooperatives. They were owned collectively (by their members), not by the 'whole people' (through the agency of state ownership).

Organization and management of day-to-day work were to take place at the level of the 'production brigade'—roughly equivalent to the HAPC— which in turn was broken down into 'groups' (*zu*) roughly the size of an LAPC.[12] The principle of distribution was socialist (according to work), not communist (according to need). Although private plots were to be gradually eliminated, private ownership of other petty productive resources (such as pigs, chickens and fruit trees around houses) and personal effects were preserved.

In addition, the party repeatedly urged prudence, caution and flexibility in the pace of the transition to, and the institutional form of, the new communes. But these admonitions were not to be heard. The last half of 1958 was one of the most radical periods in Chinese socialism. By its end almost every Chinese peasant was a commune member. Vestiges of private ownership of productive forces and even many consumer goods were eliminated. Communist principles of distribution came into use in many places, with allocation according to need (as in the 'free supply' of grain in communal dining halls) or to strict egalitarianism. Rural industries sprouted up everywhere, and with some very unlikely lines of production (including the infamous 'backyard steel furnaces'). Large contingents of workers, including a massive mobilization of female labour, were set to work on infrastructure projects both during the farming months but especially in the traditional slack season of winter., By 1959, women accounted for 40–50 per cent of the labour days outside the home, and 70 per cent of China's children were cared for in nurseries. Mass educational efforts, including part-time and evening schools, short courses, and work–study programmes, were established to disseminate industrial skills among the peasantry, and propaganda campaigns were carried out emphasizing the basic equality of peasants on the one hand and cadres and intellectuals on the other. These actually went beyond mere propaganda to attempts to prove the point in practice. For example, peasants were encouraged to write, paint and discuss philosophy. Militia work, too, was integrated with production and education. It was a time of genuine enthusiasm and very high hopes. New horizons were opened up on all fronts, as many peasants gained their first experience outside farming or outside the narrow confines of the village of their birth. As one peasant recalled: 'Those were great days! Great days! . . . Every time I recall those days I am filled with happiness' (Hinton, 1984, pp. 217–18).

In the cities, too, there was an attempt to construct people's communes—integrated units of agriculture and industry, and of political, economic and social organization. But they proved unfeasible even in the heady atmosphere of the Great Leap. Workers simply could not find enough urban land to grow crops or enough time to commute to suburbs (where the land belonged to the rural communes anyway).

This abortive movement aside, urban industry underwent its own momentous changes. First, there was a major decentralization of state planning and administration. Provincial and local authorities were now permitted to retain up to 20 per cent of certain taxes and of the profits of state industries. They were also given greater latitude in spending these funds. This amounted to a shift away from the one-sided policy of vertical rule under the First Five Year Plan toward a more balanced one of dual rule, with horizontally organized authorities at the provincial and local levels gaining some financial resources and administrative power.

Second, a similar change took place at the factory level. The heavily vertical one-man management in the factories, which had already come under attack from workers in 1956 and 1957, was replaced by a more dualistic one known as 'responsibility of the factory manager under the administration of the Party committee'. This also enhanced party authority *vis-à-vis* that of the bureaucracy and technocracy. Third was a set of factory management reforms known as 'two participations, one reform and triple combination': that is, participation by managers in manual labour and workers in management, reform of the complex factory rules established in the previous years, and the formation of teams comprised of workers, technicians and political cadres at various levels of organization and spheres of work. Fourth, more collectivist forms of distribution and material incentive were implemented, and were supplemented by non-material incentives. Fifth, mass education, propaganda and popular culture campaigns emphasizing the equality of workers and cadres and the evils of social differentiation, like those undertaken in the countryside, were carried out.

A new record for grain production was set in 1958, which may in the end have been unfortunate in so far as it masked some of the deep problems with the communes that would soon become evident. But there were also more purposive forces which acted to conceal the severity of the situation. In the flush of enthusiasm backed up by intense political pressure, a wave of over-reporting by local cadres broke out, in which the most outlandish claims—as much as 270 tons of grain per hectare (compared with an average of 1.6 in 1957!)—were made. Actually, things were much worse than before. In 1959, grain production was back to the level of 1953, 1960 was the worst year since 1950, and the 1958 level would not be surpassed until 1966. These are absolute figures; in per-capita terms matters were even more disastrous. The Chinese population suffered a net loss of 20 to 25 million people in 1960 and 1961, including both deaths and expected births which did not happen due to deferral of pregnancy, conception failures and miscarriages. Clearly the Great Leap resulted in human suffering on a gargantuan scale.

The causes of the collapse were many and varied. It proved difficult for the relatively inexperienced and untrained rural cadres to administer the finances and manage the production of units as large as the commune. Size also cut into the peasants' ability to monitor each other's work, as had been possible in the face-to-face scale of social organization of the cooperatives. Incentives suffered in other ways. With much income being distributed collectively (for example, in the form of free food in dining halls) and equally (such as in the form of free services), the link between work and reward was broken or at least weakened severely. And the combination of formerly richer and poorer coops and villages acted as disincentive for both: the poor felt less need to work since they had profited from a windfall by being thrown together with the rich, while the rich saw little point in working since they were being dragged down by the poor anyway.

But incentives were not the whole problem. The Great Leap Forward was also a time of intensification and mobilization of labour on an unprecedented scale. But some of this labour was squandered on poorly planned industrial or infrastructure projects, and some was simply not that productive. For example, in the flush of enthusiasm for these projects, agriculture was sometimes left to women inexperienced in farming or to incapable old or young people. Nature did not help: 1959–61 were meteorologically three of the worst years of the century for China, with 60 per cent of cultivated land suffering drought or flood. Even in the absence of the positive and negative effects of Chinese socialism—on the plus side, the water conservancy projects carried out beginning in 1957 and the advent of a political commitment and institutional capacity to care for the poor, and on the negative side the defects of the Great Leap—these would have been years of human disaster on a massive scale.

Industry also suffered, though somewhat differently and with much less human cost. Industrial output value rose 55 per cent in 1958, 36 per cent in 1959 and 11 per cent in 1960, and only started its fall in 1961 (dropping 38 per cent, and another 17 per cent in 1962). But output figures do not tell the full story. They were achieved at tremendous cost and at the expense of output quality. The most infamous instance was the 'backyard steel furnaces', in which peasants produced three million of the national total of eleven million tons of steel in 1958. But the steel was so poor in quality that it often proved utterly useless. Fuel and ore were used wastefully or were gathered in ways which had deleterious effects on the environment (by stripping forests of wood) or on resource reserves (by stripping mines without regard to future access). Financial costs were very high, but this was not apparent at the time since so many of them—for example, the value of locally gathered fuel and ore—went unaccounted (because they were 'free' to the commune, which could obtain them simply by mobilizing its own labour force to work in its own mines and forests). In hundreds of other, smaller ways, efficiency, cost economy and quality were sacrificed on the almighty altar of gross output.

The summary pull-out of all Soviet assistance in 1960 exacerbated the crisis (though, unlike the disastrous weather, it could be argued that here the Chinese were partly to blame for adopting industrial policies which the Soviet Union could only regard as foolhardy).

Despite all this, there were some positive results of the Great Leap Forward. Much valuable agrarian infrastructure was built. Peasants were exposed to and gained experience with industry, in what would prove to be the first steps toward China's unique and largely successful rural industrial-ization. The Great Leap also managed to break the hegemony of the Soviet-style heavy industrialization strategy that had been tried in China: light industry and agriculture would subsequently get higher priority from both Maoists and Dengists, and serious attempts would be made to integrate them in a more balanced approach to economic development. Finally, it created the integrated unit of political, economic and social organization known as the people's commune which, after some organizational readjustment, would prove to be one of the most important and successful institutions of collective agriculture in the history of socialism.

Recovery, Readjustment and Political Conflict

By early 1959, there was a consensus in the top leadership that the commune movement had developed serious excesses, but a disagreement about their seriousness and nature. At a party meeting in March, Mao himself criticized the appearance of a 'communist wind', which was manifest in 'levelling poor and rich, ... excessive accumulation and labour responsibilities, and ... "making public" all sorts of "property"'. (This last phrase was a play on the word 'communism', in which in Chinese is comprised of the characters for 'public' and 'property'.) He called for distinctions between proper and improper public ownership, and stressed that any private property taken over by the communes must be paid for, since it had belonged to peasants, not exploiters. He condemned summary movement toward ownership and management at the level of the large commune, stressing instead the need for gradual development based on the smaller brigades and teams (Mao, 1969, pp. 279-88). Others in the party—most prominently Peng Dehuai, the Chief of Staff of the People's Liberation Army—thought Mao's criticisms of the Great Leap did not go far enough. Peng condemned the commune movement outright as *'petit bourgeois* fanaticism', arguing that it had alienated the party from the people and destroyed central control of the economy.

Mao and Peng confronted each other openly in July and August at a party conference in Lushan, where both suffered political setbacks. Mao assumed the blame for many of the problems of the Great Leap, including the 'backyard steel furnaces', which he called a 'great catastrophe'. 'The chaos caused was on a grand scale and I take responsibility.' He admitted that 'I am a complete outsider when it comes to economic construction, and I understand nothing about industrial planning'. He invited criticism: 'If you don't agree with me then argue back'. But he also sought to spread responsibility for the Leap's errors among other leaders both at the centre and local levels. While he admitted that 'the one with the most responsibility is me', he also blamed others in the top leadership and especially radical cadres in the communes and counties, 'who extorted things from production brigades and teams. This is bad. The masses disliked it . . . Comrades, you must all analyse your own responsibility. If you have to shit, shit! If you have to fart, fart! You will feel much better for it'. He even held out for a more balanced view of the Great Leap: 'It is not a complete failure. Is it mainly a failure? No, it's only a partial failure'. He credited the party with having stemmed much of the 'communist wind' (that is, excessively rapid transition beyond socialism to communism) since earlier in the year, when he had criticized it (Schram (ed.), 1974, pp. 131-46). In perhaps the most stunning remark of this remarkable speech, Mao struck back at Peng Dehuai, and in the same breath threatened the party with civil war if it challenged him.

If we do ten things and nine are bad, and they are all published in the press, then we will certainly perish, and will deserve to perish. In that case, I will go to the countryside to lead the peasants to overthrow the government. If those of you in the Liberation Army won't follow me, then I will go and find a Red Army. But I think the Liberation Army would follow me. (Schram (ed.), 1974, p. 139.)

By invoking his own popular base, disarming his critics through self-criticism, reminding the rest of the party leadership of its own involvement in the Leap and, implicitly, the consequent erosion of its political base, and in general playing upon its desire for political stability and fear of civil strife, Mao was able to ride out the political storm. Peng Dehuai and his followers were removed from office and publicly vilified for organizing an 'anti-Party clique'. But Mao, too, took a fall. Liu Shaoqi was appointed Chairman of the

People's Republic, a position held by Mao until just a few months before. For the next several years, Mao occupied himself with moulding the general direction of policy and ideology, while leaving the actual administration of the affairs of party and government to others, supreme among them Liu Shaoqi. He would later complain that during these years he was rarely consulted, and in general was 'treated as a dead ancestor' (Schram (ed.), 1974, pp. 266–7).

In the context of the sharp criticisms of the Great Leap that had emerged at the party centre in 1959 and of the deepening economic crisis of 1959 and 1960, systematic retrenchments took place on all fronts. In urban areas the fleeting experiments with people's communes were abolished and, under a major financial retrenchment, thousands of construction projects were cancelled or stopped in midstream. Worker participation in management gave way to greater authority for managers. Draconian individual material incentives were put back into practice. Central planning was restored as 'trusts'—in effect, vertically integrated state monopolies—were established and held to stricter financial accountability. Urban employment was cut back by evicting the approximately twenty million peasants who had taken up jobs and residence in the cities. They were to return to their villages and get to work producing badly needed crops.

In the countryside, the communes were reduced in size by one-third through 1959 and 1960. A 1962 organizational scheme and set of regulations known as the Sixty Articles codified many changes that had already taken place (Selden (ed.), 1979, pp. 521–6). The 'basic accounting unit'—the level of collective organization at which actual production was managed, accounts kept and income shared—was lowered from the large commune to the brigade (roughly equivalent in size to the former HAPC), and then to the team (roughly the size of the LAPC). 'Private plots' were restored,[13] and strict limits set on collective accumulation and welfare funds. In important respects, then, ownership, the relations of production and distribution were similar to those of the HAPCs, but on a scale more like the LAPCs.

But there were important differences, too. The production teams were now part of a three-tiered commune structure with significant economic, social and political roles. In the economic area, the brigades and communes undertook important projects beyond the scope of the team (such as water conservancy, agricultural experimentation, rural industry, etc.). In social life they organized health care, cultural and recreational services, education and youth and women's work. Politically, they incorporated local party leadership (over political campaigns, study and propaganda, for example) and government administration and finance (coordinating economic planning, administering tax allocations and collections, and regulating commerce). Much more than in the cooperative period, the villages were formally bound up with the state and made responsible for a comprehensive and integrated set of leadership and administrative responsibilities.

Yet there was also a countervailing trend. With the devolution of responsibility and authority to the teams, and an increase in their number (from 198,000 in late 1960 to 440,000 a year later), it became difficult for the party to monitor grassroots affairs. Some teams adopted strict piece-rate labour management and other pay schemes designed to maximize incentives, at the expense of egalitarian considerations. Many teams divided up their land, contracting it to individual peasant households in return for a share of the output which the team needed to meet its tax and compulsory grain sales quotas. As the collectives lost control over production and distribution, and in the face of deep economic crisis, they atrophied in other ways, too. Work on infrastructure projects was drastically reduced, collective industries, workshops, schools, clinics and nurseries were closed or cut back, and economic guarantees and support for the poor curtailed or eliminated. In the face of the crisis, many peasants turned back to traditional 'solutions' such as witchcraft, superstition and ancestor worship. Gains obtained by women through collective organization and labour were lost. Black markets, speculation and hoarding also revived. Many peasants fled the countryside to find work in growing urban informal sectors.

These phenomena exacerbated class inequality in the countryside. Many former rich and middle peasants helped fuel the retrenchment, arguing—no doubt persuasively—that collective agriculture was a disastrous failure. Many poorer peasants turned back to them as natural leaders of the village now that the leadership associated with the revolution and collectivization was discredited (Thurston, 1977). All this, coupled with the party's new stress on raising production, elevated the political prestige of the middle and rich peasants at the grassroots. They were sometimes able to use this to gain control of the allocation of production contracts, giving themselves the most or best land. In other cases, a disproportionate share of productive resources was allocated to them because they had more labourers in their families (since the wealthier peasants could afford more children, or had been able to afford to have their children sooner after the land reform) or because, to avoid controversy, teams decided to allocate productive resources to those who had owned them before the cooperatives had been formed. To the extent that they had a disproportionate share of agricultural acumen, commercial contacts and labour power, they could also benefit the most from the expansion of private plots and household contracting.

Class cleavage did not simply run along the lines of 'former' rich and poor peasants, though. During the cooperative period new lines had been drawn, too, as some former poor peasants—including many rural cadres—prospered more than others. Some of these people were also well positioned to take advantage of the retrenchment. Grassroots cadres sometimes arranged favourable contracts for themselves. 'New middle' and 'new rich' peasants who were not cadres were able to benefit from the retreats in the same ways that 'former' rich peasants did. Meanwhile, the poorer peasants had little but the collective sector to rely on in the face of the economic crisis. But the recovery of the rural areas was taking place precisely at the expense of the collectives.

A consensus developed in the party leadership that the 'spontaneous capitalist tendencies' in the countryside were dangerous and had to be stopped. But a split developed over their significance and the attendant solutions. Where Liu Shaoqi and Deng Xiaoping saw a problem of local leadership, Mao saw a class struggle. Liu and Deng saw 'deviations' by cadres taking advantage of a specific crisis situation by lining their own pockets, ignoring their public duties or wavering in their commitment to collectivism. Mao saw all this, too, but offered a more radical analysis which traced the roots of these phenomena to incipient capitalism.

Specifically, he began to develop more fully his theory, which he had advanced in his criticisms of the First Five Year Plan in 1956, that despite the triumph of the CCP and the establishment of the People's Republic, China was still in a period of struggle between socialism and capitalism. Now he pushed the analysis further than before, though. In the past Mao had felt that the forces of capitalism operated primarily in the form of unreconstructed consciousness among certain strata (including many in the party and government leadership). He now began to develop a theory of its material basis. This he located not in *property* relations, as a Marxist analysis of capitalism would, but in *political* relations between leaders and masses. This did not mean that he was of one mind with Liu and Deng, who also emphasized the political in their concern with local leadership. Mao endowed his concept of the political conflict with all the grandeur of class struggle and, eventually, revolution, while Liu and Deng saw little more than a need for some cadre rectification.

This theoretical debate was played out in the Socialist Education Movement of 1962–65. It got off to a slow start, partly because of the relatively low priority which Liu and Deng, at the helm of concrete party and government activities, assigned to it in the face of continuing economic difficulties, and partly because of the unwillingness of the state machinery to take up a campaign that could damage many of its officials. As before, Mao had to galvanize the campaign, issuing, in May 1963, a major document called the 'First Ten Points'. It began with a critique of recent party policy on rural problems, which, he argued, failed to take account of 'other problems that have yet to be solved' and 'were not presented in a clear-cut or systematic way'. It reminded readers that Mao had argued in 1962 that 'in this stage [of history] there still exist class, class contradiction, and class struggle; and that also existent is the struggle between socialism and capitalism and the danger of a comeback of capitalism'. It went on to stress that victory in this struggle would depend, like earlier phases of the Chinese revolution, on 'the poor peasants and the lower-middle peasants'. Poor and lower-middle peasant associations should be organized at the grassroots, and these should undertake investigations of local affairs and uncover cadre abuses, which were in turn to be dealt with through mass criticism and cadre self-criticism. Mao was calling for mass mobilization (Hinton (ed.), 1980, Vol. II, pp. 952–60).[14]

Deng Xiaoping countered a few months later with his own document, which took on Mao even in its title. The 'Later Ten Points' gave the highest priority to 'organization and training of work teams'—groups of cadres from middle levels of the state apparatus which were to be dispatched to the villages to take charge of the movement. Cadre meetings were mentioned next, while mass mobilization was fifth and mass organization eighth. In general the stress was on close party leadership to identify and replace corrupt, lackadaisical and incompetent local cadres (Hinton (ed.), 1980, Vol. II, pp. 961–74). Liu followed a year later with his own 'Revised Later Ten Points', which urged more concerted action in the face of sluggish results of the movement; but the form of action was similar to that advocated by Deng a year earlier (Hinton (ed.), 1980, Vol. II, pp. 974–88).

In early 1965, Mao countered in a document known as the 'Twenty-Three Articles', which upped the previous one politically and theoretically as well as numerically (Hinton (ed.), 1980, Vol. II, pp. 989–92). It returned to the theme of struggle between classes and modes of production, this time identifying the class enemy as:

people in positions of authority *in the party* who take the capitalist road . . . There are some people in the communes, districts, *hsien* [counties], special districts, and even in the work of the provincial and Central Committee departments, who oppose socialism [emphasis added].

Mao had already decided by this time that Liu Shaoqi would have to be removed from office, though the document made no mention of this. But he had never engaged in simple Stalinist purges. So now as before class struggle was to be undertaken, and 'capitalist roaders' were to be attacked in a broad mass movement. Whereas earlier the movement had concentrated on 'four cleanups'—of work-points, local accounts, distribution of supplies, and warehouses in the teams—now the four areas were redefined much more broadly as 'clean politics, clean economics, clean organization and clean ideology'. 'We must boldly unleash the masses,' Mao urged. The work teams were not to run the movement themselves but, in classic mass line fashion, were called on to 'arouse the poor and lower-middle peasants, organize class ranks, discover activist elements and train them to form a leadership nucleus, and work together with them'. Mao went so far as to speak of forcible, even armed, political struggle:

... where leadership authority has been taken over by alien class elements or by degenerate elements who have shed their skin and changed their [class] nature, authority must be seized, first by struggle and then by removing these elements from their positions ... [T]hese elements can be fired from their posts on the spot, their Party membership cards taken away, and they may even, if need be, be forcibly detained ... In places where authority must be seized, or under conditions where the people's militia organization is critically impure, we should adopt the method of turning over the weapons and ammunition of the people's militia to reliable elements among the poor and lower-middle peasants.

So radical a mass movement did not yet break out, which only heightened Mao's resolve to break through the barriers erected by those leaders whom he felt were restraining it. Mao was feeling more angry, desperate and, at least as far as the state leadership was concerned, helpless. But he was not given to despondency and inaction: he was an activist and an optimist. He would not wait long to make one more stunning attempt to lead history forward. The analysis of class struggle under socialism which had informed the Twenty-Three Articles, and the call for radical methods of mass mobilization and even uprising which he had made there, set the stage for the Great Proletarian Cultural Revolution. Launched the following year, it was to rock China and provide the most remarkable and thoroughgoing effort at radical change yet to occur in any socialist country.

The Great Proletarian Cultural Revolution

Historically unprecedented phenomena often reveal much about history. Such was the case with the Cultural Revolution. It was played out with many of the elements of politics that had grown up since 1949: a radical supreme leader attempting to draw strength from an inchoate constituency of 'the masses'; political and bureaucratic elites advocating a more organizationally routinized and stable politics, using their control of state apparatuses to block or blunt radical thrusts; citizens being drawn headlong into mass movements with little leadership, preparation or organization, adding their own genuine spontaneity and energy, which resulted in extremism and chaos; an inability of the polity to conduct serious debate in which opposing views are aired fully and calmly, while the political rights of advocates on all sides are protected. The Cultural Revolution also gave political expression to a complex of social, economic and political cleavages that had been incubated in Chinese socialism since 1949, including those between rich and poor, former exploiters and exploited, new elites and ordinary citizens, intellectuals and politicians, and those of more and less radical ideological persuasions, to name just a few. None of these cleavages was clear-cut in practice—they were more like continua along which many people found themselves in various middling positions—and they cut across each other in myriad ways. Thus we must resist simple or simplistic conceptualizations and analyses of the Cultural Revolution as a 'two-line struggle', a conflict of 'radicals' vs. 'moderates' or 'pragmatists', mere power struggle among elites, or the like, which have been propagated in both the West and China.

There is still much to learn about the Cultural Revolution, and it will require a greater fullness of time for reflection before it can be learned. The complexity and persistent uncertainty surrounding the movement were crystallized in a conversation I had with a Chinese friend. Born a peasant, he was admitted to one of China's foremost universities during the Cultural Revolution, when emphasis was laid on recruiting students from peasant and worker backgrounds. He proved to be very adept at languages, and was now working in a high post in the Foreign Ministry. When he began to criticize the Cultural Revolution, using the standard arguments advanced in official media, I replied that were it not for the Cultural Revolution he would not be where he was and indeed would probably be working in a rice paddy. He paused, disturbed, and was unable to reply for quite some time. Finally, with a sad and serious voice and without a hint of evasiveness, he said, 'Yes, it will take us Chinese a very long time to fathom the Cultural Revolution'.

At the January 1965 Politburo meeting at which Mao had iterated the radical 'Twenty-Three Articles', he had begun to speak in vague terms of the need for a 'cultural revolution'. A 'Cultural Revolution Small Group' of five top leaders was formed, with Peng Zhen—who would soon become a victim of the movement—in the chair. At this point the party confined the movement mainly to cultural affairs, so it attracted little broad concern. Matters heated up considerably in November with the publication of a critical review of Wu Han's 1961 play *Hai Rui Dismissed From Office*, which had obliquely criticized Mao by portraying the unjustified purge of an upright official (representing Peng Dehuai) for supporting poor peasants (hurt by the Great

Leap Forward, in the modern analogy) against corrupt and high-handed officials. The author of the review was Yao Wenyuan, a relatively unknown left-wing literary critic who would later become a major protagonist in the Cultural Revolution (and one of the 'gang of four' radical leaders later vilified for their role in the movement). Yao's article was reprinted in all the major newspapers, causing a political storm that culminated with Wu's public self-criticism only a month later. Peng Zhen, speaking for the party leadership, retorted in February with a report that obliquely criticized Yao: 'We must not behave like scholar-tyrants who are always acting arbitrarily and trying to overwhelm people with their power'. Henceforth, the Cultural Revolution was to be carried out 'under leadership, seriously, positively and prudently'. Fusillades were to be fired with restraint: 'Public mention in the press of names for major criticism must be made with care, and in the case of some people the approval of the leading bodies must first be secured'. The scholarly principle of 'seeking truth from facts' was emphasized alongside that of class struggle (Hinton (ed.), 1980, Vol. III, pp. 1380–1).

The left responded publicly on 16 May 1966, with a document that revoked the February outline report, vilified Peng Zhen, and has come to mark the official start of the Cultural Revolution. It broadened the scope of the movement, locating cultural affairs squarely within a framework of political and class struggle.

[Peng's] purpose is to channel the political struggle in the cultural sphere into so-called pure academic discussion, as frequently advocated by the bourgeoisie. Clearly, this . . . opposes giving prominence to proletarian politics.

It targeted 'representatives of the bourgeoisie who have sneaked into the Comunist Party', including 'a number . . . in the Central Committee and in the Party, government and other departments at the central . . . level', branding them as 'counter-revolutionary revisionists'. Responding to the February criticism of 'scholar-tyrants', it argued: '[I]f the proletarian academic work overwhelms and eradicates bourgeois academic work, can this be regarded as an act of "scholar-tyrants"?' (Hinton (ed.), 1980, Vol. III, pp. 1408–11).

In the next several months, the struggle in the top leadership sharpened, the Maoist position became increasingly radical and, perhaps most significantly, groups of ordinary citizens ('the masses') began to participate in Cultural Revolution politics. On 25 May, a radical Beijing University philosophy instructor named Nie Yuanzi put up a big-character poster denouncing university president Lu Ping for suppressing criticism of Wu Han, and calling upon students and intellectuals to join the battle. Mao, in a classic example of the mass line principle of 'from the masses, to the masses', seized upon Nie's words as pointing in precisely the direction he advocated, and had the poster republished and broadcast nationwide on 1 June. As a result, students all over China spontaneously formed themselves into groups that came to be known as 'red guard' organizations. Educational administrators everywhere came under direct criticism from students and radical faculty. At this same time the dismissal of Peng Zhen and his associates was announced. On 18 June, college entrance examinations were postponed for six months in order to allow the student movement to blossom untrammelled.

On 1 and 2 August, the Central Committee approved a 'Sixteen Point Decision' which laid down the guidelines for the Cultural Revolution. It repeated earlier themes about the target being counter-revolutionaries and bourgeoisie in the party. It also stressed that they were to be rooted out not, as in the past, by work teams or by party rectification, but rather by self-organized, aroused organizations of red guards and new cultural revolutionary groups which were to become permanent organs of mass political power. Moreover, they were to be formed not only on campuses, but in production and administrative units of all kinds. Big-character posters were to be used to register mass criticism publicly. In fact, on 5 August, Mao put up his own poster on the door of the Central Committee meeting hall, in which he issued his famous call to 'bombard the headquarters'. On 18 August, hundreds of thousands of red guards from all over China—many of whom had reached Beijing by commandeering trains and trucks—rallied in Tiananmen Square at the centre of the capital. There Mao, donning a red guard armband, received them personally. The two-pronged attack on the state leadership—from Mao above and the radical mass groups below—continued unabated in the closing months of 1966, as President Liu Shaoqi and Party Secretary-General Deng Xiaoping came under direct personal attack as the 'leading' and 'second leading person[s] in authority taking the capitalist road'. Liu was not seen in public after November when, presumably, he was placed under house arrest.

Party and government officials, sensing quickly the need to adopt new tactics to defend themselves against the red guards, organized red guard groups comprised of their own supporters, and used them to attempt to divert criticism toward other targets besides themselves. For example, many of these groups led the infamous attacks on the 'four olds' (old ideas, culture, customs and habits) which led to the destruction of temples, shrines and historical artefacts. (This aspect of the Cultural Revolution is now being condemned vociferously by the present leadership, many of whose supporters actually fuelled it at the time.) They also directed their attack against former landlords and capitalists, which diverted attention away from the class structure of socialism. The more radical groups focused their attack on party and government officials for their corruption, authoritarianism, elitism, bureaucratism, and generally for forming a new 'bourgeoisie' under socialism. In colleges, universities, offices and factories all over China, then, the mass movement factionalized, with some red guard groups supporting local, regional and national party and government officials, and others attacking them. The situation became very confused—for observers and even participants—since groups on both sides claimed loyalty to Mao and competed in producing and iterating ever more radical language.

Up until the end of 1966, the initiative rested—albeit decreasingly—with the leaders on both sides, who were able to define the issues and provide guidance to the various red guard groups. But in early 1967 the mass movement acquired a momentum of its own, and was no longer subject to leadership control. Even Mao could not control the radicals, and he would soon criticize them for having gone too far. In January, radical red guard groups stormed the leading offices in schools, colleges, factories, farms and offices. In these 'power seizures', authorities were dismissed and often incarcerated, and radicals set themselves up in their place. Official files were opened to scrutiny, which only produced more evidence to substantiate the radicals' criticisms against the former leaders. In Shanghai, the government was reorganized as a commune on the model of the Paris Commune. In most of China, the party and government organizations simply stopped functioning completely. This was nothing less than a political revolution.

Mao and other radical leaders, not to mention less radical Maoists like Premier Zhou Enlai, began to have doubts about the mass movement at this point. In mid-February, just days after the proclamation of the Shanghai Commune, Mao summoned its leaders Zhang Chunqiao and Yao Wenyuan to Beijing, where he told them that 'the slogan of "Doubt everything and overthrow everything" is reactionary'. 'Doing away with all heads [i.e., leaders]', as demanded by the radicals and incorporated in the commune form, was 'extreme anarchism'. Mao argued that communes ought not to be established beyond Shanghai, and that even Shanghai ought to 'transform itself into a revolutionary committee' (Schram (ed.), 1974, p. 277–9).

The revolutionary committee was to be a new kind of institution based upon a 'triple alliance' of red guard groups, revolutionary cadres and the army. In proposing it, Mao was saying four important things, some of which were consistent with his previous statements and long-standing views, and some of which were not. First, he was reaffirming the importance of political leadership alongside mass participation. Indeed, the mass line had from its inception been a method of leadership.[15] Second, he wanted an end to red guard factionalism. He had stressed from the beginning, and reiterated as recently as August, that 'capitalist roaders' in the party constituted a minority, and that a broad, unified mass movement ought to be able to ascertain who they were (though he never specified how, since the masses were to 'educate themselves' in the course of the movement), and then unite with the remaining majority of revolutionary leaders to deal with them. The fractures in the mass movement had in fact made it impossible for the masses to 'educate themselves' and to identify the true capitalist roaders, and had resulted in the chaotic situation in which nearly everyone was suspect. Now Mao wanted the mass movement to act in a more unified way. Third and already noted above, Mao was stressing that not all leaders were capitalist roaders, also an old and consistent theme. Fourth, and most novel, he was giving the army the key role in forging the new coalition among factionalized masses and revolutionary cadres. This was a major retreat from his position of just a few months before when, in the August 'Sixteen Points', he had stated that 'it is the masses who must liberate themselves. We cannot do the things for them which they should do themselves' (Hinton (ed.), 1980, Vol. III, p. 1566).

Mao called on the army for several reasons. First, it was the only state organ left capable of acting in a decisive way. It had not experienced the same sort of attacks from below that the party and government had. Second, since in many places armed struggles had broken out among rival red guard groups, the job of restoring political authority was heavily military in nature. Third, the armed forces were firmly under Mao's political control. After the Lushan Plenum at which Mao purged Peng Dehuai, the former Chief of Staff, the armed forces had come under the command of Lin Biao, one of Mao's closest political allies.

The army had a formidable, and in some ways impossible, set of tasks: to reconcile red guard groups that had often become the bitterest enemies—in many places, violence and armed combat had broken out—and in this hostile context to try to make political judgements about which leaders and mass organizations were truly revolutionary and which were not. Though its very top leadership, under Lin Biao, was firmly Maoist, middle- and lower-level commanders could not be blamed for confusion about what a truly Maoist position was at this point. Since Mao had now begun to emphasize a restoration of order—indeed, it was primarily to this end that the army had been called in—many commanders sided with more conservative factions and leaders in the grassroots units they were sent to supervise. Others attempted to strike compromises between conservatives and radicals. In either event, the army was greeted with hostility and opprobrium by the radicals, who had had the initiative in January. At minimum, the army's presence gave the conservatives breathing room; in other cases, it enabled them to score victories which would have been impossible without the army on the scene. This period was later dubbed by the radicals as the 'February adverse current'.

Tensions heightened through the spring, a period of contradictory tendencies during which neither side could gain an upper hand. On the one side, Mao continued to urge power seizures against capitalist roaders, while on the other he urged stabilization under the revolutionary committees. Attempts were made to resuscitate the paralysed state apparatus at the centre, but centrifugal forces prevailed in the provinces, only four of which (aside from Beijing and Shanghai) could establish revolutionary committees by the end of April. Zhou Enlai came under attack, central government offices— including the Foreign Ministry—were raided and had their files opened, and demands for a national commune continued to be made.

In July, hostilities reached their clilmax. General Chen Zaidao, the regional army commander in the major industrial city of Wuhan, had helped the more conservative mass organization there lay siege to its radical rivals. Two top Beijing leaders, carrying orders signed by Zhou Enlai (who by this time was firmly allied with Mao), instructed Chen to lift the siege. He refused, and arrested both of Zhou's emissaries, one of whom was severely beaten. Zhou himself tried to intervene, but his aeroplane was not permitted to land in Wuhan. Ultimately, superior infantry, airborne and naval units were ordered to converge on Wuhan. Chen capitulated before they had to attack. In the succeeding weeks, the Foreign Ministry was seized by rebels who appointed their own Foreign Minister. The British Chancery in Beijing was burned down. China, already in the throes of revolution, was on the brink of civil war and political anarchy.

Mao now moved decisively to restore order. On 5 September, a joint directive of the top party, government and army leaderships, and signed by Mao personally, ordered all mass groups to turn in their arms to the army, and to obey military authority in carrying out its paramount task of restoring order. On 1 October, the eighteenth anniversary of the founding of the People's Republic, Mao greeted crowds in Tiananmen Square alongside many top military commanders who had been denounced by radical red guards in the previous months. Days later, schools and universities were ordered to reopen, and students told to get back to their studies.

Throughout 1968 the mass movement sputtered and the leadership moved to consolidate the situation. Factional fighting continued, reaching severe proportions in places. But Mao summoned red guard leaders to Beijing in July and told them that they had disappointed him and the peasants and soldiers of China. 'Mao Zedong Thought Propaganda Teams', staffed by workers and led by the army, were sent to quell campus disputes. In an attempt to narrow and then draw to a close the mass criticisms of top leadership, the arrests of major officials, including Liu Shaoqi, were announced at last. A programme for rusticating urban youth and guilty cadres was announced. An official cult of Mao, reaching new heights of deification, was propagated as a way of defusing radical mass sentiment. By April 1969, the party was able to hold its first national congress since 1958. The army took a plurality in the new central committee. To help stabilize the political situation and pre-empt a succession struggle, the new constitution designated Lin Biao as heir to Mao's leadership.

But political stability was not to be so easily found, and Lin's succession was to prove ephemeral. As Mao moved to rebuild the party by bringing back into the fold many of those criticized in the Cultural Revolution, as Zhou Enlai worked in parallel to restore the government apparatus, and as a new initiative in foreign policy was forged that involved overtures to the United States, Lin Biao and other leftist leaders became alarmed. The dispute is shrouded in mystery, and there is little more than the retrospective and no doubt biased account of Lin's opponents (including Mao) to go on. But it appears that at a party plenum at Lushan in August 1970, Lin attacked Zhou Enlai's foreign and domestic policies in a speech which he failed to clear with Mao beforehand. Lin apparently tried to divide Mao and Zhou, and also undercut the institutions of party and government by asking the party formally to deify Mao as a 'genius'. He also allegedly asked to be appointed state chairman, a post which Liu Shaoqi had held and which Mao wanted to abolish. Lin lost badly at Lushan. He and Chen Boda, who had been a major left ideologist, chairman of the Cultural Revolution Small Group, and Mao's personal secretary, were criticized. Chen was soon to be vilified as an 'ultra-leftist'. No appointment of a state chairman was made. In foreign policy, the principle of 'peaceful coexistence' was enshrined alongside opposition to the United States and the Soviet Union.

During the months after the Lushan plenum, great progress was made re-establishing party committees in the provinces and thawing Sino–US relations, both of which must have appalled Lin. In September 1971, he dropped out of sight. Only the following July would the electrifying story be revealed: Lin Biao had plotted a *coup d'état*, attempted to assassinate Mao and, when the plot went awry, fled by jet to the Soviet Union, only to have his plane crash in Mongolia!

The veracity of this official account could never be confirmed or refuted. Lin's fall opened up a very confusing period in Chinese politics, during which the struggle between the Cultural Revolution left and its opponents sputtered on. A campaign to criticize Lin Biao and the 'ultra-leftism' he represented opened the way to the rehabilitation of many of the party and government officials who had fallen from power in the Cultural Revolution, a process which went so far as to include Deng Xiaoping. The cult of Mao's personality was criticized, apparently at Mao's own behest. At the Tenth Party Congress in August 1973, a collective leadership, including elements of the Cultural Revolution left as well as representatives of the previous party and government institutions, was confirmed, replacing the unitary figure of an appointed successor like Lin. In order to assuage the left, which had been smarting under the attacks against Lin's 'ultra-leftism' and their extension to more generalized doubts about the Cultural Revolution as a whole, Lin was now portrayed as actually an 'ultra-rightist' who was left only in 'form' but not 'essence'.

The persistence of political conflict even after the Tenth Congress was manifest in the confusing and bizarre campaign of 1973 and 1974 to 'criticize Lin Biao and Confucius'. It began as a movement, probably initiated by the left, to criticize Confucius and the persistence of Confucian ideology, and perhaps to level oblique criticism against Zhou Enlai. But the crafty Zhou turned it to his advantage, broadening it to include Lin and, somewhat fantastically, portraying Lin as a Confucianist. (It was even said that Lin hung a portrait of the ancient philosopher over his bed!) This campaign never really got off the ground. Mired in confusing cross-currents and played out in the popular press in academic debates about ancient Chinese history that must have seemed arcane to most readers, it never attracted a mass following. It was mysterious even to political activists who were forced to figure out for themselves the obtuse historical allusions to contemporary events. Its only positive effect was in the area of women's equality, where it was seized upon to level criticisms against the generalized sexism of Chinese society rooted in Confucian ideology. But as an attempt by the left to formulate a political analysis and ideological critique to use as a basis for a new mass movement, it fizzled.

The left did make one more effort to formulate a theoretical basis for a Maoist critique of Chinese socialism, a feat which had eluded it thus far even during the heights of its decade of political opportunity. In March and April 1975, Yao Wenyuan and Zhang Chunqiao published major articles in *Red Flag*, the party's theoretical journal (Yao, 1975; Zhang, 1975). They struggled to formulate an argument about the material and historical-dialectical basis of bourgeois recidivism and capitalist restoration under socialism. Zhang harkened back to Marx's concept of the persistence of bourgeois right—for example, private ownership of consumer goods, circulation of money, and commodity production—in only partially transcended form during the post-revolutionary transition. He argued, in a tone more balanced, measured and analytical than previous analyses by him and others on the left, that bourgeois right was bound to be a part of Chinese socialism, and that the best that could be done was its gradual restriction. His short article attained a degree of sophistication that surpassed anything the left had previously put forward. Yet it was still just a kernel of an idea that required much more development and critical debate, not to mention testing in the crucible of political practice.

Unfortunately, the opportunity for this never materialized. Even if historical contingency had not got in the way, it is far from clear that the polemical, polarized political culture of China in 1975 was hospitable to the reasoned disagreement that can lead to a theoretical breakthrough of the sort that may have been immanent in Zhang's argument. But events soon overtook what slim possibility may have existed. A series of deaths of major party figures soon brought the Chinese polity to a crossroads at which it would have to confront and resolve the disagreements that had simmered for so long. Dong Biwu, the last surviving founder of the Chinese Communist Party, and Kang Sheng, a long-standing close associate of Mao, died in 1975. Zhou Enlai, the irrepressible and adroit administrator and diplomat, and one of the few top leaders who occupied something of a middle ground on the political spectrum and could therefore help forge compromises, finally succumbed to his cancer in early 1976. Zhu De, the Red Army leader and another widely venerated figure, died in the middle of the year.

Tensions were running high throughout China in 1976, as Zhou's death and Mao's impending death—he was visibly ill and feeble—posed in the most urgent terms the problem of the future direction of Chinese socialism. On 5 April 1976, a ceremony was held to lay wreaths in Tiananmen Square at the centre of Beijing in honour of Zhou Enlai. This was no doubt an affair planned and supported by more centrist leaders and their mass supporters. A crowd of those with more leftist sympathies moved in to try to remove the wreaths, and a riot broke out. It was quelled by the army and militia, and the left agitators were duly condemned. But Acting Premier Hua Guofeng attempted to strike a middle ground by having Deng Xiaoping—who had been making his comeback and by then had inherited Zhou's position as the leading figure of the political center—dismissed from all his posts two days later. In August the left sought to capitalize on Deng's second fall with a press campaign against rehabilitated cadres.

In this context of renewed conflict between the left and its more centrist opponents, Mao's death on 8 September provoked a furious struggle. The manœuvring in the succeeding weeks was intense, though the details remain shrouded. But on 6 October, Hua had the four most prominent leaders of the left—Jiang Qing (Mao's wife), Wang Hongwen, Yao Wenyuan and Zhang Chunqiao—arrested on a charge of trying to foment civil war by allegedly arming the Shanghai militia and planning an attack on the organs of state. Hua soon formally drew the curtain on the Cultural Revolution, which he declared to have lasted an entire decade.

Failed Compromise, 1977-78

For the next two years, Premier and Party Chairman Hua Guofeng attempted to find a middle ground between the rival policy positions and their respective leaders and followers. He presided over a campaign to criticize the 'gang of four' leftist leaders and their supporters, but at the same time continued to pass favourable judgements on the Cultural Revolution. In agriculture he associated himself squarely with the Dazhai/Xiyang programme of advanced collectivization that had dominated the 1960s and 1970s. Hua also supported the left industrial model of the Daqing oilfields. He put forward a new ten year plan which resonated strongly to the Maoist emphases on labour intensity and relative balance of industry and agriculture, with high targets to be achieved mainly by dint of great sacrifice and effort. But Hua tempered all this by setting it in the context of economic modernization—actually, not one but 'four modernizations' (of agriculture, industry, science and technology, and the military), a slogan then associated with Zhou Enlai and now with the post-Mao reformist leadership. And Deng Xiaoping made his second political comeback in mid-1977. In general, then, these were years of attempted compromise.

But a middle path between the left and centre was not meant to be. At the Third Plenum of the Eleventh Party Central Committee in December 1978, Deng Xiaoping and his supporters scored a decisive victory, and the path was cleared for a subsequent programme of reform. The Cultural Revolution and the campaign to criticize the 'gang of four' were now relegated to history, and the emphasis was shifted to socialist modernization. Deng's supporters—many of whom were soon to advance to key leadership posts—were restored or promoted. Even Peng Dehuai, Mao's bitter enemy and critic who had been vilified at the Lushan Plenum in 1959, was posthumously rehabilitated. This, together with a statement that Mao had made some unspecified mistakes, opened the way for a subsequent criticism of Mao and Maoist political economy, and for a new alternative, not yet fully visualized even by many of the new leadership, to be forged.

The Triumph of 'Reform': 1979 to the Present

The criticism of Mao and Maoism, and the establishment of an alternative, moved rapidly. Wu Han's play *Hai Rui Dismissed From Office* the criticism of which had been the opening salvo of the Cultural Revolution, was re-evaluated positively. More middle- and high-level officials criticized during the movement were rehabilitated. At the Fifth National People's Congress in mid-1979, Hua toned down the grandiose plans and targets of his earlier ten year plan, called for a transitional period of readjustment and consolidation, and stressed material incentives and income-raising measures, such as side-lines in the countryside. In a speech at the end of the year commemorating the thirtieth anniversary of the founding of the People's Republic, which was approved in advance by the party at its Fourth Plenum, Ye Jianying criticized the Cultural Revolution as having been a calamity. Mao was praised, but three key incidents in which he had been prominent—extending the 1957 anti-rightist campaign, making rash plans during the Great Leap, and strenu-ously attacking his enemies at Lushan in 1959—were criticized, all without mentioning Mao. At the next plenum a few months later, prominent leaders associated with Mao were demoted and Dengist replacements—Zhao Ziyang and Hu Yaobang, who would soon accede to the top government and party posts respectively—were promoted. Liu Shaoqi's record was posthumously cleared. In July 1980, Hua Guofeng was replaced as Premier by Zhao, and soon after Hu took over the party. Deng shrewdly contented himself with a vice-premiership (and also with heading up the Party Military Affairs Com-mission that oversees the armed forces, just to be sure). But he has clearly been the key figure in Chinese politics since 1980, and remains so as of this writing in late 1985, with no apparent threats save old age on the horizon.

No large-scale campaign of vilification was launched against Hua and other surviving Maoists. At the Sixth Plenum of the Eleventh Central Committee, in June 1981, Hua Guofeng was demoted from the chair of the CCP and its Military Affairs Commission. But the move was presented as a 'resignation', and he retained a vice-chairmanship of the Party Central Committee, as well as a seat on the Standing Committee of the Politburo. At this same meeting, a major document entitled 'On Questions of Party History', which had been drafted and debated in the party for the previous fifteen months, was issued (*Beijing Review*, 6 July 1981, pp. 10–39). It criti-cized Mao's political ideas in relation to the Cultural Revolution.

[T]he history of the 'cultural revolution' has proved that Comrade Mao Zedong's prin-cipal theses for initiating this revolution conformed neither to Marxism-Leninism nor to Chinese reality. They represent an entirely erroneous appraisal of the prevailing class relations and political situation in the Party and state.

Mao's actions, too, were criticized. He was taken to task for his attack on Peng Dehuai at Lushan, and especially for becoming 'arrogant' and elitist during the Cultural Revolution, when he 'divorced himself from practice and the masses, acted more and more arbitrarily and subjectively, and increasingly put himself above the Central Committee'. Nevertheless, Mao is still hailed in the document:

Comrade Mao Zedong was a great Marxist and a great proletarian revolutionary, strategist and theorist . . . [I]f we judge his activities as a whole, his contributions to the Chinese Revolution far outweigh his mistakes. His merits are primary and his errors secondary.

Clearly, the post-Mao leadership chose to deal with its political enemies very differently than had Stalin or Mao. Though its balanced assessment was no doubt motivated by a political desire to maintain as broad a base of support as possible during a very risky break from the past, it was nevertheless a refreshing change from the Manichaean and polemical approach to problems that has stifled serious debate on key issues of the socialist experience in China as well as in many other socialist countries.

This is not to say that post-Mao China is yet a model of socialist democracy, or that it is becoming one. But the first halting steps have been taken, both in opening political discourse and in exploring new political directions. Under the post-Mao leadership, China has moved in a direction that is as iconoclastic and unorthodox as anything witnessed in any socialist country (including China's own Maoist innovations), but also different from even the most thoroughgoing 'reform' models like Hungary. To these developments we shall turn in the chapters that follow.

3 The Trajectory of Chinese Socialism

Since socialism is shaped by and changing through history, comparative analysis of socialism needs to address developmental pathways as a subject of study. Socialism in China has developed along very different lines from those in the Soviet Union. A look at the distinctive features of the Chinese route to and through socialism thus far will help elucidate its dynamics, and contribute to both an appreciation of the wide range of socialist experience and to the theoretical understanding of the dialectics of socialism more generally.

This chapter will emphasize two themes. First, the trajectory of Chinese socialist development has been very different from that of the Soviet Union. This is hardly a controversial point, but the nature and explanation of the differences remain in need of greater analysis than they have been given by scholars more concerned with country studies than with comparative analysis. Second, the familiar argument that Chinese socialism has been playing out a repetitive pattern—the usual metaphor is that of a pendulum swinging between right and left—is a distortion, and as such not analytically helpful. Though, to be sure, successive phases have occupied different positions along a simplistic 'left–right' continuum, they have not occupied the same position as their antecedents, and each phase has been achieved in a distinctly different way. Successive 'left' phases have differed markedly from each other, as have successive 'right' phases. The trajectory of Chinese socialist development has been more dialectical than linear, with each phase incorporating elements from different historical moments in a new synthesis that did not simply reproduce the past. If metaphors are needed, the pendulum needs to be replaced by a spiral, and a rather asymmetrical one at that.

The socialist transition began slowly and gradually in China. From 1949 to 1952, nationalization moved gradually, encompassing mainly those sectors already under the control of the Republican government or those whose owners had abandoned them. This is in sharp contrast to the developmental trajectory of the Soviet Union, which in its earliest days of War Communism undertook rapid nationalization and centralization of authority. In agriculture, too, the CCP moved gingerly, by and large leaving peasants and the agricultural sector alone to recover. Though the Soviet Union likewise delayed agricultural collectivization, its appropriations of grain to feed the cities and armies stood in sharp contrast to the CCP's more benign neglect of rural appropriation.

Part of the difference can be explained by the fact that the Soviet Union was in the midst of foreign and civil war at the time of its birth, while the founding of the CCP marked the end of civil war. Indeed, with the end of the civil war, the Bolsheviks were able to move to the more moderate New Economic Policy (NEP). Still, this explanation does not go terribly far. Although the Guomindang was being routed in 1949, CCP control of the mainland was not completed until 1950, and the Guomindang did manage to gain a new lease of life by consolidating its control over Taiwan, whence for many years it made credible threats to invade the mainland and renew the civil war. Moreover, China was soon drawn into direct armed confrontation with the United States in Korea. These threats to its sovereignty could easily have provided a pretext for the CCP to clamp down on the peasantry in the name of national and socialist survival, as the Bolsheviks did in the Soviet Union.

Yet the CCP never seriously considered such options. The rural base of the Chinese revolution, and conversely the relative weakness of its urban base, accounts partly for the difference. Despite the mutual ambivalence of Sino-Soviet relations, the existence of the Soviet Union as a socialist ally which could help guarantee the security of the new People's Republic of China may also have helped reduce the urgency of the threat which might have led to more draconian and radical policies during the socialist transition in the countryside and the cities.

The next phase of China's socialist trajectory corresponded more closely with that of the Soviet Union. Both countries came to an economic peak produced by the intersection of two contradictory vectors: first, a concern with industrialization and a concomitant need to finance it with high rates of domestic accumulation; and second, a decline in the very high rate of growth during the post-war recovery. Both governments also experienced relatively high levels of political stability and support, as peace had been restored, the economy put back on its feet, and the relatively flexible and relaxed policies of the previous period (NEP in the Soviet Union, the 1949–52 years of 'rest and recovery' in China) had struck a positive chord with much of the citizenry. In both countries, the state apparently concluded that the time was right to begin to undertake the bold yet arduous steps that would be necessary to build up industry. These included completing the nationalization of industry and commerce, establishing central planning of the economy, accumulating capital at a high rate, building a heavy industrial base, and collectivizing agriculture. In the Soviet Union this was the period of Stalinist industrialization beginning in the late 1920s, when NEP was abolished and agriculture was collectivized in order to facilitate the appropriation of a surplus to finance industrial development. In China it was the period of the First Five Year Plan (1953–57).

At first sight it is somewhat surprising that China followed such a route at all. The centralization of state power, administration and resources which it required contradicted the more decentralized and less firmly Leninist proclivities and experiences of the CCP. The dominant guerrilla military tradition of the CCP did not require as strong an industrial base to defend the country as the more conventional Soviet military strategy did. And certainly the rural base of the Chinese revolution together with a genuine appreciation of and revulsion at the horrors of Stalinist collectivization mitigated against the extraction of enormous surpluses from agriculture by force, while its flexible, graduated class policy conflicted with the kind of rash move against rich peasants that made Stalin infamous.

In fact, the Chinese First Five Year Plan period differed from the Stalinist industrialization era in some important ways. As we have argued in Chapter 2, appropriation from the peasantry was carried out less ruthlessly; the rich peasantry was handled much more skilfully; collectivization of agriculture followed rather than preceded the start of the industrialization drive. In fact, the most ardent proponents of Soviet-style industrialization were also the most cautious and reserved about collectivization. They were content to extract some of the agricultural surplus through taxation and trade rather than through direct appropriation using the administrative apparatus of collectives. On the other side, Mao, who spearheaded China's break with Soviet-style industrialization, most strenuously fostered agricultural cooperativization; and he did so for reasons which had much less to do with surplus extraction and much more with his ideological and political concerns and methods. So the Soviet collectivization proceeded from very different motivations, and in a very different relationship to industrialization, than did the Chinese cooperativization.

In other important respects, though, there was a marked similarity between the Stalinist and Chinese industrialization drives. Both emphasized the priority of heavy industry, of large projects, financed by agriculture and by high rates of accumulation (with concomitantly low wages). Both were premised upon central planning and state ownership.

Why did China adopt such a strategy? In part it did so for some of the same reasons that the Soviet Union had: the need to build up a defence industry, the view that this was the fastest route to industrialization, the concern with economic independence in the long run (which meant the capacity to supply one's own producer goods). China also possessed some of the same basic attributes required for this approach: it is a large country rich in natural resources and with a capacity for economic accumulation. In addition, the Chinese case was influenced by the Soviet model, which was impressive in important respects: within the space of two decades, the Soviet Union had been converted from a largely agrarian and industrially backward and dependent country to an economic and military superpower capable of fending off fascism and contending with the United States. And the economic strains of the industrialization had been survived with no serious internal political crisis. Moreover, there was no other model for China to follow, and the Chinese leadership was fully cognizant of its own inexperience in industrial development. The Chinese case demonstrates, then, how a Stalinist approach to economic centralization and heavy industrialization could become attractive even in countries where it resonated much less well to domestic objective and historical factors.

After the initial movement toward economic centralization and heavy industrialization that both China and the Soviet Union undertook, their trajectories of socialist development parted company, and have not coincided since. The Soviet Union held to the Stalinist path for several decades. Even since Stalin's death, while some elements have changed—accumulation rates have declined and consumption risen, while production has diversified away from heavy industry—others, including tight central planning, hegemonic state ownership, and a low priority for agriculture, have not. By contrast, China has been anything but constant in its devotion to the directions of the First Five Year Plan. It has undertaken some of the most radical experiments in political economy—both toward the left and the right—of any socialist country.

Why did China renounce the Stalinist pathway which it had pursued through 1957? Some of the reasons have already been mentioned. The political and administrative centralization, bureaucratism, elitism and urban industrial bias which it engendered were less well suited to the Chinese situation—with its tradition of mass line democracy and participation, regional and local economic self-reliance, rural political base—than they had been in the Soviet Union. Another difference has to do with the capacity of each country to withstand the contradictions of Stalinist-style industrialization. In both China and the Soviet Union, it produced a serious sectoral imbalance between industry and agriculture. As industry grew much more rapidly, it needed continued infusions of rurally generated capital as well as rural markets for its products. But slow growth in the rural agricultural areas made it increasingly difficult for them to supply either, posing obstacles to continued industrial growth. Stalin could overcome these obstacles through the application of draconian administrative and coercive measures, forcing surpluses out of agriculture (and industry, too, as low wages financed high rates of reinvestment) and overpriced commodities upon reluctant buyers. In China, whose revolutionary history and ideology were so different, such policies were never an option; neither Mao nor any other Chinese leader ever seriously suggested them. Discomfort with the strategy of the First Five Year Plan was also motivated by an increasing tension in Sino–Soviet relations, particularly after the 1956 invasion of Hungary and surprise denunciation of Stalin. China had to find another way to deal with the contradictions of Stalinist industrialization.

Before examining the route China did take, it is interesting to look at those it did not take. A reformed version of the First Five Year Plan, with lower rates of accumulation and greater emphasis on agriculture, was proposed by some less radical leaders. Since this was an evolutionary strategy that broke little new ground and therefore had the advantage of familiarity and relatively little risk, and since it presumably had the support of the powerful party and government bureaucracies, it is surprising that it was not adopted. The answer seems to lie with the extraordinary figure of Mao and, just as important, the unorthodox and popular radical impulses and proclivities born of the Chinese revolution which he represented and which provided his political base. At the level of *central politics*, Mao was shrewd enough to outfox and outflank those advocating a reformed Second Five Year Plan. In *popular politics*, the radical impulses among grassroots cadres, combined with the belief among many peasants in an imminent communism of prosperity for all, were able to propel the Great Leap Forward into reality, sweeping aside the more incrementalist plans.

There is another historical alternative which was never even considered at this juncture: a programme of 'reform' like that eventually pursued two decades later, involving economic deregulation, reorganization of the state and collective enterprises, and limited privatization. Why did such a programme, which raced into reality after 1978, not even reach the political agenda in 1958? To some extent the factors already mentioned apply here, too: the radical, pro-collectivist tendencies shared by Mao, other political leaders, and so many local cadres and citizens, would also rule out 'reform' as they had Stalinism. But why was 'reform' not even proposed? The answer can be found in both the domestic and international conjunctures. China in 1958 was simply incapable of producing such a plan on its own. The Leninist and Maoist ideological traditions were too <u>hegemonic</u>: though different and in some ways contradictory, they combined in their opposition to any such 'revisionism'. Ideas, experiments and experience that would produce a praxis of 'reform' would have to develop first in the rather different political and ideological atmosphere of Eastern Europe. They had not done so by 1958. Even if they had, it is unlikely that China would have been prepared to adopt them until such time as the Leninist–Stalinist and Maoist models had been discredited—the former by the latter and the latter by itself.

If the Leninist and reformist roads were not taken, why the Great Leap? Though it turned out to be a disaster in many respects, there was an underlying rationale for it. One basic tenet of this rationale was the *primacy of human labour*. This may have drawn inspiration in a simplistic way from the Marxist principle that labour is the source of all value. It also stemmed from the Maoist revolutionary belief—itself a product of the Chinese revolution—in the power of organized and committed human energy. It also made great economic sense for a country like China which lacked capital but had a superabundance of labour.

A second and related tenet underlying the Great Leap was the *primacy of politics and organization* over 'objective' economic factors. Labour could make its contribution to economic development only if organized on an appropriate scale and motivated by means other than purely material incentives, the economic resources for which China did not have and could not afford for some time (given the need for continued large doses of investment). The 'appropriate' scale would have to be rather large—hence the communes—to undertake the major infrastructure projects that were needed to make an agricultural breakthrough (such as water projects to 'weatherproof' against drought and flood and bring unused land under cultivation). Large scale also, it was thought, would enable agriculture to gain greater efficiency through rationalization of existing resource use, as had already been experienced under mutual aid and cooperativization. And for labour motivation the Great Leap returned to the wellspring of mass mobilization which had served the party so well in earlier days.

A third basic tenet was *the unification of industry and agriculture*, and of *rural and urban* areas. If agriculture could not be ransacked to finance urban industry, perhaps peasants would willingly finance a local industry under their own control. Such rural industrialization located and controlled locally would also help supply agriculture and peasant consumers with the products they needed and demanded, just as urban-based, centrally controlled industry could not because of planning and transport problems in China's vastness and complexity. Other rural–urban linkages would also make their contributions: if a shortage of labour during busy harvest seasons in pre-mechanized Chinese agriculture posed a bottleneck to agricultural growth, then urban populations would be mobilized to help out. Urban industry would also provide technical advice to inexperienced peasant workers and industrialists. In short, then, in 1958 one could have made persuasive arguments on ideological, political and economic grounds for something like the Great Leap Forward. In embarking on it, the Chinese leadership had not taken leave of its senses.

These plans were not converted into reality, for reasons discussed in Chapter 2. The retrenchment and recovery phase which followed the Leap involved only a partial return to the organizational forms of the 1950s. In urban industry, centralized planning and control were reasserted, but the new 'trusts' signalled a desire for greater integration and efficiency than the central ministry system had been able to attain. In the rural areas, communes were disaggregated into smaller units like the former coops, but the commune form was retained to help promote large-scale projects, run and develop the surviving rural industries, and maintain political control over agriculture. This last objective was desired by most leaders in order to help promote collective production, resist 'spontaneous capitalist tendencies', and assure state access to the agricultural surplus. A greater sectoral balance between industry and agriculture was also pursued. In short, China in this period abandoned the radical organizational forms and policies of the Great Leap, yet did not simply return to the *status quo ante*.

The nature of this shift is not hard to explain. The Great Leap had been founded upon a deep and widely-held concern with the problems of the previous period. The failure of the Great Leap did not obviate this concern, but it did discredit the radical Maoist approach to it. At the level of state power this left the leaders and bureaucrats associated with Liu Shaoqi with a licence to try their hand, while at the grassroots level it opened the way for anti-collectivist opposition in the countryside. These latter forces would again go on the offensive after 1978, spontaneously charting new directions which went beyond the leadership's plans. Then the state would prove willing to tolerate and give its imprimatur to them as 'reforms'. But in the post-leap years, these same impulses and forms met with the hostility of leaders of both Maoist and Liuist persuasions, so 'reform' was still blocked at the level of state leadership. But unlike the immediate pre-leap period, it had now gained an active popular constituency.

This popular challenge to socialist organization in agriculture was serious enough a problem in itself, but it became even more so as it provided a setting for open rivalry among competing groups in the state leadership. Maoists advocated a mass movement to combat 'spontaneous capitalist tendencies', while Liuists, less favourably inclined towards mass movements and perhaps even perceiving that some of the masses might not be fully on the socialist side, opposed it. The Maoists then conflated the anti-collectivist tendencies among the peasants and the Liuist opposition to a mass movement against those tendencies into a unitary class enemy, against which they unleashed a mass mobilization during the Cultural Revolution, the next phase of China's socialist trajectory.

In one sense the appearance of mass opposition in a socialist country is not very surprising at all. Popular discontent has found expression in major mass movements of political protest in Hungary, Czechoslovakia and Poland. What gave the Chinese counterpart its distinctively radical character was the unique fact that it was led by the country's pre-eminent revolutionary and state leader. In no other socialist country did the leader of the revolution have such strong popular, anti-bureaucratic proclivities. Mao was able to shape the politics not only of the radical side of the Cultural Revolution, but of the movement as a whole. That is, even the state apparatus which Mao and his radical supporters were trying to attack was forced by the hegemony of Mao and Maoism to mimic Maoist tactics by forming its own red guard groups, finding implacable enemies and undertaking broadsides against them. Hence, both sides in the Cultural Revolution undertook a tactic of mass-based radicalism, which helps explain how the movement became so extreme and got out of control even of its own leaders. This distinctive character of the Chinese Cultural Revolution, therefore, may have had less to do with the existence of greater popular discontent in China than in other socialist countries—there is no evidence to that effect, anyway—than with the specific character of the Chinese leadership in relation to that discontent.

This period, though animated by some of the same leftist impulses that had lain behind the Great Leap, had very little in common with it. This had partly to do with the different problems of the time. In 1957 the main concerns were rural–urban imbalance and dependence on the Soviet Union; now they were opposition to collective organization and the nature of state leadership. But it also had to do with lessons learned the hard way in the Great Leap. In agricultural policy, for example, there was never any attempt to resuscitate the large communes as basic units of production, management and development; the emphasis was rather on the much smaller brigades. In other words, more attention was being paid to graduated (if accelerated) socialist transition.[1] In this and other areas, then, the leftism of the Cultural Revolution was no return to that of the Great Leap.

The Cultural Revolution did resemble the Great Leap in one important respect, though: it failed to live up to its radical promise. It never found a firm theoretical base for its criticism of Chinese socialism or for its own political actions designed to address its concerns. Its critiques of authority, bureaucracy and elitism simply could not square with Mao's own commitment to a Leninist party structure or with the high-handed methods of the left's leadership. The movement largely discredited itself in a bizarre combination of anarchism and elitism.

But this authoritarian anti-authoritarianism had a dialectical effect upon the next period of China's socialist development. The demise of the Maoist left did not produce a simple return of a triumphant bureaucratic elite. The leadership formerly associated with that elite have emerged from the Cultural Revolution with a changed political programme that in significant ways resonates to many of the themes of the movement. The Dengist leadership has been as vociferous as the Cultural Revolution left opposition in denouncing bureaucratism. It, too, has criticized the stultifying effects of overweaning state power in economic affairs. It has stressed the need for greater democracy. None of these concerns was apparent in the political programme associated with Liu Shaoqi and Deng Xiaoping in the mid-1950s and early 1960s, periods when they held greatest sway.

Of course, this is not to minimize the vast differences between the Cultural Revolution left and its successors in power today. The former sought to cure bureaucratism with mass mobilization, the latter with privatization. The left emphasized local economic initiative by self-reliant collectives, and the Dengists by expanded room for individual entrepreneurship. The left advocated direct, mass participatory democracy, while the Dengists prefer tamer experiments with electoral representation.

The point here is simply that the present leadership is now putting forward policies that differ markedly from those it advocated and pursued before the Cultural Revolution. These differences seem to reflect the effects of some of the critiques levelled during the Cultural Revolution at that leadership and its policies. In this sense, then, the pendulum has not simply swung back to where it was in 1962–65 or 1953–57.

Today China is experiencing many of the phenomena of elitism, bureaucratism and economic centralization that it did in earlier days and that Mao criticized at the time. Many of the political institutions of those days—including most prominently the Communist Party but also many government organs—remain unreformed. Many of the officials of those days have also returned to power—especially at middle levels of organization—largely unchanged in their policies or styles of work. To some extent they form an obstacle for the ambitious reform plans of the Dengist leadership.[2]

Hence it is not accurate to view the present period as one in which the conservative side of the old 'two-line struggle' has triumphed. Though the left has fallen, it has been replaced not by a monolithic right but by a variegated group of leaders among whom there are significant disagreements on politics and policy. These do not simply replay old disagreements; the pendulum has not just swung back to where it used to be. Although the present contours of Chinese politics have something in common with the past, they are in other important ways (such as the Dengist programme of economic reform) completely unprecedented. In the chapters that follow, we turn to analysis of China at its present historical conjuncture.

4 The State and Politics

The Chinese state is founded upon the same principles of Communist Party political monopoly and 'dictatorship of the proletariat' that underpin state socialism in the Soviet Union, Eastern Europe and many Third World socialist countries such as Vietnam. But in China these principles have found theoretical, institutional and practical expression in distinctive ways that distinguish China from the Soviet model. In mid-1985, Chinese politics and political institutions resemble that orthodoxy as closely as they ever have. In some ways—such as the effective silencing or pre-emption of dissent—they have even outdone the Soviet Union. But in others Chinese socialism has evinced a rather different and distinctively participatory pattern which continues to have significant legacies and implications for the future.

This chapter addresses these issues in the following order. Since the party has always been a key institution, we begin with it. We then turn to the question of the government institutions. This lays the basis for a discussion of the party–government relations.[1] To balance this discussion of elite politics and institutions, there follows a section on political participation.

The Chinese Communist Party

The Chinese Communist Party was founded in the Leninist mould—and with considerable direct Soviet influence—as a revolutionary vanguard that would operate according to tight internal discipline and would provide close leadership over the revolution. Table 4.1 shows that, in the original 'vanguard' mould, it is still a very small organization, barely attaining a membership of 4 per cent of the Chinese population in 1985 (though to be sure there has been meaningful and, overall, quite steady expansion of its membership since 1949). Its basic Leninist structure (see Figure 4.1), rather standard for ruling communist parties in state socialist countries, is still intact. Formally the party consitution vests power in the rank-and-file of party members who at each level elect delegates to local congresses; these in turn elect both the party committees at their own level and delegates to congresses at the next higher level (who in turn choose their own party committees and higher-level delegates, etc.). In fact, of course, in the Chinese Communist Party, as in most others, power really resides at the centre and flows downward. The key organs are the central standing committees—especially that of the Political Bureau—which meet regularly, carry out day-to-day business, and prepare the agendas and decisions which the larger bodies (such as the Central Committee and the Party Congress) adopt at their infrequent meetings. One institutional innovation created by the Dengist leadership is the Central Advisory Commission, a vessel used to 'kick upstairs' elder party statespersons who are to be moved out of key positions.

But the similarities of the Chinese Communist Party with other ruling communist parties have not always been matched by its actual style of operation. With the failures of its proletarian-based revolutionary strategy and the party's turn to a rural base, it developed a distinctive repertoire of participatory methods and institutions that were grafted on to but never really threatened or displaced its Leninist structure. These democratic and authoritarian elements coexisted uneasily after 1949 in what, at the risk of attributing too much explanatory power to the elite level, could be called a Maoist model of the party.

This model always enshrined the cardinal principle of democratic centralism common to Leninist parties. In theory this means that the party is to arrive at decisions democratically, but that once reached decisions are to be carried through wholeheartedly by all party members, including the minority who opposed them. In practice, of course, most Leninist parties have been more centralist than democratic. The Maoist model attempted to

Table 4.1 Chinese Communist Party membership, 1949–present

Year	Membership (millions)	Membership as % of population
1949	4.5	.83
1956	10.8	1.72
1961	17.0	2.58
1969	20 (estimated)	2.48
1973	28	3.14
1977	35	3.69
1980	38	3.85
1982	39.65	3.90
1985	40	4.0

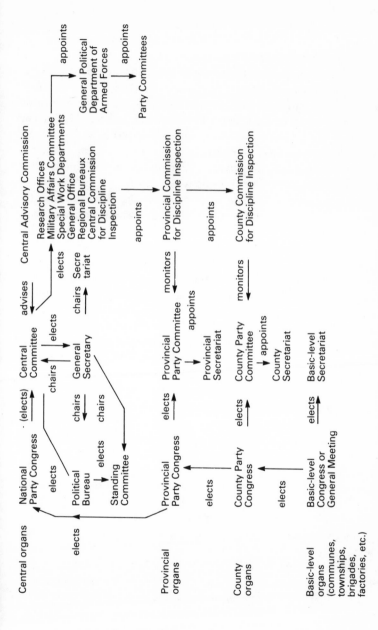

Figure 4.1 Organization of the Chinese Communist Party (as of party constitution adopted at Twelfth National Congress, September 1982)

enhance the democratic element, based on the Maoist concept of popular democratic participation known as the mass line.

This involved four elements. First, party members and officials were to maintain close contacts with the masses on a regular basis, by participating in productive labour and regularly soliciting their opinions and views.[2] Second, party members were to subject each other to criticism, and themselves to self-criticism, during rectification movements. Third, the party was to be made subject to mass criticism, a principle which would have shocked Lenin. For example, experiments known as 'open door rectification', in which villagers who were not party members were invited to criticize local party officials as part of a rectification movement, were tried in the late 1940s (Hinton, 1966, Parts IV and V). Mass criticism of the party was encouraged by Mao during the Cultural Revolution, this time in the form of a broad mass movement. Fourth, institutional methods for upward flow of views and criticisms were built into the party. Constitutional provisions permitting party members to appeal directly to the party chair were adopted at party congresses during the 1970s.

Democracy aside, the Maoist concept of the party also emphasized the internal development and maintenance of party control and discipline through ideological work. A basic tenet of Mao's political theory is that attitude matters more than institutional arrangements, and that exercise of administrative authority or coercion on its own is not a satisfying way to achieve results. Accordingly, under Mao, improving the ideological predispositions of party members through regular propaganda and study campaigns (as well as criticism and self-criticism) was emphasized, while control through institutional hierarchy and command was de-emphasized. This is not to say that these elements were abandoned. Institutional reforms, such as cadre participation in labour and periodic transfers of cadres to grassroots work, were made in order to weaken the authoritarianism and elitism which Mao knew were inherent in the vertically-structured, centralized party. Still, no attempts were made to flatten the vertical structure of the party (as was tried, for example, in the army with the abolition of ranks) or to challenge the centralist elements of democratic centralism. None the less, Chinese practice concerning party democracy was a significant departure from Leninist and Stalinist practice.[3]

Mao was ambivalent towards the party in terms of the question of class relations. On the one hand, even at moments when he was issuing his most vehement criticisms of the party, he viewed a reconstituted party as an important bulwark against a triumph by counter-revolutionary class forces. But, on the other, he saw the party as a breeding-ground for a new 'bourgeoisie'. Ultimately Mao condoned the rapid reconstitution of the party after the attacks on it during the Cultural Revolution. But it was to be revitalized in ideology and personnel, and was to share power with government and mass organizations through the revolutionary committees. In raising questions about the class nature of the party and in attempting to reduce its power *vis-à-vis* non-party political institutions (such as the revolutionary committees), Mao strayed furthest from the orthodox Leninist conception of the party.

Finally, the Maoist conception and form of the party was affected by the Maoist strategy of economic development, which emphasized mass mobilization over central planning and technological advance. This de-emphasized the party's role in exercising political control over functional ministries and technical experts, which would entail political bureaucracy to supervise economic bureaucracy. Instead, it stressed the communicative and popular organizational roles which the party had acquired and perfected in pre-revolutionary days, and which it maintained after 1949 in its leadership of mass movements such as land reform, cooperativization and the Great Leap. Different roles called for different personnel: the Maoist party preferred the revolutionary generalist (the 'red') to the administrative or technical specialist (the 'expert').

The post-Mao leadership shares some of the criticisms of the party advanced by the Maoist left. It is concerned with bureaucratism, in the form of bloated personnel roles and unwieldy procedures. It has criticized elitism, by which is meant a structured separation from the experiences and views of the masses. It has been critical of corruption by party officials, too.

In other respects it has offered new twists upon Maoist themes, or emphasized particular elements for its own purposes. It has put forward a critique of 'feudal' vestiges in the party, perhaps paramount among which is the deification of the supreme leader. To be sure, Mao, too, ultimately became critical of the cult of his personality. And, in the context of a partial criticism of Mao himself, the new leadership's stand has a political as well as structural component. That is, they are objecting to the content of the cult of Mao's personality as much as, if not more than, to the phenomenon of a personality cult itself. But the structural element is there, too, in the emphasis on consensual, collective leadership rather than the dictatorial and divisive pattern of party leadership dating as far back as the cooperativization debate of 1956. To this end, the post of Party Chairman has been replaced by that of Chairman of the resuscitated Party Secretariat.

Another Maoist theme which has been amplified so as to be put to different purposes is the emphasis on practice. While Mao posited that theory could only be 'correct'—that is, useful in promoting revolutionary progress—if based upon practice, the post-Mao leadership has derogated the value of theory further, adopting a hyperpragmatist position under the slogan 'practice is the sole criterion of truth'. This has meant, among other things, that what people think is less important than what they do, which in turn has reduced concern with ideology in general. Behaviour can now be regulated directly—for example, through political authority or economic incentives and disincentives—without worrying so much about underlying ideological motivation.

In party affairs this new hyperpragmatist orientation has had several implications. Gone is the reliance on ideological campaigns, propaganda, criticism and self-criticism as ways of enforcing discipline and political purity of the party and its members. Party members are expected to demonstrate their political virtue through the concrete results—often in the form of economic indicators—of their work. And those who cannot produce satisfactory results, or who resist the new rules of the game, are now to be dealt with not so much by ideological reform as administrative methods, including retraining, close evaluation, retirement, demotion or explusion. Party schools have been established or strengthened to help familiarize members with the new tasks before them and equip them with the skills they will need to fulfil them. Discipline commissions have been resuscitated to identify recalcitrant members and to 'help' them get in line. Lifelong tenure of party members and officeholders has been abolished, and advisory commissions have been set up as receptacles for aged party cadres for whom demotion or expulsion would not be seemly.

The scope of inner-party democracy has also been reduced. Party members may still appeal upward to levels above their immediate superiors. But this is now to be done in an orderly way, and criticisms are to be restricted to those which do not challenge the basic principles of the current policy line and which—another way of saying the same thing—serve the goal of the four modernizations (of industry, agriculture, science/technology and the military—the overarching policy theme of the post-Mao leadership).

If the internal mechanisms of party control have changed, the external mechanisms of the Maoist days have both changed and been devalued. The Dengist leadership believes that the problems encountered by the party during the Cultural Revolution had a great deal to do with the rise of extra-party methods of control over it. Liu Shaoqi and Deng Xiaoping have long spoken for many in the party with their view that in a socialist country the party's affairs are best monitored and put in order by the party itself. To be sure, this view about organizational self-supervision is common to self-serving organizations everywhere. In the case of defenders of the Chinese Communist Party, though, it rests on additional arguments about the strategic position of the party as defender of the revolution against hostile forces. This argument could be made more convincingly in the 1950s and 1960s, when external threats to China's sovereignty and internal threats to its socialist transition were more palpable and were recognized in the dominant Maoist paradigm within which even Liu, Deng and their supporters operated. But since the present leadership believes that there are no serious class-based challenges to Chinese socialism any longer—certainly not from within the party—it is harder to argue that the party needs to remain sacrosanct and immune from external criticism or challenge. This problem has not been faced squarely by ideologists of the present leadership.

But ideological consistency and elegance have not prevented the post-Mao leadership—including both Dengist reformers and more old-fashioned bureaucratic regulars—from eliminating their *bête noire*: mass criticism of the party. Gone are 'open-door rectification', mass movements like the Cultural Revolution, and anything else vaguely resembling them. This is not to say that external checks have been abandoned altogether. Perhaps the most searing criticism offered by the post-Mao leadership is that the party lost prestige and legitimacy during the Cultural Revolution. In its programme to restore these, the Dengists could hardly avoid erecting some mechanisms for popular expression about the party, if only as a way of alleging the reconstructed legitimacy of the party. It has, therefore, developed an experimental programme of local elections to representative congresses up to the county level. In these elections, several Communist Party candidates are nominated for office, and voters may choose among them. Since the offices to which they are elected are in the government and not the party, and since they are not particularly powerful government positions anyway, these elections represent a thin democratic reed and one that does not affect the party directly. But it may have some indirect effect by forcing it to put forward candidates with some popular sensibilities and broad appeal.

Finally, the developmental programme of the Dengists has called for a new type of party member. As economic incentive and technological advance have replaced ideological commitment and massive organization of labour as the linchpins of economic development, the party has come to require members and officials who are more technically or administratively expert and competent, while also respecting such expertise and competence enough to defer to it. It has sought to upgrade the skills of its members in these areas, and to attract to itself younger technical experts.[4] At the same time it has tried to demote, retire or expel members judged to be technically incompetent. In

Table 4.2 Age distribution of Members of Twelfth Party
Central Committee

Age	Number	Percentage
40–49	5	3
50–59	38	23
60–69	45	28
70–79	62	38
80–89	13	8

Source: Compiled from data in Bartke & Schier, 1985. The table only includes those officials whose ages were reported; data on forty-seven of the 210 officials were not available.

part, this has entailed much-heralded efforts to rejuvenate the party and its leadership. This has not been an easy task, for three reasons: (1) many old leaders have firm bases of power and support in the party; (2) in Chinese culture it remains a serious affront—and therefore involves high political risk—to attack the elderly; and (3) the spearhead of the party rejuvenation campaign is Deng Xiaoping, himself in his eighties. Thus, the average age of the Twelfth Central Committee was over 73, and the Politburo over 75. (The overall age distribution for those officials whose age was known appears in Table 4.2.) Yet, progress is being made, mainly by bringing in younger members rather than expelling old ones. The average age of those elected to the Twelfth Central Committee at its Fifth Plenum (1985) was 50.

There have also been efforts to raise the educational level of the party. While no data on the party as a whole have been published, the educational levels of those newly elected to the Twelfth Central Committee are indicated

Table 4.3 Educational levels of new recruits to
Twelfth Party Central Committee

Educational level	Number	Percentage
Primary	5	9
Junior middle	11	21
Senior middle	3	6
Normal school	2	4
Tertiary	32	60

Source: Compiled from data in Bartke & Schier, 1985.

Table 4.4 Percentages of party recruits from intellectual
and professional backgrounds

Year	Province	% of new recruits who were 'intellectuals' or 'professionals'
1981	Shanxi	36
1979	Beijing	15
197–82	Beijing	20

Source: Saich, 1983, p. 759.

in Table 4.3. Seventy-seven per cent of those newly elected at the Fifth
Plenum had college educations. Fragmentary data (Table 4.4) suggest,
though, that the number of new recruits with college educations has been
much lower—at least for earlier years—at lower levels of the party structure.

But these changes in recruitment criteria and membership composition
have not been motivated by purely technocratic concerns. They are also part
and parcel of a broad effort to shift the political orientation of the party by
ridding it of those with leftist views who joined during the Cultural Revolution. Those who are clearly associated with the 'Gang of Four' or who led
factional disputes during the Cultural Revolution (on the 'wrong' side,
mainly) are targets for expulsion. Thus the number of mass organization
representatives on the Twelfth Central Committee (CC) of 1982 declined by
more than half compared with the Eleventh (1977). In an effort to consolidate
central control of the party and its transformation, the percentage of State
Council officials on the CC nearly doubled in 1982, while that of provincial-
level officials dropped 20 per cent. (Female representation too has declined;
see Chapter 5, Table 5.2 and attending discussion.) But it is proving much
harder to transform the party as a whole. A major political battle at the
middle levels of the party between leftists who rose during the Cultural
Revolution and the Dengist leadership which seeks to replace them has been
underway for several years now. One indicator of this are the numerous
delays in the Dengist campaign to re-examine the membership rolls of the
entire party and the behaviour of each and every member.

Despite all these changes in political and developmental orientation and
the institutional changes they have brought in tow, the overall structure of
the Chinese Communist Party has not changed. The Leninist-Stalinist principles of political monopoly and centralized, vertical organization have not

changed at all. The primacy of the party as the locus of overall political and ideological leadership (in the state) and over civil society remains as firm a principle as ever. The substantive content of that leadership has changed, as we have seen. So has the way in which it is to be exercised *vis-à-vis* the state and society. The Dengist leadership believes that the party can best exercise its leading role of guiding the country toward its vision of socialist modernization by allowing greater latitude to non-party forces—by reducing its regulation of government organs and of civil society more generally. We take up these questions below, beginning with a discussion of government organization and turning them to relations between party and government and between the state and society.

Government

Constitutional Provisions and Changes

The constitutions of the People's Republic reflect and define the basic character of the Chinese state as well as the shifting political currents that have swirled within and around it. The first, adopted in 1954, declared the government 'a people's democratic state led by the working class'. The role of the CCP was formally downplayed, due to the continuing united-front policy of the day under which 'democratic parties' were permitted and allowed representation in the newly created National People's Congress (the successor body to the Chinese People's Political Consultative Congress, the transitional legislature). Private ownership rights were guaranteed. The document ran to 106 articles, elaborating in detail the structure of government and the mutual responsibilities of state and citizenry. The latter were guaranteed rights including due process of law, political expression, privacy, employment, education and social welfare assistance.

This constitution lasted over two decades, long past the time when many of its key features had come into disuse—of course, many others had never been implemented in the first place—or had become inappropriate due to the changing political situation. Ironically, the rapidity and radical character of those changes themselves prevented the political consolidation that would have made it possible to draft and approve a new constitution. By 1975, it appeared that the dust of the Cultural Revolution had cleared sufficiently to permit new constitutional efforts. (In retrospect we can see that it had not; the new document lasted only three years.)

The second constitution was the child of the then still dominant left, and it reflected the left's general distrust of state institutions. Only thirty articles in length, it was much less detailed about state organization and procedures than its precursor. In such institutional terms as it did recognize, it exalted the party above the government (in line with its view that politics ought to be 'in command'). It declared, in language which had no parallel in the 1954 constitution, that 'the Communist Party is the core leadership of the whole Chinese people' (Hinton (ed.), 1980, p. 2503). The position of Chairperson of the Republic—the functional head of state, a post last held by Liu Shaoqi—was abolished, leaving the Party Chairperson unchallenged. The Party Chairperson also replaced the Chairperson of the Republic as commander-in-chief of the armed forces—a change which reflected both the politicization of the military itself and also the key role it had played in the national and local politics of the Cultural Revolution. Locally, revolutionary committees—on which, as we shall see, the party held sway—were legitimated as local governments.

The defeat of the left in 1976 of course necessitated revisions in this constitution, which were made in a new document approved in 1978. This prefigured several subsequent political developments. While the leading role of the party was reiterated, some distance was begun to be put between the party and the government: now there was no mention, as there had been in 1975, of the National People's Congress being under party leadership. More latitude was to be given to intellectuals: 'letting a hundred flowers bloom and a hundred schools of thought contend' was once again to be the official order of the day. The key task of the government was to be the promotion of the 'four modernizations' (agriculture industry, science/technology and the military).

The 1978 Constitution, though a radical change from the one which preceded it, was nevertheless a compromise document promulgated during a period of political flux. It was adopted in March (and therefore drafted earlier), well before the key Third Plenum in December at which the Dengists would triumph. As such, it embodied many features with which the Dengists were dissatisfied and which they were soon in a position to change.

The 1982 document deleted the adulation of Mao which the previous one had retained, recreated the position of head of state (though in a more purely ceremonial role than had been enjoyed by Liu), and placed the military under firmer state control. The rule of law was emphasized. Rights of free speech and expression, which had been used primarily by critics of the post-Mao leadership, were deleted. The new constitution also reflected the changing policy priorities of the post-Mao state by diminishing the political and governmental role of the people's communes (now to be transferred to township governments), and by establishing mechanisms for creating 'special administrative zones' to accommodate the hoped-for return of Hong Kong and Taiwan to Chinese governmental control.

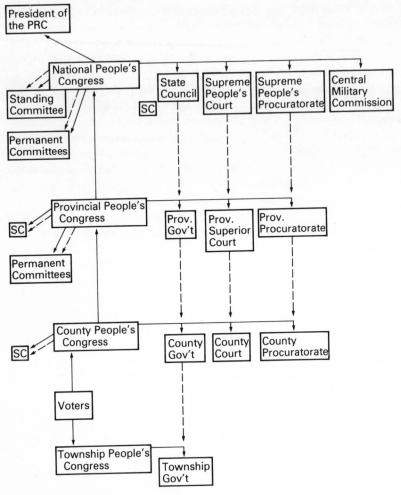

Figure 4.2 State structure of the PRC 1982 Constitution

Sources: (1) 'Constitution of the People's Republic of China', *Beijing Review*, vol. 25, no. 52 (27 December 1982). (2) Townsend and Womack, 1985, p. 96.

Government Institutions

The structure of the Chinese government under the 1982 Constitution is depicted in Figure 4.2. The supreme organ of government remains the

National People's Congress, which since 1954, has been the closest thing China has to a legislature.[5] It is a large body—the second session of the Sixth NPC was attended by 2,700 delegates—comprising representatives of provincial assemblies (which in turn are elected by the counties and municipalities below them), as well as certain functional organizations like the army. It is reconstituted every five years or so (though during the Cultural Revolution a full decade elapsed).

In the past, the NPC served little in the way of a genuinely representative or legislative function. As in other state socialist countries, it mainly rubber-stamped policies made by the Party and imparted to them the legitimacy and formal status of 'laws'. Lately there have been some efforts to strengthen the role of the NPC and its delegates. Where in the past it was disabled partly by its lack of an internal committee structure, the 1982 constitution provided for six 'specialized committees'—on nationalities, law, finance and economics, foreign affairs, overseas Chinese, and education, science, culture and public health—which are to 'examine, discuss and draw up relevant bills and draft resolutions' (*Beijing Review*, 2 December 1982, p. 21). While in the past service as a delegate was a part-time position—which meant that delegates were mainly government officials serving primarily in other posts—now the position of delegate is to be a full-time post. Annual sessions, held only occasionally in the past, are now to be regularized. Delegates have also been given the right to initiate legislation themselves.

They are also now chosen on the basis of a strengthened system of popular elections. Popular election of delegates to county-level People's Congresses has been instituted (see pp. 132-3). These county bodies in turn elect provincial People's Congresses which, in similar fashion, elect delegates to the NPC. Thus while there is only the most indirect popular election of NPC delegates, presumably such delegates have originally had to be directly elected to their positions in the county-level Congresses.

It is difficult to say precisely what effect these changes will have. To be sure, China—with its one-party system and its conflation of party and government—is still a very long way from anything like a representative parliamentary system. But with the recent changes in the organization of the NPC and the role of its delegates, some gains in this direction have been made. At minimum the NPC serves as a way for the top leadership to have personal contact with a large number of the most important regional and local leaders.[6] This is not entirely a one-way process either. At the NPC, regional leaders have the opportunity to make their case to each other and to the top leadership. Of course, the issues that they raise are, as in any political system, largely circumscribed by the prevailing ideology and structure of power. No delegate to a Chinese NPC would question basic socialist values or the party's current approach to them. Indeed, the delegates themselves are party members who have been chosen because they accept the prevailing parameters of political discourse. (Exactly the same could be said of the Democratic and Republican members of the United States' Congress, or of most British MPs.) But they do use the forum of the NPC to press their particular concerns—for example, the needs of their region, sector or organization for more resources, administrative support or even for policy changes. At the second session of the Sixth NPC, no less than 2,501 'suggestions and criticisms' were put forward; it is inconceivable that all of these could have been prepared in advance by the party or government leadership.

Both formally and in practice, the NPC is not an administrative body. Government administration is overseen by the State Council, which is elected by the NPC upon recommendation by the party. The State Council consists of the Premier, one or more Vice-Premiers, and the heads of the various vertical ministries, bureaux and commissions that comprise the Chinese government's administrative apparatus. The number, type and relative importance of these organs has varied over time in a pattern reflective of the policy emphases of the day. For example, the anti-statist themes of the Cultural Revolution, which informed specific demands for administrative simplification, found expression in a reduction in the number of ministries from forty-nine to twenty-nine. With the end of the Cultural Revolution, organizational restructuring tailored to the modernization programme has been carried out. The emphasis on streamlining administration continued: in 1982, forty-three of the organs under the State Council were consolidated into a mere fourteen. This round of simplification was intended, of course, not to reduce the power of the state in the spirit of a relatively abstract anti-bureaucratism (as during the Cultural Revolution), but to facilitate the economic modernization programme. That is why the restructuring has also involved creation of new institutions. For example, responsibilities for agriculture and forestry, formerly grouped under one ministry, were divided among two to give each greater prominence and attention; the People's Bank has been subdivided into specialized banking institutions; a State Commission for Restructuring the Economic System and Ministries of Electronics and Foreign Trade have been established.

Another area of expanded government institutions and activity is legal affairs. The post-Mao leadership has emphasized the restoration of 'socialist legality', partly because of its general commitment to procedural regularity and partly because of its direct experience with the irregular 'justice' of the Cultural Revolution, during which many people were imprisoned or punished without anything resembling a trial or even formal charges. The 1978 Constitution restored the People's Procuratorate—abolished during the Cultural Revolution—which is empowered to evaluate evidence against those arrested by the public security organs, on the basis of which it decides whether to approve the arrest and prosecute the case in a people's court. The first (!) criminal code of the People's Republic was approved in 1979.

An expanded legal apparatus has also been a necessary accompaniment to the economic reforms, which have emphasized contractual relationships in commerce and agricultural production. One-third of all civil disputes in the rural areas in recent years have concerned contracts and other economic matters. These reforms went ahead without clear institutions and legal guidelines concerning the ways in which contracts were to be drawn up or the means of resolving inevitable disputes about them.[7] By mid-1985, law offices had been established in over 20,000 townships, to notarize and help write contracts and to settle contractual disputes.

This brings us to the question of local government. Below the centre are three levels of government. The first consists of twenty-one provinces, five 'autonomous regions' (administratively identical to provinces, but located on China's borders and populated heavily by minority nationalities—hence the different name), and three cities—Beijing, Shanghai and Tianjin—which are so large that they are treated like provinces directly under the national government. The next level is the county and county-level municipality, of which there are around 2,300. Below them are townships and communes. Here the situation is in flux. From their inception during the Great Leap, the communes were combined units of production and government (as well as of social organization). The post-Mao leadership, as part of its programme to separate politics and economics, has sought to strip the communes of their political and governmental functions and to vest them instead in township governments, like the situation that prevailed during the cooperative period in the 1950s. (In many places the communes have actually been abolished.) By 1983, about half of China's counties had completed the process, which was scheduled to finish by 1985. At each of these levels, a people's congress is to be elected, which in turn appoints people's governments to administer concrete affairs.

Reform of Government and Party-Government Relations

The government has proved to be the part of the Chinese state most vulnerable to attack from other political forces, including the party and the masses. It had its heyday during the early and mid-1950s. The pressing tasks after 1949 were administrative and institutional rather than political. Governmental organizations had to be established and begin to function throughout the country. For example, the People's Bank had to issue currency, bring hyperinflation under control, absorb existing banks and their assets, and set up procedures for handling and transmitting funds. The Ministry of Commerce had to get control over prices and markets as well as establish mechanisms for receiving and distributing commodities under planned exchange. The Ministry of Communications had to build up networks for the collection, transmission and distribution of information through printed and electronic media. And so forth. China's First Five Year Plan, modelled on the organizational forms and economic strategies of the Soviet Union, vested power in the hands of central ministries with strong, vertical control over the economy. The 1954 Constitution made relatively little mention of the party.

Reaction to the political effects of the First Five Year Plan manifested itself in a major decentralization of power to the provincial level. There the bureaux of the vertically organized government ministries were weak, since they required central approval for the most important decisions and since their purse strings were held by their superiors in Beijing. Provincial party committees, by contrast, were quite strong. In part, this was a legacy from the revolutionary past, when the party operated in a relatively decentralized fashion because of the existence of numerous base areas. There was also a functional side to the strength of the provincial party committees. Since they were charged with supervising the political 'correctness' of the government as a whole, they were preoccupied with coordinating relations among government administrative and mass organizations (such as unions or the Women's Association). As a result, they had greater manœuvrability at the provincial level than any one functional bureau could. The decentralization of late 1957 gave greater power not only to the provinces, then, but (and more significantly) to the party as well. It was this organizational change that paved the way for the innovations of the Great Leap Forward, when 'politics' was put 'in command' of administration and when the party itself undertook to coordinate the large-scale mobilization of governmental organs and human energies in a crash programme of economic growth.

When this failed, power did not simply return to the central ministries. Rather, centralization was tempered with yet further and finer decentralization down to direct producing units. For example, we have seen that in the countryside the small production teams became the basic units of production and accounting, and many of them went further in subdividing control and management of production to individual households. Expanded scope for rural markets meant reduced power for the Ministry of Agriculture, the Ministry of Commerce and others. Experiments with expanded enterprise autonomy in industry were tried as well. In this period, the government faced serious challenges from the market and from the direct producers.

In the Cultural Revolution the government (as well as the party) faced its most serious challege, this time from a deadly combination of an un-organized but radicalized civil society and a supreme leader bent on ridding China of the bureaucratism, elitism and authoritarianism of which the government administration was a breeding-ground. Different elements of civil society attacked the government in different ways: radicals and others with more parochial complaints criticized it, self-interested workers took advantage of it for 'free rides' (collecting pay while keeping the factories closed or at least not showing up for work), and ordinary citizens often ignored it, doubting its legitimacy and authority or fearing pressure from anti-statist activists.

A semblance of order was restored starting around 1968 through the establishment of revolutionary committees, an institutional innovation consisting of representatives of the party, the government and mass (initially, red guard) organizations. In the meantime, party committees, too, were gradually being resuscitated, albeit in the hands of a phalanx of leftist leaders and recruits. The party, the only participant in the revolutionary committees that was also organized outside them, became the predominant political institution. The distinction between party and government became very indistinct during the Cultural Revolution decade. In many senses the party came to function as the government, getting involved in many of the small details of administration, while also dominating the larger issues of debating and setting policy directions. In terms of the latter, the ideological move-ments and counter-movements, and the political manœuvrings that domi-nated Chinese politics through 1976 were in any event within the functional purview of the party more than the government. In sum, then, during the Cultural Revolution the party reached its apex of political importance, while the government, and with it the party-government distinction, descended to its nadir.

The post-Mao leadership—including the reform-minded Dengist top leadership, the intelligentsia, and the pre-Cultural Revolution party and government regulars—is determined to change this. All the groups in the present coalition were greatly hurt by the unbridled predominance of the party during the Cultural Revolution. This was partly a matter of the leftist political ideology and programme that dominated the party. But it also had an institutional side. For many the party had never been their main organizational home. Deng and his associates had in the past found more undifferentiated support in the government than the party. Intellectuals, of course, viewed the party with suspicion. And old party and government bureaucrats learned the hard way of the need to maintain the institutional separation between party and government, if only to provide an institutional counterweight to the party that could help prevent a renewed leftist thrust, and to provide an alternative institutional refuge if the party undertook such a thrust. Thus there is a strong consensus among the various elements of the post-Mao leadership coalition that the distinction between party and government must be restored and that the predominance attained by the party during the Cultural Revolution must be changed.

In this area, as in many others, the Dengist leadership has not been able fully to match its political practice with its proposed policies. There is still considerable interpenetration of party and government leadership (Table 4.5). To be sure, it is something of an achievement that three of the five Party Politburo Standing Committee members—Chen Yun, Deng Xiaoping and Hu Yaobang—held no high government position as of 1986. But the other two still did: Li Xiannian was President and member of the State Council Standing Committee, and Zhao Ziyang was Premier, Minister in Charge of the State Committee for Restructuring the Economic System, and a member of the Science and Technology Leading Group. Moreover, of the remaining fifteen full members of the Politburo, only two did not hold high government positions, and one of these (Yang Shangkun) was a PLA General.

Beyond the issue of party–government relations are strong differences over the institutional shape of the Chinese polity, as well as the larger question of the relationship of the state as a whole to society. The Dengist leadership, strongly committed to its programme of economic reform based on expanded market forces, private and public sector entrepreneurship, and enterprise autonomy in some non-key sectors, has emphasized both depoliticization of the state (that is, a reduced role for the party *vis-à-vis* government administration) but also, and more significantly, a marked reduction of the power and authority of the state *vis-à-vis* society. The state is repeatedly urged to stop 'interfering' in many aspects of economic life, so that the productive energies unleashed by the reform programme be unrestrained in the pursuit of modernizing the economy. Political institutions at the grassroots have been reorganized so that they do not reside as closely to local society. In particular, the rural collectives have, as we have seen, been stripped of much of their political and administrative roles, which now repose in

Table 4.5 Party and government posts held concurrently by Members of the Politburo (as of October 1985)

Name	Politburo position	Other Party positions	Government positions
Chen Yun	SC Member	First Secretary CDIC	
Deng Xiaoping	SC Member	Chair, CAC Chair, CMC	
Hu Yaobang	SC Member	General Secretary, CC; Chair, CCGPC	
Li Xiannian	SC Member		President; SCSC Member
Zhao Ziyang	SC Member		Premier; Minister, SCRES; Member, STLG
Fang Yi	Full Member		State Councillor; Minister, SSTC; Chair State Council NADC (1980)
Hu Qiaomu	Full Member	Director, CEPWMZ	Honorary President, CASS; Chair, State Council NADC (1983)
Hu Qili	Full Member	Member, CC Secretariat; Director CC General Office	
Li Peng	Full Member	Member, CC Secretariat	Vice-Premier
Ni Zhifu	Full Member		Chair, ACFTU
Peng Zhen	Full Member		Chair, NPCSC
Qiao Shi	Full Member	Alternate Secretary CC; Director, CC International Liaison Dept; Member, CC Secretariat	
Tian Jiyun	Full Member	Member, CC Secretariat	Vice-Premier; Secretary-General State Council

Table 4.5 (*Cont.*)

Name	Politburo position	Other Party positions	Government positions
Wan Li	Full Member	Member, CC Secretariat	Vice-Premier; Chair, National Committee for Promoting Social Ethics
Wu Xueqian	Full Member		Minister of Foreign Affairs; Member, State Council
Xi Zhongxun	Full Member		
Yang Dezhi	Full Member	Deputy Secretary, CC Military Commission; First Secretary, General Staff Department Party Committee; Member, CMC	Chief of PLA General Staff
Yang Shangkun	Full Member	Vice-Chair, CC Military Commission; Member, CMC	
Yao Yilin	Full Member		Vice-Premier
Yu Qiuli	Full Member	Member, CC Secretariat; Member, CMC; Deputy Secretary-General, CC Military Commission	State Councillor; Director, PLA General Political Dept.
Chen Muhua	Alternate Member		State Councillor; Minister of Foreign Trade and Economic Relations; Chair, CPSCC
Qin Jiwei	Alternate Member	Second Secretary, Beijing Military Region Party Committee	Lieutenant-General and Commander, Beijing Military Region

Abbreviations:	ACFTU	All-China Federation of Trade Unions
	CAC	Central Advisory Committee
	CASS	Chinese Academy of Social Sciences

township governments that have a much greater distance from, and therefore reduced capacity to regulate, the peasantry.

This programme has not found enthusiastic support among some top leaders and much of the officialdom that staffs the party and government bureaucracies. In ideological, political–stylistic and programmatic terms, many of these people are deeply committed to a statist socialism in which central planning of the economy and political–administrative regulation of social life are paramount, and they are just as deeply suspicious of the rise of uncontrollable 'capitalist' forces and tendencies. To some extent this is an expression of an abiding Confucian elitism and authoritarianism, and also of the continuing attraction of the Soviet model. Many of China's leading and middle-level officials of the 1980s were trained in the Soviet Union in the 1950s. And though they may be duly critical—at least in public—of the ways in which central power is used and the purposes to which it is put in the Soviet Union, they are still believers in the efficacy of centralized state power to achieve rapid results.

Ideological and political style aside, there is a functional dimension to the concerns of many Chinese leaders about the Dengist programme. It aims to deprive them of some of their power and authority, and it has also complicated the tasks with which they remain charged. For example, officials involved in economic planning and administration would, under the reforms, have less to plan, fewer and less authoritative levers of control at their disposal with which to execute plans (for example, they must now use prices and incentives rather than commands), and more uncontrollable forces

---

Table 4.5 Abbreviations (*Cont.*)

CC	Central Committee
CCGPC	Central Commission for Guiding Party Consolidation
CDIC	Central Discipline Inspection Committee
CEPWMZ	Committee for Editing and Publishing the Works of Mao Zedong
CMC	Central Military Committee
CPSCC	Central Patriotic Sanitation Campaign Committee
NADC	National Academic Degrees Committee
NPCSC	National People's Congress Standing Committee
PLA	People's Liberation Army
SC	Standing Committee (Politburo)
SCRES	State Committee for Restructuring the Economic System
SCSC	State Council Standing Committee
SSTC	State Science and Technology Committee
STLG	Science and Technology Leading Group

Source: Bartke & Schier (1985).

(such as competition in alternative markets, both legal and illegal) with which to deal. As another example, the Dengist attack on rural collective institutions has made it much more difficult for state agencies charged with regulating population movement to carry out their task of preventing peasants from migrating to urban areas (Solinger, 1985). At a September 1985 special party conference called to consolidate the Dengist leadership, no less a figure than Chen Yun, China's leading economic thinker and planner, made an oblique attack on the Dengist reform programme when he stressed the need for continued state vigilance over the economy.

Thus there are several axes of political contradiction in the Chinese state at present. First, the Dengist leadership has attempted to bring into the party many intellectuals and reform-minded, middle-level officials at the same time as it has urged a greater separation between the party and the government institutions in which they serve. Second, it has brought them into the party while simultaneously urging the party to reduce its authority *vis-à-vis* the government and civil society—a great deal to expect from leaders newly admitted to the sanctum sanctorum of the state. Third, and related to the previous point, the Dengists, like the Maoists before them, face the fundamental contradiction of having to use levers of state power to minimize state power. Specifically, they are urging the party to cut back its own role in the state and to lead the state as a whole in reducing its role in managing civil society. Their opponents in the state are, as the Dengists frequently complain, using their positions of power in the state to oppose these plans. *Thus the struggle for depoliticization of the state becomes politicized*.[8]

Fourth is the contradictory nature of the economic tasks facing China. It is no doubt true that strengthened economic incentives and expanded privatization and decentralization to enhance entrepreneurial flexibility and autonomy can play positive roles in economic growth. But many of the grandiose plans for economic modernization (four modernizations, actually!) which the present leadership has put forward, and on which its political fate will ultimately depend, also require a continuing forceful role for centralized state economic planning and administration. Energy, transportation and education are key sectors requiring massive expansion and development. In capitalist countries, states have found it very difficult to run these profitably or in a decentralized manner. And even the Dengist advocates of privatization of certain economic sectors are not ready to tolerate private enterprise on the scale that would be required to run great utilities or universities. It is also doubtful that the amounts of capital that would be required to do so could be raised even in the climate of investor reassurance that the Dengists have tried to create. Finally, it seems unlikely that the vast number of state apparatuses that would interface with such private firms would not make strenuous efforts to undermine them through exercise of regulatory and extortionary measures as well as outright political pressure.

In short, then, China's four modernizations will entail a large role for a centralized and subsidized state sector at the commanding heights of the economy. At the same time, the reform programme is fostering privatization and profitability as economic principles and practical modalities. This contradiction is already finding political expression in innumerable conflicts over investment, pricing, management and planning policies (as well as economic expression in inflation, overheated growth rates, and black markets, to name just a few). Some of these take place within the state: for example, the state banks have recently been chastised for supplying excessive lines of credit to the relatively autonomous state firms as well as to private enterprises. Some of these take place between the state and society: for example, government agencies have taken to levying all manner of *ad hoc* taxes and fees on private firms, and in some cases to extorting funds from them. This state–society contradiction resonates back within the state, too, as these practices incur criticism from the Dengist leadership.

Thus, political relations within the Chinese state, and between it and society, continue to face serious contradictions in several respects. They will not disappear. A goal shared by almost all those in the post-Mao leadership coalition—most of whom suffered during the Cultural Revolution—is to find a way to manage them in an orderly and regular manner. One aspect of this search has been the attempt to strengthen institutional and procedural guarantees, such as socialist legality and constitutionalism. And since a major source of political instability and personal difficulty for the post-Mao leadership historically has been mobilization of discontented and radicalized citizens, major efforts have been undertaken to regularize and strengthen the political relations between the Chinese state and its people.

Popular Participation and Organization

Mass Organizations

In some ways mass organizations in China have differed little from their counterparts in other state socialist countries. They begin from the assumption that there is no fundamental conflict of interest—much less class or class-like struggle—between their mass constituents and the state. They also have no political autonomy from the government; indeed, they are official parts of it. Accordingly, they serve mainly to organize various social groups to carry out the policies which the state has formulated for those groups. Their representative functions are decidedly secondary and minor.

For example, the All-China Federation of Trade Unions (ACFTU) includes fifteen labour unions which together take in 80 per cent of China's state-sector industrial and commercial labour force (which numbered 115,150,000 in 1983); the remaining 20 per cent are simply new workers whose membership applications have not yet been processed. In functional terms, Chinese unions can be likened more to a labour relations department of a capitalist firm than to a trade union. Their major activities are in the areas of social welfare, adult education, recreation, and helping management organize and discipline the labour force. They administer welfare subsidies for workers in economic straits, hold after-work vocational and general classes, run factory libraries, recreation rooms and sports leagues and facilities, and help promote safety and productivity drives. They are not to call strikes, and in fact are responsible for helping to settle such strikes as occur rarely and spontaneously by mediating between striking workers and factory managers. Yet they occasionally do act on behalf of labour by bringing official complaints about working conditions and workers' rights. The ACFTU claimed full credit for exposing the details of official malfeasance which resulted in the death of seventy-two people when the Bohai No. 2 Oil Rig capsized in 1979. (In contrast to the advocacy model, though, it is just as likely that in this instance the state chose to publicize the issue through the ACFTU in order to enhance the appearance of its power.) It should also be noted that Chinese labour unions have thus far not organized at all among the burgeoning sector of rural industry.

The Women's Association too is an official organization of the state. Membership figures are difficult to find, though the Federation did have over 100 million before the Cultural Revolution. At the grassroots, it is not really an organization so much as a social category—all women automatically belong, and there are no regular dues or meetings. It does have local cadres appointed or recruited by higher levels of the association, and their job is mainly to organize festivities on 8 March (International Women's Day) and propagandize on issues like female hygiene and birth control. They may also help promote female labour participation, through exhortation as well as by organizing day-care facilities and special projects or work groups. In general the emphasis is on women's contribution to the state and the economy rather than to examination and pursuit of women's particular interests.

Other mass organizations serve this same purpose of integrating the masses into the state on the latter's terms. The Communist Youth League, with 48 million members in 1978, helps communicate approved values to young people, and identifies and coopts the politically inclined among them for leadership roles. The Young Pioneers, a mass organization for children aged 7–14, has around 130 million members, 80 per cent of the eligible age cohort; recently a goal of raising that figure to 100 per cent has been set. The militia is an arm of China's defence apparatus but it also functions politically to propagate and mobilize active nationalist sentiments among the people.

This manipulative pattern aside, China has experimented with more genuinely representative forms of mass organization in ways that are quite different from other state socialist countries. They were related to the Maoist belief that socialism had not eliminated serious social conflict—including class conflict—and that accordingly the masses needed institutions to represent their interests within and even against parts of the state. During the Socialist Education Movement, Poor and Lower-Middle Peasants Associations were formed in villages to organize opposition to 'spontaneous capitalist tendencies', criticize local cadres for their participation or acquiescence in these (or for more banal sins like corruption), and reconstitute village political authority. The most prominent examples of mass organizations which undertook to represent society rather than the state were, of course, the red guard groups. Following the early and most radical period of the Cultural Revolution, revolutionary committees were formed as an attempt to find an institutional form that could reconcile representation and advocacy of social interests with the exercise of state power.

In the post-Mao period all these institutional innovations have vanished, while other political forms not important in the Maoist state have appeared or, more accurately, reappeared. The post-Mao leadership has encouraged the reactivation of 'democratic' political parties and interest associations—such as the Revolutionary Committee of the Guomindang, the China Democratic League, the China National Construction Association, the China Association for Promoting Democracy, the Chinese Peasants' and Workers' Democratic Party, the 3 September Society, and the Taiwan Democratic Self-Government League—and has provided them some representation in the resuscitated Chinese People's Political Consultative Conference (CPPCC). None of these parties and groups was particularly important in Chinese politics even in the pre-1949 period. The largest of them was the China Democratic League, formed in 1944 out of the former Union of Comrades for Unity and National Reconstruction and its successor, the League of Democratic Groups. It was a loose federation of various small political parties, associations and clubs comprised of students, intellectuals, writers, poets, journalists and political activists. What united them was a commitment to promulgating liberal political values and institutions similar to those of the West. Even before 1949, the Democratic League had a very small following nationally, and nothing approaching a political organization capable of competing for or exercising political power at the national level.

In September 1949, the CCP convened the CPPCC, ostensibly to represent the 'united front' of anti-Guomindang political groupings such as the Democratic League. In fact it was the CPPCC—only sixteen of whose 662 delegates were Communist Party members—that actually proclaimed the establishment of the People's Republic of China. It went on to serve as China's legislature until the first NPC was convened in 1954.

The CPPCC, as well as the various groups that comprised it, gradually atrophied even further in subsequent years. Formally the CPPCC remained in existence until the mid-1960s, presided over by Premier Zhou Enlai and serving as a way of linking non-Communist political figures to the state. It was not heard from during the Cultural Revolution. But it reappeared in 1978, this time with Deng Xiaoping as its president. By 1982 it had over 100,000 members and 1,600 organs at the provincial and county levels.

According to the *Beijing Review*, the CPPCC

consists of the various democratic parties, non-Party democrats, people's organizations, public figures of national minorities as well as patriotic personages from all walks of life, including compatriots in Taiwan, Xianggang (Hong Kong) and Aomen (Macao) and Chinese nationals residing abroad. [*Beijing Review*, 20 December 1982, p. 5.]

This report failed to mention that 40 per cent of the members of the CPPCC are also members of the Communist Party. CPPCC national meetings are held concurrently with those of the NPC. It operates according to a corporatist principle of organization (Womack, 1984, p. 430), under which delegates are chosen not by the members but rather by each of its constituent organizations.

The revival of the CPPCC and its present role serve several political functions. It is a way of coopting such non-Communist political forces as have survived in China into the state. It lends a veneer of popular legitimacy to the state. As suggested by the passage quoted above, it is especially useful as a way of institutionalizing linkages between the state and overseas Chinese, especially wealthy business persons, who are given membership on the CPPCC in order to win their support to help smooth the reunifications with Hong Kong and Taiwan and to promote foreign investment. Finally, the CPPCC no doubt serves to percolate opinions and information upward, thereby keeping the state leadership abreast of the range of political interests and concerns of various strata and groups.

Popular Political Expression

The Maoist Period

Chinese politics are also distinctive from those in many other state socialist countries in their attempt to develop channels by which the masses can express their views to their leaders. This had its origins in the mass line of Yan'an days, when party and government cadres undertook intensive political work at the grassroots: persuading peasants to cooperate with and participate in the revolutionary movement, identifying potential activists and leaders, and so forth. The land reform was carried out with a very heavy component of mass democracy, as the party stressed the importance of the peasants themselves confronting their oppressors. As we have seen, this democratic element reached so far as to involve mobilization of popular criticism against local cadres, including party members. The movements for mutual aid and cooperativization—at least through the latter's initial stage—were not only voluntary but also strongly democratic in character, as peasants were involved intimately in the details of establishing and operating the new institutions.

It is frequently argued that the Great Leap Forward was a period when this democratic tradition was abandoned in favour of high-handed state authoritarianism.[9] This argument ignores the strong popular impulse with which the state leadership approached the Great Leap, and the strong popular support it enjoyed early on (Hinton, 1983). The Chinese leadership genuinely believed that the Chinese people would be enthusiastic about the Great Leap, and in a sense they were right. In political terms,[10] the problem was that the popularity of the Leap was heavily manufactured by the state through hyper-mobilization and propaganda rather than the careful and thorough grassroots work which built support and helped shape and revise policy and institutions flexibly into workable forms. The Great Leap, then, was a case not only of state authoritarianism but also of blunt, crude, rash and spontaneous popular participation mobilized by an excessively optimistic and careless leadership which allowed it unbridled latitude.

The political dynamics of the institutional and political changes that took place in the wake of the leap remain shrouded by the lack of detailed and dispassionate evidence from a period of economic disaster. But internal party documents from local levels suggest that there was something of a return to the grassroots investigative and participatory political processes of earlier days (Chen & Ridley, 1969). In any event, once the immediate economic crisis was resolved and the communes disaggregated into smaller sub-units, local politics settled down to a combination of bureaucratic state authority and local autonomy based on popular direct democracy.

State authority set the parameters for local democracy, but did not eliminate it. For example, while certain methods of collective operation (such as subcontracting to households) were forbidden, production teams were also given a definite latitude to conduct their affairs as they wished among a meaningful range of choices. They could choose time- or piece-rate distribution, set their own norms for allocating work-points, and adjust their accumulation rates and welfare spending within lower and upper limits. They could also choose their own officials, even to the point of ignoring party nominees. They arranged their own work on a day-to-day basis.

Within the teams, these functions were often carried out quite democratically. Team meetings were held frequently, and they were often scenes of lively debate over how to organize and run local affairs. Team cadres were ordinary peasants from the village who earned their livelihoods by working in the team, so there were few obstacles (save personality and leadership style) to prevent peasants from approaching them with questions, complaints and suggestions. This they did in many circumstances: when the villagers congregated informally in the evenings, during rest breaks or even while working, on the way to work in the fields, at local shops, and so forth. Peasants also made conscious use of indirect methods, such as village grapevines and anonymous big-character posters, to make known views which they expected to be unwelcome to their leaders. A wide range of peasants used these various channels of political expression. They could, and frequently did, bring up issues of concern to them (rather than restricting themselves to agendas set by their leaders), frequently disagreed with their leaders (not to mention each other), and were often successful in influencing the outcome. In general, strong norms of consensus operated within Chinese production teams, and the most effective leaders were those who could forge such broad agreement (Blecher, 1978a, 1978b, 1983).

There were also numerous channels by which peasants' views could reach the ears of leaders beyond their villages, at higher levels of the collectives (that is, the brigade and commune) and the state. They could have their views represented by delegates to the meetings frequently held at the brigade, commune or county levels. They could write letters to local officials or newspapers. Like those operating within the teams, these modes of expression fall broadly within the category of what is known in political science as 'political participation', that is, activity initiated by citizens to communicate their views and interests to political leaders and influence political decisions.

But the Chinese state did not always wait for its citizens to take the initiative. It frequently solicited their views through numerous mechanisms which provided the main conduit for expression of popular opinions and sentiments to leaders beyond the village. For example, work teams periodically visited villages, often with the express purpose of ascertaining the contours and nature of mass political discontent. Higher-level cadres were regularly sent down to villages to 'squat on the spot' (*dun dian*), which meant that they moved into villages for extended stays of several weeks or even months, during which they lived in peasants' homes and worked in the fields alongside them. They were also sent to villages for shorter visits to conduct interviews or to attend mass meetings. 'On the spot conferences' (*xian chang huiyi*) were held to investigate particular matters. In these ways, the views and concerns of peasants who lacked the inclination or ability to make themselves heard could be ascertained, and their situations experienced, by local and middle-level leaders. As a result, the state did not merely receive information from its own sympathizers or from those with greater political resources and energies. It could tap into a wider range of mass expression (Blecher, 1978a, 1978b, 1983).

The situation in the urban areas differs from the countryside in that there is a greater separation of work and home, the unity of which in the countryside helped promote participatory politics there. There were experiments with the mass line, such as the famous constitution of the Anshan Steel Mill, lauded by Mao, which institutionalized the two participations (of workers in management and managers in work) and triple combination (of managers, workers and technicians) in workshop organization. During the Cultural Revolution, the Beijing General Knitwear Factory, where a management committee was comprised of equal numbers of political and production cadres, and where factory officials regularly rotated jobs in and out of the office, became an exemplar of new forms of management based on participatory politics and management solicitation and investigation. But such experiments were short lived. Worker participation along Yugoslav lines was never broadly pursued in China.

Urban neighbourhood committees are another institution with potentially participatory political functions. But they have generally been preoccupied with carrying out propaganda and public health and information campaigns, and with exercising social control and mediating disputes. The extent to which they have provided the means for political expression within the neighbourhood or between it and higher levels of governance remains little studied.

The Post-Mao Period

Although scholarly research has not yet caught up with the recent changes in China, in all likelihood there has been a sharp decline in the participatory character of local politics in the Chinese countryside. During the 1960s and 1970s it depended on the existence of processes and institutions of collective production, which provided the substance of local politics (the issues about which people concerned themselves), its institutional forms (elections, meetings, investigations, etc.), and the context within which it could flower (such as relatively high social and economic equality among citizens and between them and local leaders). It also depended on a commitment to mass participation and close leader–mass relations which emanated from the dominant Maoist values of the day.

Under the reforms, production and income distribution have lost much of their collective character. Peasants spend their days working on household plots and other individualized work processes, or else in much smaller and more authoritarian group settings (such as small firms). They are much less interdependent during work and in the processes that determine their income. In addition, the scope of political life has been reduced by the general depoliticization pursued by the post-Mao leadership. Moreover, political institutions have been hived off from economic ones and transferred to the more distant township governments. In short, today in rural China there is less going on in the political arena, and fewer opportunities and greater obstacles to popular expression about what is going on.

But the post-Mao leadership has not done away with the idea of democratic participation in political affairs. It has put forward a programme of popular elections up to and including the county level, which is unprecedented in Chinese revolutionary politics. This is another sense in which the present leadership has not, as the pendulum model would suggest, simply returned to practices which its top officials put forward in previous periods when they had influence (a theme discussed more fully in the previous chapter). There is no evidence that either Liu Shaoqi nor Deng Xiaoping ever seriously advocated such elections in the mid-1950s or the early to mid-1960s.

People's Congresses have been established at the levels of the township and the county, and elections to them were held in 1980 and 1984. By the second round, two-thirds of China's counties held elections, though only one-fifth actually convened the congresses so elected. Voters were given the opportunity to select among multiple candidates nominated by the Communist Party and even by mass organizations and 'democratic' parties.[11] The power of these People's Congresses, and the democratic character of the elections of representatives to them, cannot be discussed without further research. At minimum, they are a means for coopting local activists and legitimizing state policy. They will help the state identify popular and politically adroit local people. They may also serve as a way for local concerns to find expression at higher levels of the state, as delegates bring to township and county government People's Congresses the views and demands of their constituents. To the extent that these delegates have their own electoral constituencies to which they are accountable in competitive re-elections, they may have reason to try to represent those who elected them. Having an electoral constituency may also provide delegates to local assemblies a certain autonomy from local governments (Womack, 1984). Finally, it should be noted that local government has never been an insignificant level of political power and administration in socialist China. Particularly with the effort to trim the power of the central state, township and county governments may even gain new developmental roles and levels of manoeuvrability (Meisner & Blecher, 1982).

Dissent

China has not produced the sort of persistent, semi-organized, underground opposition that has become a permanent fixture of the political landscape of the Soviet Union and Eastern Europe. In 1978, the 'Democratic Wall' movement attracted attention in the West. It consisted of a very small group of young workers and a few students who put up posters on a prominently located wall in downtown Beijing not far from the offices of the foreign press corps. Some underground magazines and political tracts were also published, though they never approached the circulation of the Soviet Union's *samizdat*. The movement was suppressed by the state in 1981, and has not been heard from since. That it lasted three years may have less to do with its strength or support within the leadership or the populace at large than with the post-Mao leadership's desire to appear accommodating in its early years of consolidating its power. The state may also have been trying the risky tactic of drawing its opponents fully into the open before smashing them.

There are several reasons for the weakness of popular dissidence of the Soviet type in China. Some have to do with the relationship of intellectuals to the state. In the Soviet Union and Eastern Europe, dissidents have mainly been intellectuals. Chinese political culture has for centuries emphasized the role and obligation of intellectuals to serve the state, as functionaries and sometimes as loyal advisers who can offer suggestions and constructive criticism. During the early part of this century, many intellectuals did take up the cudgels against the imperial state, but others did not; and in general their level of activity was strong enough to challenge but not destroy the older values about the proper political role of intellectuals. To this, of course, must be added the hostility which the Chinese Communist Party has shown regularly to intellectuals. Thus most Chinese intellectuals are simply disinclined to get involved in politics at all, or seek to do so only on the state's terms. That leaves very few with the inclination or the temerity to participate in dissident activities.

This points to a second set of factors which concerns the class basis of dissent. The disinclination of intellectuals to take part in dissidence helps explain why workers rather than intellectuals have led the small dissident movement that did appear after 1978. This in turn accounts in part for the weakness of the movement in general. The Chinese working class is somewhat economically privileged but also politically weak, two characteristics which help make it politically quite passive. So worker-dissidents could count on little broad support from other members of their class. They are even less likely to garner support from intellectuals, for reasons stated above and also because of the elitist condescension with which so many intellectuals regard the working class. And peasants are an equally unlikely source of support, because of the cultural and geographic chasms and the rather different political situation that separate them from the working class. Hence, in class terms the dissident movement in China has had weak leadership and real constituency problems.

A third set of factors has to do with the ways in which the Chinese state has allowed and encouraged opposition in the past. Discontented persons and groups have not lacked opportunities to express themselves, from the Hundred Flowers Movement and the Socialist Education Campaign to the Cultural Revolution and its follow-up campaigns. Such periodic openings for public expression of criticism pre-empted the coalescence and formation of an underground opposition movement.

Finally, the strength of Chinese patriotism, combined with China's long hostility to and separation from the West, have weakened dissent. One of the most potent sources of support for dissident movements in the Soviet Union and Eastern Europe has been the citizenry and governments of the United States and Western Europe. For twenty-five years potential dissidents in China were deprived of such potential support by the utter absence of contact between Chinese citizens and the West. And because Chinese dissident leaders were drawn more from the working class than the intelligentsia, they would have a more difficult time establishing such contacts anyway. More-over, to the extent that a dissident movement in China would draw upon the support of the West, it would offend the strongly patriotic sentiments of most Chinese, thereby drawing opprobrium and disgrace upon the dissidents for encouraging foreign interference in China's affairs.

5 Society and Socialism: Class and Gender

Class

The problem of social class has vexed analysts of and participants in Chinese socialism alike. More than any other socialist country, China has attempted to face the question of class directly. While political leaders and official ideologists in the Soviet Union, Eastern Europe and elsewhere have held steadfastly to the position that, with the abolition of private ownership of the means of production classes too have disappeared, Mao and other left-minded political leaders have argued that class cleavages and conflict continue to exist and even develop under socialism. Middle- and local-level leaders as well as many Chinese citizens have also raised the question repeatedly, both in discourse and practice, from the early days of land reform and cooperativization through the Socialist Education Movement, and, of course, into the Cultural Revolution. Western analysts of Chinese socialism, too, continue to debate the issue. At the end of the day, no conceptualization of class relations under socialism could be found that was both theoretically coherent and effective in guiding political action. As a result, the controversial issue of class in socialist China remains. But even if no satisfying solutions have yet been found, it is probably the case that more progress in thinking about the issue has been made, and more experience garnered, in the Chinese case than in any other socialist country. Practitioners and students of socialism elsewhere might well look to China as an aid to analysis and political practice concerning the class dynamics of socialism.

Social Class in Socialist China

The major classes of post–1949 China, and some of the important changes among them, are summarized in schematic form in Figure 5.1. (As a summary of Chinese society only, it excludes specific reference to state officials.) This figure also sketches in some of the lines of class cleavage which have been suggested by analysts of Chinese social strucure. They are: a political-sectoral cleavage between those working in the state sector (which includes mainly urban residents) and those in the collective sector (mainly rural dwellers); a cleavage between state and society; and the differences among those people with different economic endowments (such as peasants in rich or poor villages). These are discussed more fully in sections that follow.

Movements among various classes, denoted by the directional lines in Figure 5.1, reveal much about the nature and policies of the Chinese state, which engineered or permitted them.

Former 'Bad Classes'

We have seen (in Chapters 1 and 2) how the CCP led a very skilful attack on the dominant classes of pre-revolutionary society by adopting a flexible and pragmatic class policy that included alliances with exploiting classes at perilous moments and by pursuing its attacks on them in a gradual and phased way. As a result, the political and economic power of the landlords, rich peasants and capitalists was, to use the Chinese phrase, 'basically' destroyed before the end of the 1950s. In Chinese parlance, 'basically' means 'mainly' but also 'not completely', and in fact the former dominant classes did retain some economic resources and political clout even after the first decade of Chinese socialism. In the wake of the Great Leap Forward, former

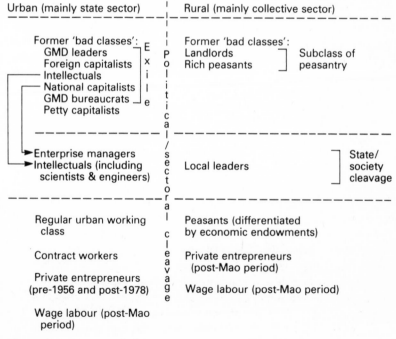

Figure 5.1 Summary of Chinese class structure, 1949–present

landlords and rich peasants were at the forefront of decollectivization at the village level. Even where collectivization was not reversed, their political position in the villages was often strengthened as fellow villagers now turned to them to exercise the farming and entrepreneurial skills which they often possessed in disproportionate quantities and which were so badly needed to pull out of the crisis of the Leap (Thurston, 1977).

Even through the 1970s, former rich peasants and landlords were in many villages still regarded with a certain measure of respect, fear or deference. Rich peasants in particular were often felt to be especially knowledgeable about agriculture. Both they and even former landlords were also utilized as sources of information and informal contacts needed in the development of rural industries (to help obtain scarce supplies (often illicitly), identify markets, manage the workshops, design the products, repair machinery, etc.; see Blecher, 1978, pp. 115-19). At the same time, these former class enemies—particularly the landlords—have been ostracized and victimized in specific ways. They were excluded from regular political meetings, and often forced to attend special ones for former class enemies. They were subjected to regular political surveillance, and were ostracized from the social life of many villages. Former landlords usually received 10 per cent fewer work points for the same work as other peasants, and were regularly made to work in the fields on holidays when everyone else had a day off. Even the children of former landlords and rich peasants were objects of discrimination, in areas such as educational advancement, selection for special employment or training opportunities and so forth.

On the urban side, of course the top Guomindang leadership retreated to Taiwan, where they remained in an exile that continues to the present. Foreign capitalists too left, some immediately and some after a period of several years during which they remained in China, ran their businesses under increasing state regulation, and negotiated compensation for the eventual nationalization of their enterprises. Many intellectuals, national capitalists and state bureaucrats, fearing for their personal fortunes in an uncertain future under the CCP, went into exile on Taiwan or abroad. But many others stayed on the mainland, often more out of patriotic than pro-Communist sympathies. Their talents were needed for the economic recovery and the development of the new state apparatus. Hence the CCP, continuing its flexible and pragmatic class policy, kept many of them on, tolerating some and attempting to coopt others. For example, many capitalists were kept on as managers of their former firms which had been nationalized. Indeed, many capitalist enterprises were only partly nationalized, i.e., converted into joint public-private firms, part of whose profits were paid as interest on the part of the stock which remained privately owned. (These interest payments continued until the Cultural Revolution, and were restored retroactively after 1978.) Many scientists and intellectuals too stayed at their posts or were brought into new positions under new state organs, where, to be sure, they now found themselves under the close supervision of party officials. Under meritocratic admissions criteria the children of formerly dominant urban classes continued to be admitted to colleges and universities. But when it came to allocations of scarce resources such as the most desirable job placements or housing, those with 'bad' class backgrounds were often discriminated against by state officials, who favoured political activists (including sometimes their own cronies) from 'good' class backgrounds. And during political campaigns the 'bad classes' were periodically subjected to public criticism and ostracism.[1]

Petty capitalists, including shopkeepers, traders and service providers (such as barbers and tailors), were regarded as having a contradictory class position—not really class enemies but not strong supporters of the revolution either. Under the CCP's flexible and pragmatic class policy, they were allowed to continue to operate through the early 1950s. Socialization of this class's means of production came in 1956, but most of its members were permitted to continue working in their former businesses that had come under state control. Hence they were incorporated into the state sector as employees (and often supervisors) of their old enterprises.

The pressures built up by the contradictory situation in which former class enemies in the countryside and the cities were preserved and required for economic construction, but at the same time treated with disfavour, exploded in the Cultural Revolution. When Mao called for mass criticism of and uprisings against 'those in authority', his words struck a responsive chord among former 'class enemies' who had been victimized by the state officials and institutions which Mao was now criticizing. This explains in part why state officials so often tried to shift the focus of the Cultural Revolution to struggles against former capitalists, landlords and rich peasants. Moreover, many former class enemies and their offspring had leadership skills that were valuable in developing the mass movements of the Cultural Revolution. The Maoists even went so far as to protect them and legitimate their role in the Cultural Revolution by condemning 'blood theory'—which held that class character was indelibly determined by birth—and by arguing that the key determinant of class was attitude and behaviour—which were change-able—rather than one's parents' (or even one's own former) class status. As a result, the Cultural Revolution provided a medium for the expression of animosities of former class enemies and their families against the state which had been discriminating against them. A statistical study of the social bases of participation in the Cultural Revolution found that former class background proved to be the most significant correlate of faction membership, with people of capitalist or landlord background disproportionately represented among the rebels (Blecher & White, 1979b).

The continued importance of those with 'bad class backgrounds' is difficult to measure. As late as the early 1970s, peasants from Guangdong Province still often regarded former rich peasants as particularly knowledgeable about economic and production matters. They were regularly drawn into collective deliberations of such issues. The collectives also made use of former landlords' and rich peasants' personal contacts to find scarce resources or develop extra-state commercial contacts. In some places collective fields were still referred to by the names of their former owners, and it was reported that property stones used to demarcate plots before land reform were still buried in place. Whether former landlords and rich peasants or their children have been able to benefit disproportionately from the responsibility systems and commercial and employment deregulation in the countryside is an important but largely unresearched question.

In any event, it is significant that one of the first steps taken by the present leadership in implementing the reforms was the abolition of formal class categories. The official Chinese position today is similar to that of most other socialist countries: that classes do not exist. This position is more difficult to sustain in the Chinese case, since the argument that this is as a result of the socialization of all productive resources cannot hold.[2] For on the question of class relations, the present leadership has largely refused to face the theoretical implications of the rise of a small but growing sector of private ownership of the means of production. To be sure, they will have much greater difficulty ignoring the effects of class cleavages and conflicts in practice. This raises the problem of understanding where those cleavages lie.

Movement of Societal Classes into Leadership Classes

In addition to recruiting officials and functionaries from the Guomindang government, the People's Republic has, of course, also continuously recruited new cadres and officials from the ranks of the working class and the peasantry. This movement of citizens into leadership positions was encouraged by the Maoist emphases on mass participation and the tendency to place political above technical qualifications in leadership recruitment. In the countryside peasants were continuously drawn into the ranks of a burgeoning group of local grassroots cadres. Especially with the advent of cooperatives and then communes, a large number of peasants took up positions of responsibility ranging from team warehouse attendant to commune leader. As many as one person in ten, and sometimes even more, held some sort of official position in the collectives during the 1960s and 1970s. Up to the brigade level, all leaders were local peasants; many commune-level cadres were, too. Indeed, many leaders at county, provincial and even national levels were former peasants. Their presence in the state was symbolized by the accession of Chen Yonggui, a former poor peasant and brigade leader of Dazhai Brigade—which became a national model—to the post of Vice-Premier. Workers, too, could enter positions of leadership as factory forepersons and leaders of neighbourhood committees. Many factory managers, too, were former workers.

Local Leaders, Intellectuals and Enterprise Managers: Between Society and State

These local leaders stand right on the cleavage between state and society. Many are party members, and even those who are not are expected to support state policies and directives. Yet they also have definite ties to local society. During the Maoist period all team and brigade cadres, and some commune cadres, too, were on the payrolls of their collectives rather than the state. Like other peasants, their income was determined by work-points, whose value depended on the health of the collective economy. Therefore they had a direct material interest in the economic well-being of the villages. Moreover, team and even some brigade cadres were elected by the villagers, who had real autonomy in their choices, even to the point of being able effectively to oppose party nominees (Blecher, 1978; Burns, 1978). So in addition to their economic identification with the locality, grassroots cadres were politically responsible to and based in it.

That is why they have sometimes acted to protect local interests against the state when they deemed the latter's demands to be harmful to the former. For example, during the Great Leap Forward there was a rash of over-reporting of production results by local cadres who sought to protect their villages against criticism from the state for not living up to the high expectations of the day. At other times local cadres under-reported their villages' output or production capacity, so that the locality could retain more of its output or so the state would lower the production targets which it expected the locality to meet. The campaign to emulate Dazhai was resisted in many places because cadres felt the concrete methods involved in doing so were inappropriate to their villages' material conditions.

Local cadres have also been active in communicating the wishes and interests of ordinary citizens at the grassroots to the state, while also carrying information and instructions to them from the state. At countless local meetings which they regularly attend at the commune or county seats, they are able to voice the complaints and concerns of villagers—with whom they are regularly in touch on a face-to-face basis—to higher-level officials who are also present there.

Intellectuals, too, occupy an ambivalent and sometimes contradictory position between state and society. Maoist, Liuist and Dengist leaderships alike have hoped for an intelligentsia which, like that of imperial days, would be unquestionably loyal to the basic values of the state even when offering criticism of it. But many intellectuals have not been especially inclined to the political left, and many of those who were had different conceptions about socialism and the contours of the good society than did the state leadership. Accordingly, many intellectuals have found themselves partly in the state—working for state agencies and trying to contribute to it—and partly out of it—in quiet or even active opposition or else exorcised from the state by the latter's periodic attacks (as we have seen in Chapter 2). Other intellectuals—particularly many scientists and technicians—have worked within the state for various specialized agencies, but have tried to remain apolitical.

Even enterprise managers, like rural local leaders, have often been caught between the conflicting interests of their grassroots 'constituencies' (their factories and the workers therein) and the demands of the state. During the recent period of reform, for example, they have often ignored state directives by expanding their factories beyond the parameters desired by the state. (The attendant rash of factory expansion has caused serious shortages of construction materials, which in turn produced inflation and black markets.) Other factory managers have distributed bonuses—intended by the state to foster labour incentives—to all workers (regardless of labour performance) in order to maintain factory morale, reconcile the current policy of material incentives with the Maoist or simply socialist commitment to economic equality, or protect themselves from criticism from the work-force for practising favouritism or trying to increase labour discipline.

Conceptualizations of Class and Socialism in China

Maoism

Perhaps Mao's greatest, most innovative and radical contribution to the theory and practice of socialism was his theory of continuing revolution based on class conflict under socialism. Unfortunately, Mao and the theorists and politicians he influenced were never able to formulate a concept of class that could provide a basis for clear political action to move China closer toward socialism. The present-day rejection and abandonment of the Maoist concerns about class conflict and revolution under socialism is a dialectical product of the Maoist failure.

By the mid-1960s, after some casting about, Mao came up with the concept of a new dominant class as 'persons in authority taking the capitalist road'. He spoke of a restoration of capitalism in the Soviet Union, and of capitalist-roaders in China as a new bourgeoisie. The thrust of this class formation had less to do with an argument about the bureaucracy exercising the functional equivalent of ownership prerogatives than with an argument about leadership: the leaders' attitudes, the sectoral balance of their policies, their relationship to the masses. For example, his criticism of the Ministry of Public Health was focused less on the relatively high incomes of doctors and ministry officials than on their preference for ministering to the health needs of the urban rather than the rural residents. He was not concerned so much about state officials' incomes *per se* or as examples of simple inequality. Nor did he conceptualize them in terms of a Marxian economic logic adapted to the socialist mode of production, which would refer to the process of bureaucratic appropriation of surplus value and exploitation. Rather, he was principally concerned about the effect of these incomes in creating and reproducing a political barrier between leaders and masses. For Mao the causes and effects of inequalities between leaders and led lay more in the realm of politics and consciousness than in economics.

The major problem with this formulation was its practical indeterminacy. During the early days of the revolution a landlord or a capitalist could be identified with some certainty; during the Cultural Revolution a capitalist-roader could not. Of what did proletarian consciousness or attitude consist? And how could it be determined whether a particular person had it, or enough of it? In the absence of clear criteria and in the maelstrom of the Cultural Revolution, these questions could not possibly be posed or deliberated in a serious and constructive way. All leaders and many masses became suspect and the movement quickly degenerated to the level of personal and parochial charges, defences and counter-charges.[3] 'Class' and 'class struggle' became tools in these idiosyncratic politics rather than the basis or focus of politics.

A related and resulting problem was anarchism. By focusing on political leadership as the locus of class formation and domination—'persons *in authority* taking the capitalist road'—but failing both to specify how the members of the new class were to be identified and to limit the attacks on them, Mao invited a general and thoroughgoing attack on all authority. The palpable anarchism which appeared in the Cultural Revolution was a product in part of the failures of the Maoists to theorize and guide the class struggle.

There is evidence to suggest that at least some Maoists recognized these problems and attempted to do something about them. In his major 1975 essay, Zhang Chunqiao made a serious if primitive effort to articulate a materialist basis for class conflict in the socialist mode of production (Zhang, 1975). Specifically, he argued that it was the continued existence of commodity production that 'engendered' the production and reproduction of a bourgeoisie. He admitted that this could only be gradually restricted, not eliminated in one fell swoop, and intimated that this could be done through a combination of institutional and organizational changes in the socialist economy as well as through political movements. To be sure, Zhang's position on the pernicious effect of commodity production is controversial. It is arguable that markets can serve the development of productive forces under socialism without endangering its class basis. The problem was that in the highly charged environment of Chinese politics it was difficult for a meaningful debate on this issue to take place. And in the absence of the results of such a debate, a political practice on the class question that would advance socialist development and transition was even more unlikely. The efforts of Zhang and other Maoists to correct the problems with the Maoist approach that shaped the earlier and more extreme phases of the Cultural Revolution were too little too late. The tragic result has been that serious discussion of the class dynamics of socialism has been utterly discredited and abandoned in the one socialist country which raised it most forcefully and where, with the resuscitation of a growing private sector, it may be most apposite and necessary.

State, Economy and Class

If discussion of this question is practically impossible in China, it is still alive among Western scholars interested in the class dynamics of socialism. One approach—which could be called political-sectoral—identifies a major social class cleavage in Chinese socialism as that between employees in the state sector—the government administration and state-run enterprises—and those in collective or private-sector enterprises. In this line of thinking, one class employed directly by the state has enjoyed benefits of urban residence, guaranteed employment, retirement pensions, more easily available and affordable consumer goods, and social services such as health care and education which are provided by the state and of higher quality than in the non-state sector.[4]

One major element of this cleavage has to do with income levels and their mode of determination. Those employed in the collective sector have had to depend for their incomes on the success of collective endeavours, which in turn depend on the quality of management, collective solidarity, labour input and productivity, price structures, and unpredictable factors such as weather. Moreover, the state has forced collectives to produce in accordance with its own plans, often requiring them to concentrate on lines of production to which they were ill suited and for which it did not pay them very well anyway. The most notorious example is the policy of 'taking grain as the key link', under which many communes already engaged in profitable cash-crop production were forced to switch to grain, from which the income was much lower. Meanwhile, the state has guaranteed income and employment to its employees regardless of their level of work or productivity or the effects of external factors.

A second element concerns state policies on consumption. The state has set prices and allocated scarce commodities in favour of itself and by extension in favour of those it employed. For example, it has assured guaranteed supplies of inexpensive foodgrain to the cities, passing the cost along to the collectively organized peasants in the form of artificially low procurement prices. It has also subsidized profits of state enterprises by setting ex-factory and retail prices of their products high while not enforcing quality standards. The costs of this have been borne by the peasantry who have to buy the high-priced and shoddy products.

Finally, through its system of household registration, the state has created strict social and political barriers between its employees—most of whom reside in towns and cities—and those of the rural collectives. Specifically, peasants are classified as rural residents. Rural households are forbidden from taking up employment or residence in towns. Without a card verifying one's status as an urban resident, one cannot qualify for urban housing, jobs, health care (unless referred by a rural clinic or hospital) or education (unless specifically assigned by virtue of demonstrating great talent). One may not even purchase foodgrain at the state-run outlets.

The political-sectoral approach, like the Maoist approach, sees the state as central in structuring society into classes. But it differs from it in some important respects. Whereas the Maoist approach emphasized the cleavage between state and society, this one concentrates on cleavages within society created by the structures and policies of the state. Hence it allows for the possibility of state action to ameliorate or reinforce class cleavage and social inequality. By contrast, the Maoist approach located the key agency of changing class structure and relations in the actions of society—specifically and, in conceptual terms, rather grossly, the actions of 'the masses'. The political-sectoral approach is a response to the lessons of the Cultural Revolution decade, in which the unorganized 'masses' of 'society' proved unable even to take up seriously, much less to act constructively and self-consciously upon, the class contradictions of Chinese socialism.

Class could also be conceptualized in terms of what could be called economic endowments.[5] In this approach class inequalities are understood as those based upon the ability to command returns to unequal endowments of productive resources. For example, it could be argued that Chinese industrial workers have on average enjoyed incomes two to three times those of Chinese peasants in part because the higher organic composition of capital in industry, which in turn makes for its higher labour productivity and per-worker output and income, and provides the material basis for paying industrial workers more. As another example, the higher incomes of peasants who work in areas blessed with more fertile land, better transport facilities or greater proximity to urban markets for cash crops are seen as a form of rent collected by those peasants on their more valuable land (since they do not necessarily work harder—and may actually work less hard—than their fellow agriculturalists who have to scratch out a living on rocky mountainsides or remote steppes). This way of thinking about class has something in common with a Marxian economic approach, in that it attempts to identify in socialist China—specifically in the ways in which it determines income—the functional equivalent of prerogatives of ownership of productive resources and appropriation of their output.

The economic endowment approach is not at all inconsistent with the political-sectoral one. It shares with it the concern with finding class cleavages within society and it also sees these as the result of state structuration (and therefore subject to reduction through state restructuration). But the economic endowment approach emphasizes the question of class relations *within* sectors as well as *between* them. For example, it proposes a way of conceptualizing class inequality among peasants themselves, not just between them and state workers or government staff. And it does so in a way that does not rely upon the largely anachronistic categories of poor, middle and rich peasants. It also resonates to the socialist principle of distribution according to work. Put differently, it views socialist society as having class stratification insofar as it distributes the social product according to criteria other than labour input (Blecher 1985a).

Both these approaches to class under socialism are analytical, in the sense of defining in objective terms those cleavages that shape social contradictions that could form a theory of the dialectical 'laws of motion' of socialist society.

In Marxian terms, they are ways of thinking about class 'in itself'. Of course their real utility lies only in the extent to which they correspond to the actual political and social struggles that are playing themselves out in China. This is a difficult area to study, both because of the difficulty of carrying out research and also because of the constraints on expression of social conflict which operate in the context of Chinese society and politics.

But there is evidence that each of these concepts of class is a reality among the Chinese people. For example, the political–sectoral approach suggests that peasants would understand that a definite cleavage exists between themselves and workers on the state payroll, and that this understanding would under certain circumstances influence their political actions. In fact the peasant–worker cleavage is deeply embedded in the language, culture and consciousness of the Chinese people (Potter, 1983). Moreover, it was frequently the case during the Cultural Revolution that peasants who had been hired as temporary contract workers in urban industrial enterprises were among the most radical participants in the movement, and that they demanded equal pay and employment conditions, and sometimes even abolition of the rural–urban householder distinction. Recent reforms have had the effect of lifting mobility restrictions on the peasantry, resulting in new flare-ups. For example, there have been reports of employees of state enterprises attacking peasants who have set up urban enterprises that compete with their own (Oi, 1986). It appears, then, that the 'objectively' defined classes of rural and urban householders posited by the political–sectoral theory do indeed correspond to a subjectively understood reality at the levels of consciousness and political action.

It is harder to find evidence of the subjective character of the economic endowment concept of class. But it is also very difficult to imagine that, for example, peasants who have ended up with contracts for poorer land or for less capital–intensive sidelines do not feel resentment against those who have. It seems that the contracting process in the villages, during which productive resources are allocated for use, has caused its share of controversy among peasants—between, for example, those with high household dependency ratios, who advocate allocation of land on a per-capita basis, and those with low ones, who advocate per-worker allocation (Lin, 1983).[6] It is also reasonable to suppose that some of the incidents reported in the Chinese press, in which productive resources such as fruit orchards are vandalized, are not the result of hooliganism by young people who have come under the negative influence of the Cultural Revolution (as the official interpretation would have it), but more likely expressions of anger by peasants against what they take to be the private appropriation of formerly collective resources, at least for a contracted period.[7] To the extent that the inequalities resulting from uneven distribution of productive resources are causing resentment that could become politicized, they pose a great potential danger to the political stability on which the present reforms are predicated and which they propose to reinforce. The economic endowment theory of class, then, suggests some of the lines of contradiction that are likely to be evident in Chinese socialism at present.

Economic Equality and Inequality

The significance of any of these lines of contradiction for social and political conflict and action depends in part on the magnitudes of economic inequality involved. One of the greatest accomplishments of Chinese socialism has been rapid gains in economic equality, which were achieved alongside very respectable rates of economic growth (discussed in Chapter 6). In this respect Chinese socialism differs markedly from the modal pattern of capitalist development, in which the early and middle period of economic modernization produced increased inequality (Adelman & Morris, 1973).

In China this achievement had several dimensions. The land reform eliminated the inequalities resulting from tenancy, under which the landlord class, comprising just 1 or 2 per cent of the population, appropriated an economic surplus in the vicinity of 30 per cent of national income (Lippit, 1978). Cooperativization eliminated all inequalities resulting from unequal ownership of productive resources within the village-sized coops. With the nationalization of industry and commerce in the 1950s, urban employment was broadened and wages standardized, reducing inequalities among the urban population. Inequalities among villages and regions remained more daunting, although the state took several steps to reduce them. For example, in the 1950s it used the state budgetary process to redistribute financial resources from rich to poor provinces (Lardy, 1978). It targeted inland provinces for industrial investment, seeking to broaden the geographical distribution of industry and correct the imbalance—inherited from colonial days—in which industry was heavily concentrated in coastal cities and Manchuria. It standardized prices geographically, which in effect provided a subsidy to the generally poorer remote areas. It adopted a rural development strategy which at least formally gave the highest priority to the poorest areas (though whether it had this effect is the subject of a scholarly debate which will require much better data before any resolution can be found).[8]

But also embedded in the structures and policies of the first three decades of Chinese socialism were forces which operated to restrict the scope of economic equality. Some of these were designed to provide production incentives. For example, rural taxes were regressive, with more prosperous coops and then production teams paying a smaller percentage of their crop than rich ones. The size of the basic unit of collective accounting and income distribution was kept small, a lesson from the Great Leap when excessively large units proved to be unmanageable and hurt labour incentives.[9] Peasants were forbidden to move to cities or to richer villages—both of which would have increased equality—for fear of the social disruptions and abandonment of poor but still marginally productive land that would result.

The overall effect of the economic structures and policies pursued in the first three decades of Chinese socialism was heavily egalitarian. By the mid-1970s, economic equality within villages was extremely high and virtually all residual inequality at that level was due to the unequal labour capacities of individual households. Moreover, steps were taken to reduce the effect of these residual inequalities by offering welfare benefits and long-term loans to guarantee minimum living standards. Inequalities among villages in a given region were higher than those within villages, but still very low in comparison with other Third World countries. For example, in 1978 in Hebei Province (which, with 50 million people, was larger than many countries), the poorest 40 per cent of the peasantry received 25 per cent of distributed income (compared with an average of around 13 per cent in other Third World countries) and the richest 10 per cent only 18 per cent of income (compared an average of 39 per cent in the Third World).[10]

The effect of the post-Mao reforms on economic equality is another subject of debate among scholars which is hampered by inadequate data. There is broad agreement among Western and Chinese analysts that they would most likely show a definite rise in inequality within villages. Official Chinese criticisms of the pre-1978 policies as fostering excessive egalitarianism, together with their repeated arguments about the virtues of 'letting some get rich first', suggests that the post-Mao policies have indeed increased economic inequality overall, or at least that Chinese leaders expect them to have done so. Chinese press reports on peasant income are dominated by the accolades given to those able to buy automobiles, computers and even aircraft (!), but less is heard there about the village poor, who are increasingly subject to recidivisms such as tenancy (based on sub-renting of large tracts leased from the village on a long-term basis by a few peasants) and debt (due to crop failures or insufficient output relative to the quotas and fees charged: see Kelliher, 1986). In one unusual report, 11,000 households in Chuxian Prefecture (Anhui Province) achieved annual incomes in excess of Y5,000 by 1983, but 9,900 households still earned less than Y100. Despite certain relief efforts and development assistance to them, half of this latter group could not look forward to breaking through this level by 1985, according to local officials (*Beijing Review*, 27 February, 1984, p. 9).

The effect of the reforms on inequality among villages and regions is much more difficult to assess. There is little doubt that overall urban–rural inequality has declined, as rural prices have risen and irrational plans which kept many villages from planting in accordance with their comparative advantage have been lifted. The ratio of average per capita incomes in urban and rural areas was 4.58:1 in 1978, but only 2.74:1 in 1984 (*Far Eastern Economic Review*, 20 March 1986, p. 78). Changes in provincial and sub-provincial distributions are harder to assess. Places which were poor partly because of the policies of the Maoist period—such as those which had an excessive build-up of rural labour that could not be released to urban areas, or those which were forced by the emphasis on grain production to abandon profitable cash crops—will have seen improvements since 1979. But those which could benefit from those policies—such as those which needed collective institutions to organize infrastructure development or rural industry, or to retain needed labour power, as well as those which were receiving such development assistance and income subsidies as was available—will have stood to lose from the present policies.

Before 1978, intra-village inequalities were due largely to unequal labour endowments among households. These tended to even out over the life cycle (as children grow into income-earners) and were also subject to amelioration through collective welfare and credit policies. Unequal labour endowments still shape inequality within the household-based responsibility systems. But now they are supplemented by property-related factors, too. Some of these are in the public realm. Peasants who farm the best land or use the best productive resources can earn more income from using them, even if they apply the same amount of labour as their neighbours who are working less good land with less capital. In a sense, they are collecting rent on the land and interest on the capital. Then there are inequalities resulting from unequal private ownership of productive resources, including private firms that hire labour, where direct profit and labour exploitation (in the strictest Marxian sense) are taking place. This is also beginning to happen without formal ownership: for example, in Long Bow Village, Shanxi, one peasant who contracted for the village's vegetable plot was hiring wage labour to work it (Hinton, C., 1986). There is also, as noted above, the phoenix-like return of tenancy and usury. Meanwhile no steps at all have been taken to do anything about regional inequalities resulting from factors beyond the peasants' control, such as quality of land, proximity to lucrative urban markets or transport routes, and the like. In this light, the justifications of the new inequalities set out by the present leadership that they do not result from exploitation, are becoming increasingly untenable. Even where peasants have access to unequal endowments of collectively owned productive resources, and certainly in cases where they actually own such resources privately, it is clear that the new inequalities rest on more than differential work effort.

The Chinese government could take steps to reduce these property-based or economic endowment-based inequalities, through tax policies, differential rent charges, or direct income redistribution programmes. It has thus far shown no inclination to do so. Part of the reason for this, no doubt, is that these inequalities have not yet become politicized in ways or to degrees that would force some political response. It is difficult enough for discontent to organize itself against the state in any socialist system of the Soviet or Chinese type. And while memories of the Cultural Revolution remain fresh, it may continue to be even more difficult in China than elsewhere. But the Polish experience shows how social discontent can coalesce even in a one-party socialist state. The Chinese revolutionary tradition of mass participation and mobilization may in the long run prove to help the process along. Everything about Chinese history in this century suggests that the peasantry will not brook inequality and exploitation forever.

Gender Inequality

The Chinese Communist Party has always accorded revolution, nationalism, socialism and economic development higher priority than gender equality. Its policies on women's issues have generally been determined by the require-ments of its policies on these and related issues. To be sure, the Chinese revo-lution and Chinese socialism have meant great progress for women; there can be no doubt that they are better off today than in 1911 or 1949. But the contours of the gains, and the processes by which they have been achieved, have been determined by male-dominated political leaderships that have not valued gender equality for its own sake and have pursued it only in so far as it was consonant with, and not threatening to, their political positions and programmes.

During the Chinese revolution, Mao spoke of women 'holding up half the sky' and being more oppressed than men because they were subject to male domination. And while some women did join the party and the revolutionary armies, by and large women were relegated to the roles of providing support for the revolutionary movement in ways that suited their traditional roles: providing food, sewing uniforms, and so forth. While the party, through the

Women's Association, organized campaigns against foot-binding and wife-beating, it pulled up far short of the kind of consciousness-raising and mass mobilization of women around women's issues that it used so skilfully and extensively during the struggles against the Japanese and the landlords.[11] It did so partly because of the lower priority it placed on women's issues, and partly because of its recognition that doing so might cost it support among its male constituencies. This could be interpreted variously as male insensitivity to women's issues, male cynicism and opposition to women's liberation, or as consistent with the party's long-established policy—which proved so important to its revolutionary triumph—of never dividing the masses and only drawing lines of political conflict between vast coalitions and small, isolated enemies.

The arguments about party insensitivity or cynicism seem to be called into question by the simple and very important fact that one of the party's first actions after establishing the People's Republic in 1949, and its first major piece of legislation, was the promulgation of a Marriage Law. It outlawed 'bigamy, concubinage, child betrothal, interference with the remarriage of widows, and the exaction of money or gifts in connection with marriages'. It made divorce legal and available on demand by mutual consent (or by court decree if reconciliation failed and grounds—which were not specified—were judged warranted). In any event, men were not permitted to divorce their wives when they were pregnant or within one year of the birth of a child. Women were granted 'equal rights in the possession and management of family property', including rights of inheritance. They were to possess 'the right to free choice of occupation and free participation in work or social activities'. Infanticide, which had predominantly affected baby girls, was outlawed (Marriage Law, 1950). Of course, legislation never translates directly into practice. Bride prices have never disappeared, for example. Nevertheless, this law marked a sharp break from the past, by making it clear that the state would throw its weight against some of the worst depredations perpetrated by men and traditional patriarchy against women.

This has been coupled with a clear ideological position that women are the equals of men. Of course, state ideology never translates directly into practice either, and sometimes can even provide an excuse for the failure to undertake actual change. Still, the official position of the Chinese state that women are the legal equals of men is well ahead of many other countries in the Third World and even in the more economically developed part of the world (including the United States, which after decades of debate still does not include a statement to this effect in its constitution). Moreover, other ideological proclivities of the Chinese state operate to women's benefit, though this is not their intention. For example, the puritanical morality for which Chinese state ideology and propaganda is so well known has the effect of preventing women from being exploited as sex objects in public iconography.

In other respects the state has done little to help women. Perhaps most serious is its persistent failure to do anything about China's oppressive structure of family relations. One of its core elements, and a major factor in female oppression in China, is patrilocal exogamy coupled with a taboo against intra-village endogamy. The dominant pattern of marriage throughout the socialist period has been for the bride to hail from a different village than her husband and to move to his home upon marriage, losing contact with her natal family and village.

This has several very important implications for women, all negative. First, it makes a girl a poor economic investment for her parents, who have to bear the expense of bringing her up only to lose her just when she could begin to make a productive contribution by working (on the farm or at home) or by bearing children. This lies at the root of the universal preference for boys in Chinese families. (It also explains the persistence of the bride price, which functions to recompense the girl's parents.) Second, women are outsiders to the villages in which they spend their adult lives. Cultural suspicion of outsiders is strong in China (as elsewhere), and this affects women in many ways. In particular, it has proved to be an obstacle to their accession to political office or responsibilities. Third, they are outsiders to the families in which they spend their adult lives, and so are subject to mistreatment by their in-laws and husbands. The party has never made a serious offensive against patrilocal exogamy and so this root cause of social, economic and political oppression of rural women has remained almost completely intact after nearly four decades of Chinese socialism.

In part the party's failure to do so has resulted from its dependence on the traditional family structure as part of its programme of socialist transformation, or on the positive functions which that structure could play for the process. For example, by continuing to place the burden of reproduction of the labour force (including feeding, housing and clothing present workers as well as future ones (that is, children)) on the household, the coops could shepherd their financial resources for production and accumulation. Indeed, the only attempt to socialize the processes and costs of labour force reproduction occurred during the disastrous Great Leap (though the leap's failure was not particularly attributable to this).

Moreover, the extended family has proven well suited in several ways to the mobilization of women into labour outside the home. First, it has provided a way for children to be tended at no cost to the collective—that is, by grandmother—during the day. It has also provided the collective flexibility in labour management which is so important in highly seasonal and variable agriculture. Women have been drawn into collective work as needed (for example, during busy planting and harvest seasons), and then shunted back to their homes when work slackened. The male-dominated household has proved an excellent device for extracting the maximum labour from women in another sense, by helping enforce the double burden of work outside and inside the home. Finally, the fact that income has consistently been shared by the family has made it possible for collectives to pay women less than men for the same work—a Chinese version of the family wage.[12]

If the traditional family structure has been well suited to the needs of collectivization as the Chinese leadership has pursued it, those collective forms have in turn helped reinforce patriarchy. The emphasis and political latitude given to the small, village-sized collective unit to run many of its own internal affairs vested considerable local power in the hands of village men, who could effectively obstruct feminist offensives waged by local women. It also provided an obstacle to the progress of women's issues during the rare moments when the state raised them seriously. The most prominent of these was the offensive raised by the recently resuscitated Women's Association to use the campaign to criticize Lin Biao and Confucius in the early 1970s to press for matrilocal marriage.

This is not to say that women have fared terribly. In the rural collectives of Maoist days, the most capable women earned an average of around 80 per cent of the most capable men's work points (and in places where more egalitarian methods of point allocation were in use, even a higher percentage). This is far better than, for example, the figure of around 65 per cent in the United States. They were given special consideration as needed in job assignments (for example, during menstruation they were given less strenuous jobs closer to home). By the 1970s each team had a position known as the women's team head; the person filling it was elected by the women of the team, sat on the team management committee, and served as an advocate for women's interests in team affairs. Women were increasingly elected to other positions of responsibility in production teams during and after the Cultural Revolution. In one sample of several hundred team cadres, women comprised between 8 and 12 per cent from 1958 to 1966, but between 16 and 21 per cent from 1970 to 1974 (Blecher, 1978, p. 61). Perhaps the greatest gains for women have resulted from the efforts to control population growth, which have reduced the tremendous burdens imposed by having to see many children through pregnancy, birth and childhood. (Yet even here sexism operates: Chinese population-control planning has heavily emphasized the role of women in birth control.) Reductions in infant mortality have also reduced the number of pregnancies women have to endure.

The policies of the post-Mao leadership have helped women in some ways and hurt them in others. On the positive side, they have, as part of the general policy of reducing the direct dominance of the state over society, perhaps imparted a certain latitude for the Women's Association to express women's interests in various national political conclaves, though the latitude is in all likelihood narrow and the effects so far little in evidence. Opportunities for lucrative employment in sidelines and light industry, sectors in which women are concentrated, have expanded. The one-child policy has further relieved women of the direct burden of reproduction.

But in each of these areas there are also negative effects for women. The one-child policy, for example, has increased the psychological and social pressure on women, who now have only one chance to bear a son. Hence there are reports of women being harassed and abused for giving birth to baby girls. These babies, too, have suffered: the one-child policy has resulted in the hideous recrudescence of female infanticide perpetrated by fathers who demand a son. There can be little doubt that decollectivization has hurt women in certain ways. Women who in the past found some representation, however meagre, in their teams through the agency of the women's association or women's team head are now atomized in their individual households, where they are subject to the more unbridled authority of the male household head. With the decline of small rural schools, women face even greater obstacles to gaining an education. They have also lost other forms of collective support, including welfare benefits, health care, collective child care in some places and, perhaps most important of all, the diffuse but palpable solidarity among the women in the village who often worked and socialized together in the context of the production team.

At the national level, change has been very slow and limited, but the situation is not static or retrograde. Until recently, the only women who gained positions of national political power or prominence were the wives of senior male leaders. Most notorious among these was, of course, Jiang Qing, Mao's wife, who was a major figure of the Cultural Revolution left and later was condemned as a ringleader of the 'gang of four'. But Deng Yingchao and Wang Guangmei, married to Zhou Enlai and Liu Shaoqi respectively, also achieved political influence in the top leadership ranks. So did Song Qingling, Sun Yatsen's wife, who became a major figure in the CCP's united front efforts to attract support from patriotic non-communists as late as the 1980s. This pattern, which is sexist in its own way (since it admits women to position of national prominence because of their husbands' power), has

Table 5.1 Women in the Party Central Committee

Central Committee	Full members	Alternates	Total
Seventh (1945)	1 (2%)	2 (6%)	3 (4%)
Eighth (1956)	4 (4%)	3 (4%)	7 (4%)
Ninth (1969)	14 (8%)	10 (9%)	24 (9%)
Tenth (1973)	20 (10%)	21 (17%)	41 (13%)
Eleventh (1977)	14 (7%)	23 (17%)	37 (11%)
Twelfth (1982)	11 (5%)	13 (9%)	24 (7%)

Source: Bartke & Schier, 1985, p. 73.

begun to change under the post-Mao leadership. Chen Muhua, a recent Minister of Foreign Trade, and Hao Jianxiu, the new Minister of Textile Industry (and member of the Secretariat of the CCP Central Committee), exemplify the ability of capable women to achieve important leadership positions on their own.

But despite this shift, the Chinese national leadership—like those elsewhere—is a very long way from complete gender equality. Twenty-one per cent of the delegates to the Sixth National People's Congress in 1983 were women, a figure which was actually down on the 23 per cent for the Fourth NPC in 1975 (though still far better than anything the United States' Congress has ever been able to muster). The party has done worse: Table 5.1 shows that female representation on the Central Committee (CC) declined from a high of 13 per cent on the Tenth CC (1973) to 7 per cent on the most recent Twelfth CC. Party spokesperson Zhu Muzhi characterized the present situation as 'unsatisfactory' and attributed it to the 'historical reasons' (*Xinhua News Bulletin*, 24 September 1985, p. 38). These must be long-term ones, for Table 5.1 shows that the Cultural Revolution produced real gains in female representation which have now been reversed. On the Ninth Central Committee (1969), the number of women more than tripled, and the percentage doubled; further gains were achieved in the Tenth CC of 1973. But Zhu's remark is not utterly cynical, for throughout the People's Republic period, including the heyday of Cultural Revolution radicalism, women have always had higher representation among CC alternate than full members, and never achieved representation even approaching their percentage of the population. There is still much to be done. Commenting further on female membership in the CC, Zhu continued: 'Of course our party has always paid attention to this problem and is trying to change this as soon as possible.' Still, the fact that

the party was much more successful at its September 1985 national conference in lowering the average age of its top leadership than at raising its female
representation reflects its differential priorities. And the post-Mao leadership, like its predecessors, has shown no particular inclination to the raising of
feminist issues as a distinct set of concerns.

6 Political Economy

Perhaps more than any other socialist country, China has experimented with a wide range of economic policies and organizational forms. Many of these have been bold innovations. There is not one but several Chinese models. In a period when socialism is being pursued in so many different countries, and when dissatisfaction with elements of past economic performance is becoming manifest in almost every socialist country, leading often to radical challenges to the fundamentals of theory, organization and policy, the Chinese case may have much to offer to analysts and practitioners of socialism. China has accumulated valuable experience about the range of possibilities that can potentially be accommodated under the broad umbrella of socialism, and about some of their implications under specific circumstances.[1]

Economic Structure and Organization

Ownership

Throughout the socialist period, there have always been three forms of ownership in China: state, collective and private. Of course, their composition and relative weight have changed over time, but none has ever been fully obliterated. State ownership refers to assets owned, in Chinese parlance, 'by the whole people'. In theory, they belong to the country and its people as a whole, on whose behalf the state administers them. By contrast, collective ownership refers to assets which are the property of some definite sub-group of the Chinese people. Usually this is the people who work with those assets (in the case of productive resources) or who produced them or the income used to purchase them. For example, a production team's land and any tractors or television sets it may have acquired are owned by the team, not the state. Likewise, the assets of an urban collective workshop run by a neighbourhood committee or some other *ad hoc* group of residents belong to the neighbourhood denizens or the workers who purchased them and established the enterprise.

Sometimes collective ownership may also include a larger sub-group of the Chinese people than those who work on or have produced the owned assets. For example, there has been a category of industries known as 'county-run collective enterprises' (*xian ban jiti qiye*) whose profits have been retained completely by the county government rather than being transmitted upward to the coffers of higher levels of the state, and whose planning has been more subject to local control than is the case with state-run enterprises. Though the county government is a level of the state, it is apposite to think of ownership of these enterprises as resting with the people of the county (since profits are retained completely within the county) rather than 'the whole people' of China. A more precise formulation would be that the county government administers them on behalf of its own people, not the rest of China's people or the central state as a whole (Blecher *et al.*, forthcoming, Chapter 5).

What does 'ownership'—especially of productive resources—actually mean in a socialist country like China? In particular, what rights, powers or prerogatives accrue to collective or private ownership in a country with such strong state power, pervasive state ownership, and central planning? To explore this problem, it is necessary to think of ownership in several different senses. First, it may refer to formal declarations or codifications as embodied in constitutions, other state documents, contracts, deeds, and other legal instruments. Second, it may refer to the capacity to alienate the property—by selling, trading or bequeathing it—or to realize income merely from owning it—by renting, leasing or mortgaging it. Third, ownership may refer to the capacity to use the property in productive activity unencumbered by com-peting claims of others on its use or on the income derived from using it. These can be called, respectively, *formal, actual* and *practical ownership*.

Collective and private ownership have in the past embraced different forms. For example, under the rural collectivism which prevailed from around the mid-1960s through 1978—which can been referred to as 'high collectivism' (Blecher, 1985b)—production teams owned their land in all three senses. Formal ownership was legally codified in point 21 of the Sixty Articles: 'All the land within the production teams belongs to the production teams' (URI, 1971, p. 704). This document immediately went on to guarantee actual ownership, stipulating that higher levels of collective organization (and implicitly the state above them) are 'not allowed to rent, buy or sell the land owned by the production teams' (URI, 1971, p. 704). In fact, the teams were the only ones that could alienate the land, by trading it with other teams or by selling it to the state if the latter needed it to build a factory or a road. Yet the state simultaneously set limits to actual ownership of land: the teams were not permitted to sell their land to their members (converting it to private ownership), and no functioning market in land was permitted to operate. Finally, the teams exercised practical ownership: after they paid their taxes and made their quota sales, they could keep all the remaining product. Even under the responsibility systems which have replaced high collectivism since 1978, teams retain formal and actual ownership of land. But with the return of subcontracting land and hiring of labour, peasants too have begun to acquire actual ownership of land.

As another example, county-run collective enterprises constitute actual and practical but not formal ownership by the county government. Nowhere is it codified that they belong to the county, but the counties can exercise certain ownership prerogatives over them, such as retaining their profits or selling off their assets.

Private ownership, too, has taken a number of forms. The most well-known one is the so-called 'private plot' (a poor translation from the Chinese, which means literally 'self-retained plot'). These plots have never been subject to formal private ownership. Under high collectivism, teams maintained formal ownership. This was manifest every three years, when the plots reverted to the team for redistribution to adjust for changes in family size. Nor did peasants have actual ownership: they could not sell, lease or trade such plots. They only had practical ownership: they could keep everything they produced on them. But with the recent reforms, peasants are permitted private ownership of productive resources—including agricultural machinery, vehicles and even small industries outright or in part through joint-stock arrangements—in all three senses.

Economic Sectors

The Chinese economy is usually divided analytically into three sectors: industry, agriculture and commerce. Industry in turn is subdivided into heavy and light. By 1983, agriculture, light industry and heavy industry each contributed about one-third of gross value of output (GVO), a major change from 1952 when agriculture contributed over half. In output terms, then, the Chinese economy is predominantly industrial. But this is not so in human terms: in 1983, 70.7 per cent of the labour force was employed in agriculture and related occupations, and only 13.1 per cent in industry. Only 4.4 per cent was engaged in commerce.[2]

There is only a rough correspondence between sectors and ownership forms. Heavy industry is predominantly state owned, although in some economically more advanced areas it can be under collective ownership of a locality. Light industry can be state owned or collectively owned by a local government, rural collective unit, or even by its workers (in the case, for example, of a group of housewives who combined to purchase sewing machines and establish a tailoring shop). Overall in 1983 22 per cent of GVO originated from collectively-owned firms, and 77 per cent from state-owned ones. Only 0.1 per cent came from private firms.

Collective ownership has by and large predominated in agriculture. State farms, in which land and capital are owned by the state and farmers draw a wage from it, have not been very important in China. They have only been established in areas where the state wanted to bring unused land under cultivation or settlement. In 1983, they only employed 1.4 per cent of the agricultural labour force, and produced 2.1 per cent of grain output.

State ownership continues to predominate in commerce. In 1983, 72.1 per cent of retail sales volume was handled by state outlets, 16.6 per cent by collectively-owned shops, and 10.2 per cent by private traders (including sales of agricultural products by peasants to urban dwellers).

The overall picture, then, is rather different from the common stereotype of China as a poor, agrarian and increasingly capitalist economy. Though it is true that by far the bulk of the population is employed in agriculture, industry predominates in output value. And in general state ownership continues to dominate in industry and collective ownership in agriculture,[3] with private ownership playing its largest (but still relatively small) role in commerce.

Rural Industry; Urban Agriculture

Though Westerners tend to think of industry as urban and agriculture as rural, one cannot do so in the case of China. China has gone further than any other country in its development of rural industry. People's communes were originally intended to be agricultural-industrial combines. Though many of their first industrial undertakings, such as the infamous backyard steel furnaces, quickly proved infeasible, rural industrialization outlived the Great Leap and indeed proved to be one of its few positive legacies. It has received the support of both the Maoist and post-Mao leaderships and has prospered under both. From 1970–78, its output grew an average of 30 per cent per year. In 1977, it turned out 15 per cent of China's coal and 80 per cent of its building materials. Though the post-Mao reforms have included a certain rationalization of rural industry—including closing inefficient plants and consolidating small firms into larger ones—by 1983 rural collective industries comprised 77.6 per cent of China's industrial enterprises and 22 per cent of gross value of industrial output (GVIO).

Rural industry has had important implications for China's socialist economic development. Several of these have to do with labour. In a country whose huge population poses a very serious structural problem of labour absorption, rural industry has created employment for millions of peasants, thereby helping prevent rural migration to urban areas, which has been so great a problem in other developing countries. It also adds flexibility to rural labour allocation, since employees of rural industries can still be mobilized for agriculture during busy seasons. In particular it has provided an excellent opportunity for employment of rural women, on terms more comparable with men than have been possible in agriculture.

In the area of production, rural industry has helped supply the vast rural areas with industrial goods which the centralized and somewhat cumbersome and unresponsive state industrial structure could not do, or which could not reach the remote rural areas for lack of transport facilities. Some of these have been agricultural inputs which have aided its moderniza- tion. Though often inefficient in strict output–input terms by comparison with large, modern, capital-intensive plants, Chinese rural industries have been able to make use of inputs—such as agricultural by-products or coal from small, remote seams—which otherwise would have gone unused. And with their low costs, these firms have been able to operate at a profit even using very primitive technologies.

They have also made a significant contribution to rural output value, income and living standards. In Shulu County (Hebei Province), a rural area well developed in urban, state-owned industry, rural collective industry still accounted for 28 per cent of total GVIO in 1978, and a full 82 per cent of rural collective-sector GVO (Blecher *et al*., forthcoming, Table 7.3). Nation- ally, rural collective industries produced 30 per cent of income in the rural collective sector in 1979. They have also made available to peasants consumer goods which were otherwise unobtainable.

China has also witnessed the development of urban agriculture, though this has been less significant than rural industry. It too got its initial impetus from the Great Leap, when factories were urged to develop their own garden plots. As industrialization has proceeded apace, urban land use has had to give way to expansion of factories, shops and warehouses. But some small plots in many urban areas, particularly smaller ones, still remain. And even where agriculture is restricted to the peripheries rather than the cores of urban areas, it blends with urban life in social terms. In the Shulu County capital, peasants who work the land on the perimeter of the city live in the same urban neigh- bourhoods as factory workers, intermingling with them at markets, political functions, cinemas, clinics and schools.

Political Economy

The most controversial and fluctuating aspect of China's socialist economy has been in the area of political economy. This concerns a complex set of interrelated issues, such as planning (including structures (centralization and decentralization) and principles (political or economic)); allocation by plan or market; pricing (which embodies the politically weighty question of the relative value of different commodities and, by extension, the sectors and enterprises that produce and consume them); sectoral priorities; the relative emphasis on consumption and accumulation; enterprise management; the nature of agricultural collectivization; and integration of the economy, both internally (which involves the issue of specialization versus self-provision) and internationally (which involves the issue of insertion into the world economy vs. autarky). The sections below now take up these issues.

Centralization and Decentralization

Planning in the state sector of the Chinese economy has varied over two analytical dimensions. *Structurally*, it has sometimes been highly centralized, emphasizing national level coordination and locating economic authority in Beijing. At other times, it has been more decentralized, passing authority downward to regional levels of government or to enterprises.[4] The underlying *rationales* of planning have also changed. At some moments, political considerations such as regional balance or preferred sectoral priorities have held sway, while at other times economic considerations such as profitability, efficiency or comparative advantage have been more dominant.

Central planning of the Chinese economy proceeded only on a year-by-year basis until mid-1955, when the First Five Year Plan was enunciated retroactively to 1953. It can be described as emphasizing centralized planning using a political rationale. Under the plan, the state-run economy, which at the time came gradually to coincide with all Chinese industry and commerce,[5] was highly centralized, like the Soviet model it aped. Mandatory targets and norms concerning output, employment, wages, other production costs, labour productivity, profit, production techniques, innovation of product lines, and other indicators were formulated by the State Planning and Economic Commissions. These were passed down level by level until they reached the enterprise which had to abide by them. At its heart were politically rather than economically informed planning priorities and choices. For example, the desire to emulate the Soviet Union and the genuine belief among many planners and political leaders in the theory that economic development proceeds most rapidly and securely from a foundation of 'basic' industries, lay behind the plan's emphasis on development of heavy industrial sectors, to which 90 per cent of capital investment was devoted. And a political commitment to economic balance, along with strategic concerns about national security, motivated the decision to locate industry inland, away from the more prosperous, industrially developed and military vulnerable coast and north east (Manchuria).

Although this regime of centralized administration produced rapid growth,[6] it also resulted in many of the problems that have become characteristic of centralized planning throughout the socialist world. If anything, the problems in China were somewhat more daunting than elsewhere because of China's huge size and wide range of variation in natural and developmental conditions. Economic coordination on a national level was hampered by China's poorly developed transport system. Technical norms set in Beijing planning offices proved inappropriate to many factories. Planning was often carried out incorrectly, allocating resources that did not exist in some cases, and in others allocating excessive or insufficient resources. Production targets were frequently set irrationally, producing excesses of some items that were not needed, in weak demand, or unsuitable to their planned purpose, while leaving shortages of others that were essential.

As part of the overall shift in China's socialist economic strategy at the time, a major decentralization, still based mainly around a political rationale, was carried out in state-sector industry in 1958.[7] The number of mandatory targets was reduced from twelve to four: output, employment, wages and profit. Middle-level planners, in particular at the provincial levels, were given greater leeway in technical aspects of production, diversification of production lines, cost reduction, and ways of improving productivity. Coordination was to emphasize the horizontal principle of territorial integration more than the vertical principle of functional integration. Many firms producing light industrial products, textiles and agricultural machinery were put under the complete control of regional authorities, leaving the centre with only 'basic' sectors such as defence industries, iron and steel, and so forth. The primacy of political over economic planning principles remained, as in the First Five Year Plan. But their actual content shifted somewhat, for example, to a greater emphasis on agriculture and light industry.

During the Great Leap, emphasis was placed on provinces as regional units of industrial planning and economic integration. In the rural areas this same movement towards middle-level units produced a tendency towards greater centralization (away from grass-roots units), as the large communes replaced the smaller cooperatives and markets. But the initial wild enthusiasm of the Leap and the deep crisis that followed it crippled the planning mechanism altogether. The Second Five Year Plan was replaced by annual and even quarterly plans which reflected efforts to cope and survive rather than to project order and political will on the economy.

Planning began to function again in 1961, this time in a more centralized and economically rationalized fashion. During the next several years advocates of central planning began to press for a greater role for vertical (functional) rather than horizontal (territorial) coordination. They coined the slogan 'the whole country is a chessboard' to express the view that the Chinese economy was one integrated entity in which changes in any one part affected all the other parts. In the wake of the dislocations of the Great Leap, whose emphasis on local and regional autarky had heightened regional inequalities and made manifest the need for central control and resource allocation, their arguments found adherents. In 1963, 'trusts'—in effect, large public corporations organized centrally (and functionally) in various industrial sectors—began to appear. As an example of the new use of economic criteria for planning, the trusts were given authority to allocate investment capital wherever it was most profitable. They also resonated to growing concerns about technical specialization and comparative advantage. They naturally favoured the more technologically advanced firms, generally located in the wealthier areas. Consequently, this form of central planning based on an economic rationale was prone to exacerbating regional inequalities, like the more decentralized, politically motivated mode of planning which preceded it.

The trusts were criticized bitterly during the Cultural Revolution. Planning of any sort was hampered from above by red guard attacks on state officials serving in the economic administration, and from below by the breakdown of productive activity in the factories. During the early, most radical years of 1967–69, planning was rendered impossible when many factories stopped production as their workers preoccupied themselves with political matters in their factories.

It continued to be obstructed by poor labour discipline and incessant political campaigns through the early 1970s. To the extent that planning took place at all at this time, decentralization and politicization predominated. The emergence of revolutionary committees gave strong impetus to horizontal coordination, while the disruptions of the Cultural Revolution and its attacks on the state had weakened capacities for vertical control. Thus decentralization was pushed further than ever before, with even very large firms in key sectors—such as the huge Anshan Steel Complex, then China's largest—turned over to provincial administration. Profits and efficiency were eschewed vociferously. One slogan alleged to have been put forward by the left leadership of the time was: 'Better a socialist train running late than a capitalist train running on time'. Planners emphasized raising output without particular regard for costs, markets or quality control, and factory managers struggled to meet even this simple objective.

The years since 1978 have seen China's first serious flirtations with decentralization to enterprises rather than to regional or local bureaucratic authorities. This was tried sporadically during the Cultural Revolution, but the emphasis then was on enterprise politics. Now enterprises were urged by some political leaders and economists to pursue their economic interests.

Enterprise decentralization based on an economic rationale proceeded quickly in 1979 and 1980 in the glow of the Dengists' dramatic triumph at the Third Plenum of late 1978. There was much talk of emulating both Yugoslavia and Hungary—which suggests that the reformers themselves were divided since these two systems are so different. After a series of limited experiments, which made select groups of enterprises responsible for their own profits and losses, were held to be great successes, the State Council decided in September 1980 to extend responsibility over finance, marketing, personnel, procurement and production to all industrial firms. But this decision was soon rescinded as the problems accompanying rapid economic decentralization to enterprises became manifest. These included upward pressure on prices, which were not deregulated; a burst of unplanned and uncoordinated investment by factories with surpluses; increasing difficulties in meeting even reduced state plans now that firms could find more attractive uses for their production capacities and output; financial problems for the state resulting from reduced revenues; and growing pressure for price reform from enterprise managers in sectors where price distortions made profitability impossible even with the most efficient technology and management.

In 1981 advocates of a greater role for planning made a comeback. They argued that in the context of China's unbalanced economy, where certain goods and services were very scarce and therefore in high demand, reform would cause inflation and dislocation long before it would resolve the imbalances. In the language of Chinese economic discourse, readjustment would have to precede reform. And readjustment meant planning. Further extensions of enterprise autonomy were stopped in 1981. Responsibility systems, a form of contractual relations between government agencies and firms in which the latter were permitted to retain a share of profits, were used to help make planning work; but they were a very different matter from giving firms autonomy from planning.

Planning now emphasized some of the same goals and institutions it had in the early 1960s: functional specialization, amalgamation of small firms into integrated industrial combines, and even in the reappearance of trusts in the form of large state corporations which are instructed to orientate their activities to profitability rather than politically inspired planning goals. Many of these are organized regionally, suggesting a return to the bureaucratic decentralizations of the past.

As of this writing (late 1985), then, there is a certain stalemate on the question of planning in China. Clearly, the highly centralized planning of the First Five Year Plan has been set aside, as has planning based on a political rationale. The question now is between, one the one hand, regionally de-centralized coordination, vesting great economic authority in the hands of middle-level officials who are to act more like corporate managers and less like socialist planners, and, on the other, enterprise autonomy approaching something like 'market socialism'.

Whatever the outcome may turn out to be, the contrast between the halt-ing pace and ambivalence of reform of state-owned industry and commerce on the one hand and the rapidity of reform of the rural collectives on the other is striking. In the countryside, de-collectivization often proceeded faster than the state anticipated, leaving the latter in a position of having to rewrite its policies to keep up with events at the grassroots (Watson, 1983). To be sure, there has been some opposition to rural reform, both from local cadres who have now lost their political bases and also from both them and peasants in places where the collectives had been relatively successful and the material and ideological commitment to collective agriculture strong. But this has not been powerful enough to prevent the rural reforms from proceeding with astonishing celerity and thoroughness.

Until further research and analysis can be undertaken with the passing of time, the reasons for the contrast with the urban areas can only be hypo-thesized. One could be that, despite Maoist goals and rhetoric to the contrary, the urban areas were relatively favoured before 1978 (in pricing policy, avail-ability of goods and services, and employment terms and conditions). Second, those classes and groups which stand to lose most from the reform of state industry and commerce—the regular state employees (with their fixed wages, fringe benefits and lifetime tenure) and the state bureaucracy (with all of the same advantages plus the political power that goes with its capacity to allocate and distribute scarce resources)—are in a good political position to hold up reform, by arguing against it and resisting implementation. The peasantry, its grassroots leadership, and even its state-connected leadership (in the party and at the commune level) has always had great difficulty resisting the will of the socialist state, from the Great Leap (and, some would argue, even the higher-stage collectivization) through the Cultural Revolution. There is even evidence that peasants and local leaders who have doubts about elements of the recent reforms have nevertheless given in resignedly, both in model areas like Dazhai and Xiyang and in more ordinary places like Long Bow (Hinton, 1986; Tsou, Blecher & Meisner, 1982a and 1982b). Third, and related to the previous two hypotheses, the rural reforms have probably been genuinely popular with many rural people, including household heads (who could now reassert their authority over production directly), males (who could resassert their authority over females in their households), those with non-agricultural skills and contacts (who can now utilize them more freely), and generally with peasants who suffered from state plans and policies (like the emphasis on grain production or the restrictions on rural commerce).

Markets and Prices

In the early years of the People's Republic, some of the greatest victories in economic policy and transformation were achieved in price and market control. The socialist government was able rapidly to bring one of the worst inflations in history under control through issuance of new currency and strict application of price controls. State-administered prices lay at the heart of the system of central planning that was erected in the 1950s. Regulation and socialization of rural commodity and credit markets were essential parts of its strategy to isolate rich peasants and promote cooperativization. Thus it is not at all surprising that free markets and floating prices have been viewed as evils by both the Maoists and the planning-minded state bureaucrats who have attacked each other so viciously.

This is not to say that planners have been utterly averse to using prices as levers of planning. In fact planning in China has combined physical planning at some times for some sectors—in which fixed quantities of physical inputs are allocated and quotas for procurement are expressed in similar terms— with price planning—in which the state allows enterprises to make their own choices among inputs (and to a lesser extent outputs) which are made available through (or sold to) government commercial outlets at state-set prices. But they have been averse to deregulating commerce by freeing markets and allowing those markets to set prices.

It is not hard to see why. Free markets and floating prices wreak havoc on planning efforts. They can create financial problems for a state used to raising large sums from appropriation of enterprise profits. They also have the potential to be politically explosive in a country where goods are scarce and consumers have become used to basic goods such as food, clothing and shelter being supplied to them at low prices. (The reverse side of this is, of course, that what can be bought for these low prices is often of poor quality and may be rationed by coupon or queue. But for people with low incomes—wages have been kept generally low and stable (or stagnant, depending on one's perspective)in China—who have no assurance that rising prices will be accompanied some time soon by rising supplies or quantity, price increases are often experienced as an alarming development.)

Price deregulation is potentially explosive for another reason. The structure of state-set prices has formed a matrix of political and social relations which is embedded deeply in the Chinese economic structure. Certain sectors facing unfavourable price structures, such as coal (whose price is set very low), have become used to operating with large subsidies. The sectors that purchase their outputs have been receiving an indirect subsidy in the form of low price. Meanwhile, others, including many industrial firms and the ministries that supervise them, have become accustomed to high profits, which in turn have provided them definite economic and political clout. Fundamental price reform would potentially upset them all. Coal mines stand to lose their subsidies, producers of high-priced industrial goods their profits. It could be argued—and has been by economic reformers—that they have nothing to fear: coal-mines will benefit from higher market prices, and industrial firms from reduced taxes and profit appropriation by the state. But these are all uncertainties from the point of view of the actors involved, who have been deeply hurt in the past by the unpredictability of Chinese politics. For this reason price reform has remained one of the thorniest and most intractable problems facing Chinese economic reformers. It has been mooted since 1978, but only in October 1984 could it be put at the centre of the political agenda by the Third Plenum of the Twelfth Central Committee, which admitted that 'reform of the price system is the key to reform of the entire economic structure' (*Beijing Review*, 29 October 1984, p. viii). Even now it is envisioned as a process that will have to proceed gradually over several years. As Vice-Premier Tian Jiyun put it, 'the [price] reform should be carried out gradually and the steps taken should be not too big' (*Beijing Review*, 28 January 1985, p. 17).

Sectoral Priorities

Price distortions in turn have been one important way of assigning priorities to economic sectors. In particular, agricultural outputs have been priced low, and industrial outputs high—the 'scissors' pattern familiar to students of Soviet economic history. So long as agriculture used few industrial outputs and peasants bought little in the way of industrially produced consumer goods—which was the case throughout the 1950s and early 1960s—scissors pricing was of limited significance. To be sure, peasants were probably receiving less than what the free market price would have been for their marketable surplus. But they were also taxed at low and declining rates and offered credit on favourable terms. But from about the mid-1960s on, as agriculture began to use larger doses of industrial inputs like chemical fertilizer, cement and farm machinery, it began to suffer more from scissors pricing. To some extent this was offset by agriculture's self-provision of some of these inputs through its own rural collective industries. Still, the problem was serious enough to attract the attention of the post-Mao leadership very early in its tenure in office. One of its first significant actions in the economic field was to raise procurement prices for quota grain by 20 per cent, and above-quota grain by 50 per cent.

Pricing aside, sectoral priorities have also been affected by a state investment policy. In general, state investment in agriculture has been very low, averaging just 12 per cent of total investment from 1953–78 (compared with 54 per cent for industry). This has varied over time: during the First Five Year Plan it was under 8 per cent, and in the years of recovery after the Great Leap (1963–65) it rose to nearly 19 per cent. Agriculture was expected to finance itself to a large degree, which it did. One scholar has recently argued that since the industry–agriculture imbalance of investment was greater than the imbalance in their growth rates, it would appear that Chinese state investment policy has been irrational: that is, 'the rate of growth of national income would have been higher if a larger share of investment resources had been allocated to agriculture' (Lardy, 1983, p. 129). Students of economic development in the Third World generally will recognize this as an instance of the common phenomenon of 'urban bias' (Lipton, 1976).

Within industry, state investment has overwhelmingly favoured heavy industry by a factor of about ten to one. As with agriculture, this has to do with the fact that light industry, whether owned by rural collectives, by their workers, or 'collectively' by local governments, has been self-financing. Though some have suggested that heavy industrial investment statistics include that for production of agricultural machinery, in fact this has not been significant: only 8.6 per cent of investment in heavy industry has gone for such production. The simple fact is that although some adjustments have been made over time, by and large heavy industry has throughout the socialist period absorbed the lion's share of Chinese state investment capital, dwarfing both agriculture and light industry.

Socialist Accumulation

This raises the issue of accumulation versus consumption. The People's Republic inherited an economy whose growth had been seriously hampered by very low rates of capital investment, due to (and in turn causing) low rates of growth and production, wartime destruction, and capital flight. But even without a serious problem of war or political instability, investment rates under the republic were far too low to catalyse modern economic development. In current prices, investment was only around 5 per cent of gross domestic product (GDP) in 1933.[8] Ironically, therefore, it was left to the People's Republic—as to other socialist states in poor countries—to depress the relative size of the consumption fund and to extract a proportionately larger surplus from the Chinese people with which to finance investment.

By 1957 it had done so: investment was up to 24 per cent of GDP. Some of this was relatively painless to most people. For example, the land reform eliminated a class which had been consuming around one-quarter of national income, and the expropriation of the small Chinese bourgeoisie helped, too. But these were one-time gains, and soon the Chinese people would begin to feel the effects. During the Great Leap, investment surged to the astronomical figure of 43.8 per cent of national income in 1959 and 39.6 per cent in 1960, which contributed to the massive declines in consumption—or, in human terms, the spread of hunger and even starvation in many places. To make up for this, accumulation declined to only 10.4 per cent in 1962. During 1967–69, the most radical years of the Cultural Revolution, it averaged 21.9 per cent, which indicates that periods of left politics cannot be associated in a simple way with excessively high rates of accumulation. Throughout the 1970s it rose again to about one-third of GDP. And although the post-Mao leadership has emphasized over-accumulation as a major cause of low incomes and economic waste during the Maoist period, it has not been particularly successful in getting accumulation down. From 1979 to 1983, accumulation averaged 30.7 per cent of national income.

The reasons for China's very high rate of accumulation are not hard to find. To some extent they are common to state socialist economies elsewhere. These economies tightly regulate consumption through strict control of income (via wage policy and restrictions on black or grey labour markets), but they are less good at regulating investment. Capital goods allocated through central plans are not costed to the enterprise, so factory managers have no incentive to limit their requests for capital. Actually they have every reason to make requests greatly in excess of their needs, since they can never be sure how much they will be allocated now or in the future, and they can easily store the excess or, still better, cannibalize it for spare parts or use it to trade *sub rosa* for other scarce goods which they did not receive in sufficient quantities through the plan. In China in the late 1970s, therefore, one saw lathes everywhere, many going unused, but still few simple transistor radios.

These accumulative tendencies inherent in state socialism were exacerbated by specific features of the Maoist strategy of economic development. In general Maoism eschewed high levels of consumption (though it was not as ascetic as its opponents frequently charged, emphasizing instead basic needs). The emphasis on collective rather than individual consumption, intended partly to foster community solidarity, also had the effect of reducing the costs of popular consumption. It was much cheaper to purchase one television set for a production team than one for each peasant household. Finally, the generally low levels and quality of consumer goods production further discouraged consumption.

The post-Mao leadership rode to power partly by capitalizing on a wave of popular sentiment that the time had come for higher standards of living. One of the Dengists' most pointed criticisms of the Maoist decades was that on average workers had not received a rise for twenty years. They identified excessive accumulation as a major culprit. Yet, as we have seen, accumulation rates have not fallen significantly since 1978. The reforms actually promoted accumulation in some respects. For example, enterprise managers who were given greater autonomy over production, management and innovation, told to act like good entrepreneurs and to be on the look-out for profitable opportunities, and allowed to retain an increased share of their enterprises' profits, could not resist the urge to expand their capital bases rapidly. Central and regional planners, deprived of many levers of economic control and told not to interfere excessively in the spontaneous economic pursuits unleashed by the reforms, were poorly positioned to regulate accumulation even if they wanted to do so. And many citizens who have experienced increased incomes have sought to invest large proportions of their new wealth in small businesses, partly because of their entrepreneurial inclinations, partly because of the strong cultural value of providing for one's family's future, and partly because consumer goods, particularly those of high quality, are still in relatively short supply.

Enterprise Management

China has experimented with participatory management, but it has never been able to institutionalize these experiments into an ongoing system of workplace democracy. In the early 1950s, the East China or Shanghai system concerned a wide range of practices under which factory managers were made responsible to management committees of workers, technicians and even factory owners. This system served a variety of purposes in specific instances, sometimes simultaneously. It could be used to win over or harness the cooperation of factory owners and technicians. It could encourage and institutionalize worker participation and mobilization. It drew in the trade unions and assigned an important role to the party committee of the enterprise.

The East China system began in 1953 to be overshadowed by 'one-man management', a form of industrial management inspired, as so much else in early 1950s China, by the Soviet Union.[9] Premised on the primacy of scientific management principles and the need to integrate the internal operations of each enterprise with the larger directions of the economy—for example, the need for uniformity of technical and labour norms—it vested authority almost completely in the hands of managers who were to run factory affairs in accordance with detailed rules and organizational principles decided by central planners. Vertical lines of authority were drawn within enterprises, with each submanager having complete authority over those below while also being fully responsible for all facets of work to those above. In this sense it replicated the patterns of bureaucratic and hierarchical authority which were used in the central planning apparatus of the day.

One-man management ran into several difficulties. It grated against the participatory and mobilizational sensibilities of many revolutionaries in the party. It required large reservoirs of scientific managerial and technical expertise and data which China lacked. It passed significant authority into the hands of Soviet advisers. These problems led many to oppose the system and to propose around 1956 that it be replaced with one that placed managerial responsibility for factory operations under party authority. The effect of this change was not to increase workplace democracy or to challenge the principles of technocratic, scientific management, but rather to put the party in overall charge of the factories. The party used its authority to ensure compliance with national plans and to shore up its own political position *vis-à-vis* its rivals in the industrial professions and the state bureaucracy.

During the Great Leap, a plethora of criticism surfaced over bureaucratism, excessive rules and regulations, irrationalities resulting from one-man management (both with and without party supervision), mind-numbing division of labour, and elitism of factory officials. The party called for 'two participations and one reform', which meant (1) participation of all cadres regularly in productive labour; (2) worker participation in management; and (3) reform of old workplace rules and structures.

Managers' participation in production was an interesting counterpoint to worker participation in management. By participating in labour, managers were to gain a different perspective on factory affairs, come to understand the workers' point of view and interests, and therefore be better able to take them into account in running the factory. This was a form of political solicitation, in which the managers would take the initiative to discover and experience the workers' situation. As such it contrasts with worker participation in management, also urged at this time, under which the workers were called on to express their views to managers through meetings of committees which included worker representatives.[10] Reform of work rules meant reorganization of factories into small, collaborative workshop-sized teams comprising managers, technicians and workers. They were given operational latitude to tackle and structure tasks collectively. The idea was that the combination of managerial, technical, practical and political perspectives from each respective group in the teams would unleash the initiative and creativity of all and arrive at the most efficient, dynamic and democratic outcomes.

With the decline in industrial production in 1961 and 1962, these management practices were called into question. The reassertion of central planning exerted definite pressure to change the 'two participations and one reform'. But no clear alternative could be found or agreed upon by the party. A return to one-man management was even more difficult since the detailed data, strong managerial authority, technical resources, and Soviet advice which it required or brought in train were now more lacking than ever. Extensive debates were carried on in these years about the proper role of worker participation in management, the relationship of political to technical values, calculus and authority (the famous question of 'red versus expert'), and the organization and division of labour in the workplace.

The Cultural Revolution saw these debates turn into, and in turn become inundated by, a radical mass movement whose scope included but transcended the issue of enterprise management. For a time in many factories there was little or no management in which to participate as production slowed to a trickle or ceased altogether. There were spontaneous attempts to institutionalize new forms of management based on some of the principles enunciated and tried during the Great Leap. But these were integrated into broader and more radical efforts to politicize workplaces more generally (for example, over issues such as political study, ideological campaigns, and recruitment and training of workers to be managers and technicians).

These experiments in broad democracy in workplaces now conceived as political communities conflicted with counter-trends toward rationalization of authority and management in the hands of managers and technicians under the supervision of the revolutionary committees, which in many places came to be dominated by former party and government leaders or their sympathizers. The situation resembled that of the post-leap period, in which there was a contradiction between the participatory and democratic elements embodied in the Great Leap innovations and the need of an increasingly complex modern industry for efficiency, predictability and standardization. This contradiction sometimes resulted in efforts to reconcile the two and in political conflicts between their respective advocates.

During the post-Mao period, there have been some experiments with limited worker participation, this time institutionalized in the form of workers' congresses and election of factory managers. Workers' congresses are not new; they existed at various times during the socialist period and were revived in 1975 after their abandonment during the Cultural Revolution. Their formal powers include the right to review budgets and production plans; specify uses of safety, welfare and bonus funds; make decisions about management structure, wage systems and training programmes; and oversee the election and conduct of cadres. But it is also specified that the higher levels of the party and economic administration are under no obligation to abide by these decisions; in other words, they are not binding.

Election of factory managers has also proceeded unevenly. By 1982, factory directors were elected in only 11 per cent of state enterprises, and workgroup leaders (like forepersons) in only 35 per cent. Not all elections have been contested or involved secret ballots. Nominations are often controlled by existing factory leaders or party officials.

In general it appears at present that workers have little power to run factories, to participate in a meaningful way in their operation, or to structure their organization. But things have not returned to the dictatorial pattern of one-man management either. The present limited levers of worker participation do give workers some control over issues of direct concern to them and of limited interest to factory managers, such as the disposition of welfare funds and housing, safety considerations, and even decisions about who shall receive bonuses. (In fact, in this last area, the state has been critical of factory managers who abnegate their responsibility for awarding bonuses to the especially assiduous by turning the issue over to the workers or by simply distributing bonuses equally to everyone. Such managers, it is argued, are not using the bonuses to promote labour discipline and motivation. Yet as long as factory managers remember the Cultural Revolution, fear the political consequences of dividing the labour force, lack strong incentives to improve labour discipline, or genuinely believe in egalitarian pay principles, they may continue to defer to workers on this issue.) Workers also have the wherewithal to take action against managers who have been particularly unreasonable or who have committed especially egregious mistakes or offences. In this way even the limited powers of workers in their factories help to keep the exercise of managerial authority within certain very broad bounds.

Collective Agriculture

If China's experience with socialist transformation of the workplace has been ambiguous and ambivalent, the same cannot be said about collective agriculture. China has probably had a more serious, elaborated and successful experience with collective agriculture than any other socialist country. Indeed, it has provided a model for many other countries to follow and a laboratory in which students of socialism have been able to analyse the possibilities for rural transformation. It has also recently gone further than any other socialist country in criticizing collective agriculture and 'reforming' (or at least re-forming) it in more individuated ways. This, too, has had important implications for practitioners and observers of socialism outside China, many of whom are now concluding that socialist agriculture is a very questionable enterprise. China has, in other words, proved to be both a positive and negative model of collective agriculture. The truth lies somewhere in between.

'High Collectivism': c.1963–78

Once the institutional and policy readjustments after the Great Leap were complete, collective agriculture in China settled down to a fairly standard pattern for the next fifteen years. This was the heyday of collective agriculture, so it can be called 'high collectivism'.[11] Within the three-tiered commune, what was called the 'basic accounting unit' was located at the lowest level, called the production team. Under the state's practice, learned first in Yan'an, of structuring grassroots institutions in conformity with the contours of civil society, teams could vary considerably in size. So their boundaries sometimes took in several small hamlets, sometimes a small village, or sometimes a neighbourhood of a larger village or town. They usually contained between twenty and forty households—roughly 100–200 people. The important point is that they were always small enough to be face-to-face groups.

The teams owned the land and most of the basic productive resources.[12] They were also the lowest level at which costs and income were accounted. Perhaps most important, they were the unit of income-sharing among team members. That is, each peasant's income was a share of the net distributed income of the team (and not the larger brigade or commune of which the team was a part). This meant that peasants in different teams could have different incomes, in part simply because they were members of teams with different levels of economic development or success. Though this built definite inequality into the collective structure, the Great Leap had taught Chinese leaders and peasants much about the dangers to incentives and consequently to production and income from sharing income among too large a collective unit.[13]

Specifically, income determination worked as follows. Each team member earned a certain number of work points each day, the amount of which was recorded by an official of the team (who in turn received work points for doing this job!). There were various methods for deciding how many work points each person had earned. Sometimes teams set piece- or task-rate norms and simply measured work performance against those norms to arrive at a work-point total for the job. Sometimes they used 'time rates', which meant that each member was evaluated for his/her skill, assiduousness, strength, etc., and then given a rating of a certain number of work points per day. Teams were given considerable latitude to make their own decisions about which rating system to use and how to apply it.[14] Since all team members had a very direct stake in these issues, in practice these decisions were made quite democratically at lively and sometimes acrimonious team meetings.

At the end of the year the total number of work points awarded by the team was divided into the team's net distributable income—that is, what it had left after paying its taxes, any other debts, and after setting aside funds for investment, next year's reproduction, and welfare (including subsidies for the poor and collective consumption goods such as a new table-tennis set for the team recreation hall). This calculation produced the value of each work point. Each team member's annual income was then calculated by multiplying his/her work-point total by the work-point value, with the product recorded as a credit on the member's account with the team. Each member could then draw his/her income, some in the form of grain (bought from the team at the same (low) price at which the state purchased quota grain from the teams), some in the form of other material commodities which the team had available for distribution (such as fish from its ponds or fruit from its orchards), and the remainder in cash.

Thus each team member's income was a dual function of the number of work points earned and the value of the work point. Work-point earnings were partly an individual matter; they depended on how much work one did, how well one did it, how much or how valuable a skill one had, and so forth. Though work performance was in some sense an objective fact, still it could not be translated into work points in a simple, objective way. This required evaluation of one's work by the team. So work-point earnings were subject to some collective (and rather democratic) mediation as well as individual determination.

If the number of work points earned was partially mediated through collective decision-making, the value of the work point was almost completely determined collectively. That is, it depended on the labour activism, organization, skills, solidarity and entrepreneurship of the team as a whole. Each team member therefore had a direct interest in the economic results achieved by the team, and by extension in the way in which all other team members conducted themselves at work.

Thus it can be seen, contrary to the stereotypical view that Maoist China relied primarily on moral incentives and political exhortation to sacrifice for the larger good, that in fact a complex web of material incentives was built into the heart of collective agriculture during the Maoist period. These took two forms. First, there were individual material incentives: the more one worked, the more one could expect to earn. These were, as we have seen, subject partially to individual factors and partially to collective mediation to evaluate those factors. Second, there were collective material incentives: the more one's team earned, the more one would earn. These can be termed collective for two reasons: they were subject almost completely to collective determination, and they affected every member of the collective equally.

To put the matter differently, collective agriculture offered Chinese peasants two major ways to raise their incomes. They could work harder themselves—the individual material incentive—or they could try to get others to work harder—the collective material incentive. The two were certainly not mutually exclusive. If anything, they were complementary. One of the best ways to encourage others to work harder was to work hard oneself. And since everyone faced the same individual and collective incentives, the two tended to reinforce each other: everyone had an interest in working hard for his/her own individual self-interest and also in order to get everyone else to work hard.

Moreover, this system of incentives could promote collective solidarity and lively collective politics. Since all members knew that their incomes depended partly on everyone's efforts, they all had reasons to support each other's efforts as much as possible. And because each member's income also depended upon successful decision-making in the team—about management, planning, investment and innovation—peasants in general took a strong interest in collective affairs.

High collectivism also had positive effects on economic equality within teams. Of course it completely eliminated any inequality resulting from ownership of productive resources within the team. Teams could find suitable employment for elderly and disabled poor people—such as guarding orchards or warehouses—enabling them to earn an income. They provided welfare benefits in the form of 'five guarantees' to any family too poor to provision itself with minimal standards of housing, nutrition, shelter, children's education and burial. Most economic inequality within a team was due to life-cycle stages—people with small children were poorer than those with none or those in the most advantageous position with grown children capable of participating fully in labour. To even this out, teams allowed their members to overdraw their work-points to pay for necessary foodgrain whether they had the work-points to pay for it that year or not. They would repay their overdrafts in later years when their children were grown and they had work-point surpluses. In other words, the teams provided a way of equalizing consumption without equalizing income in the short run. Finally, they provided collective goods—such as inexpensive education and health care, recreation facilities and programmes, and in some special cases even housing—to everyone equally.

Efforts were made in national policy to encourage production teams to take steps to increase economic equality even further, consistent with the demands of economic growth. Under the national movement to emulate Dazhai Brigade, a formerly poor mountainous village, and Xiyang County (where Dazhai was located), several concrete measures were proposed. Time-rates were to be preferred to piece- or task-rates in allocating work points, and the criteria for assigning them were to include diffuse contributions such as collective spiritedness as well as specific tasks accomplished. This would, it was thought, help to minimize work-point inequality due purely to differences in natural endowments, while also contributing to and expressing collective solidarity. Upper limits were to be placed on work-point values (individual consumption), with any further surpluses to be used for collective investment or consumption (such as team housing, better schools, or improved health care, in which all would share equally). Brigade- and commune-level industries were to be built up to the point that their per-capita profits would overshadow those of the teams, thereby facilitating some equalization among teams. This was to occur either by distribution of profits equally to all the teams in a brigade or commune or, ultimately, by amalgamation of the teams into a single brigade accounting unit whose sufficiently large financial weight would help overcome the incentive problems that had arisen from combining poor and rich villages during the Great Leap.[15] At the same time, higher-level units such as brigades, communes and even the county government were to use their surpluses to invest in the poorest areas under their jurisdiction, thereby pursuing a redistributive pattern of growth.

The Dazhai/Xiyang campaign was an attempt to extend the economic logic of high collectivism in ways that would promote greater equality while not damaging labour incentives and would pursue continued growth across the board and especially in the economically backward areas. It became the *bête noire* of the post-Mao leadership, which sought to attack the basic structures of high collectivism on which the Dazhai/Xiyang programme was built and of which it was the most advanced exemplar. Thus Dazhai and Xiyang came under strenuous attack after 1978. More important in the long run was the concurrent attack on high collectivism, to which the criticisms of Dazhai opened the way.

It has been argued that high collectivism hurt labour incentives and suppressed local economic entrepreneurship. This argument has been widely accepted by Western analysts who are prone to believe in the impracticality of socialism anyway. In fact little or no good evidence has been adduced to support the claim that high collectivism hurt labour incentives. Moreover, good theory and evidence run the other way. The economic model of rational behaviour under uncertainty suggests that the payment structure of Chinese collectives gave peasants incentives to apply super-optimal quantities of labour. In other words, since peasants did not know in advance how much their work-points would be worth, they worked harder and longer than made sense from a labour-efficiency point of view (Putterman, 1983). Former peasants and rural cadres interviewed by numerous scholars in Hong Kong during the 1970s did not complain about indolence among the peasantry. On the contrary, their complaint was that peasants worked very hard—as they always had—but did not seem to be reaping economic gains commensurate with their efforts.

Why was this? Here the post-Mao critics are probably right. The demands placed on the teams to conform to state plans for agriculture—for example, to emphasize grain production at the expense of specialized crops in which they had a comparative advantage (a policy to be discussed below)—hurt productivity and income in many areas. Restrictions on rural markets and other forms of commerce among teams made it difficult for peasants and collectives to buy what they needed for consumption and production, while also holding back their entrepreneurial potential. In the absence of careful attention by the state to technical support and cost accounting, its emphasis on rapid, labour-intensive construction by rural collectives of infrastructural projects such as dams, canals and reservoirs led to considerable wasted effort, as these projects piled up high costs or ultimately failed to produce the intended benefits.

But none of these problems was inherent to high collectivism itself. That is, there is every reason to hypothesize that high collectivism could have achieved much better economic results under a different set of state policies on commerce, planning and investment.[16] Since the post-Mao leadership has made changes on all fronts at once—by eliminating some of the most extreme applications of the local grain self-sufficiency policy and encouraging some specialization in planning, by freeing up rural commerce, by being more careful in calculating costs of production and investment, and also by attacking high collectivism—it is impossible to say for certain whether the impressive economic results that have been achieved in recent years are due to the new, less collectivist organization in the countryside or to other factors. It can certainly be said that any claim that high collectivism had to be eliminated for economic reasons rests on very spurious logic.

This raises the question of why the post-Mao leadership attacked it. At this moment in history, and with the information presently at hand, it is impossible to say. Perhaps high collectivism was viewed as a potential source of political radicalism which the present leadership wanted to excise from the body politic. Perhaps careful analytical distinctions were not made in undertaking the reform, either due to muddy thinking or to a desire for very rapid results to help legitimate the post-Mao regime. It is also possible that evidence exists that would call the practicality of high collectivism into question, but that for some reason it has not been adequately brought to light.

There is also the question of the apparent popularity of the movement away from high collectivism. This, too, requires much more study than has been possible so far. Analysts have decided that high collectivism was unpopular from the fact that it was so quickly replaced: indeed, it appears in many places peasants and local leaders moved more rapidly than national leaders in abolishing it (Watson, 1983). But this deduction involves logical and methodological problems. It is entirely possible that the rapid move away from high collectivism after 1978 was more the result of the power of a limited group of influential peasants and local leaders than of widespread popular dissatisfaction. Indeed, this was the case in the early 1960s when former rich peasants and other opponents of collectivism seized the opportunity presented by the failure of the Great Leap to move toward household subcontracting. The difference is that now opponents of collectivism have the support of the state, something they lacked in the 1960s. It is also possible that peasants were responding to what they took to be clear cues from the post-Mao state about its desired new directions. The very same scholars and observers who correctly expressed doubts that the rapid spread of Maoist policies always reflected their popularity may now have made this same error.

Another possibility is that peasants throughout China really did want to abolish high collectivism because they failed to distinguish between it and the policies that were distinct from but associated with it, or because they felt that in political terms the best way to reverse those policies was also to expunge high collectivism. Yet another intriguing and more theoretically complex hypothesis has to do with the structure of the responsibility systems themselves. Their early forms restricted peasants' claims on land but expanded their ability to own agricultural capital (in the hope that this would encourage investment). This produced a contradiction: peasants could hardly be expected to invest in land which they might lose in the next round of contracts. Thus it may have been necessary to move toward giving peasants firmer and more long-term control over the land (still short of outright ownership)—as the most extreme and now common forms of responsibility system have done—in order to resolve this contradiction and encourage investment in improving and maintaining the land.

Whatever the case may be, the implications of this line of argument are that collective agriculture of the sort practised in China during the years of high collectivism cannot be dismissed as a failure based on the evidence now at hand. It would be a mistake for Chinese socialists, political leaders and citizens in other socialist countries, or analysts of socialism to relegate it to the scrap-heap of history, as the post-Mao leadership has tried—successfully, so far—to do. In the absence of more careful analysis, there is a great danger that one of the most original and progressive innovations achieved by socialism in its infant years will be lost.

'Contractual Collectivism': 1978 to the Present

The agrarian structure that has replaced high collectivism has been regarded by many observers, including ideologues of various right and left persuasions, as capitalist, or at least as the end of collectivism. It has been defended by others, including the post-Mao leadership, as conforming to the basic definition of socialism. Again, the truth lies somewhere in between.

In formal terms the collectives have not been abolished. This has not always been, and in many places is still not, a mere formalism. So long as contracting was done on a relatively short-term basis (as in the early 1980s when contracts were renewed annually, biennially or triennially), it was difficult for peasants to alienate the land (in order to acquire unearned income from it) by selling or leasing it. In the terms introduced earlier in this chapter (pp. 159–60), they did not have 'actual ownership' of land. But this has begun to change with the rise of long-term land contracting—for fifteen to thirty years—in the mid-1980s. In some places today peasants with long-term contracts to land are sub-letting it; land markets, rental payments and tenancy relationships have reappeared (Kelliher, 1986).

Nevertheless, there are still restrictions on 'practical ownership' of land— that is, the ability to use it in production as one sees fit unencumbered by competing claims or regulations. Chinese contracts for agricultural land differ from those in capitalist countries in two very important respects. First, they specify not only charges for the land but also the crop to be grown on it. Second, contract terms are not really negotiable; they do not reflect market prices or values. Thus, even in the face of renascent land markets, rural China today is some distance from reintroducing capitalist tenancy. In fact, in some places—where peasants who have contracted for land sub-let some of it because they cannot afford to farm it all—the return of land markets has actually been based on the restrictions on practical ownership. (There are even instances of land abandonment in China today—a truly astonishing development in a country with such a dearth of arable land (Kelliher, 1986).) Insofar as the peasants have not acquired complete private ownership of land (using a complex concept of ownership), and since collectives still act in significant ways to restrict such privatization, it may be best to identify and describe the hybrid form that has emerged since 1978 as 'contractual collectivism'.[17]

Land aside, peasants have from the outset of the reforms been permitted— indeed, encouraged—to own agricultural capital goods like trucks, tractors and other agricultural machinery. These can be used on their own plots or to provide services to other peasants for a fee. Under the latter, hired labour can be used to work this equipment. Peasants have also been permitted to own small manufacturing and service businesses, and to hire labour to work in them. In the area of capital, then, something more closely tantamount to capitalist productive relations has begun to prevail.

But here too there are new hybrids. In some places collective industries are being sub-contracted to peasants. In others peasants are forming joint-stock companies with their collectives or even with state enterprises. (In Taiyuan, the capital of Shanxi Province, there is now a restaurant owned and run jointly by the provincial Bureau of Heavy Industry and a rural production brigade (Jacobson, 1986)!) Some of these use wage labour and involve, at least primarily, private appropriation of profit. But the terms on which these contracts are let, or under which these firms must operate (specifically, prices and production plans) are not always set on market-based terms. They are still under considerable state control (for example, of their supplies of inputs, credit arrangements and production plans).

In the face of all this, what, if anything, remains of the collectives? In some places—including, surprisingly, parts of rural Guangdong (thought by many Western and Chinese analysts to have had a weak base of collective institutions)—the collectives still appear to be functioning in a meaningful sense. Though land is subcontracted, local enterprises are owned and run collectively, with their operations and profits under some form of popular control. The collectives also continue to provide social services such as schools and clinics (Johnson, 1986). In these places, the funds retained by the collectives under the land contracts might even be thought of as collective dues or investment shares rather than rent.

But in other places the social services provided by the collectives have withered or been abolished, and collective enterprises have come under greater private actual or practical ownership. There the relationship of the peasant to the collective has become much more attentuated, and the attendant productive relations less socialist in character. Accordingly, it seems reasonable to hypothesize that the level of collective solidarity and the democratic character of village politics have declined as their existential and material bases have been undermined. Peasants now spend most of their time working on family-sized plots leased from the team. They are in much less frequent contact with each other on an hour-by-hour, day-by-day basis. Since work points have been abolished under most of the responsibility systems, peasants' income is not collectively mediated as before. There is, in short, less opportunity for collective politics to take place, and less substance to it in terms of concrete issues that affect the lives of its members in ways they experience as important. Yet there are certain issues that continue to bring team members together and around which a lively form of politics seems to take place. There are indications, for example, that the terms of the contracts which the teams sign with their members have caused serious controversies, particularly since much of what is being leased out is collective property that was produced by the accumulated labour of the team members over many years.

Thus questions remain about what the collectives are, what they are and are not doing, and what kinds of politics their activities and characters engender. Until these questions can be answered, it will continue to be difficult to evaluate the nature of collectivism in China today, or to make confident pronouncements about whether or not it even exists in any meaningful sense. Even if the answers to these questions could be known, contractual collectivism would probably prove difficult to characterize in any simple way, since it combines elements of a more fully socialist high collectivism with more privatistic ones that have affinities to capitalism. The best answer we can probably give, then, is that simplistic definitions of the new developments in rural China—whether capitalist or socialist—should be avoided and efforts made to understand them as a new kind of hybrid with its own special characteristics and contradictions.

Economic Integration and Self-Reliance

Chinese socialist development is noted for its emphasis on self-reliance. Domestically, this has meant creating local or regional units that would provide broadly for their own needs. Internationally, it has meant minimizing external trade. China's efforts to create self-reliant economies at both levels have attracted widespread attention from students of economic development in the Third World. For those concerned with the depredations wrought on peasants by agricultural specialization—for example, the common phenomenon of peasants who produce large surpluses of coffee or cotton but still hunger for basic foodgrains—China has appeared as a model of a country which has got its priorities straight by producing 'food first' (Lappe & Collins, 1977). And for those who believe that integration into the world economy can only leave Third World countries dependent and underdeveloped, China has been a model of autocentric, independent development.

It is not so clear that Chinese leaders or planners have thought of their self-reliance policies this way. Both domestic and international self-reliance was founded partly upon concerns with national security. The communes—the original units of industrial and agricultural self-reliance—were to some extent a response to China's worsening international relations as the Sino-Soviet split was growing and tensions were running high in the Taiwan Straits. Chinese leaders sought to disperse industry away from the major centres so that no invader could choke the vast majority of the people in the countryside by occupying them (as Japan had done in the 1930s). The same reasoning lay behind the emphasis on 'taking grain as the key link'; a concurrent slogan urged people to 'store grain everywhere' to hedge against invasion. The international dimension was that China should never lay itself open to international threats or pressure by having to import food. The domestic dimension was that each locality should be able to provision itself so that it could not be starved out in the event of occupation of itself or of other areas on which it might depend for food.

It could be argued that the emphasis on self-reliance was less a choice made by Chinese leaders than a policy imposed on them. Indeed, when the international situation presented possibilities for expanded economic relations with foreign countries, China took advantage of them. Mao himself went to Moscow in 1950 and endured considerable personal humiliation at Stalin's hands in order to get commitments for trade and assistance. Self-reliance in international economic relations began to receive serious theoretical emphasis only after Sino-Soviet relations had deteriorated. In the early 1970s, China did not hesitate to improve its relations, including trade, with the United States.

National security aside, regional and local self-reliance was also based on a realistic approach to the low level of development of China's transportation infrastructure. It was and still is very difficult to move large quantities of commodities from place to place over the vastness and complexity of Chinese geography. While local production of various goods might be less efficient and more costly than concentrated production in a few larger, more modern plants, the differential could often be more than made up for by the high cost and unreliability of shipping the goods from their production centres to their large number of widely dispersed consumers. Local self-reliance also helped supply collectives and peasants with simple producer and consumer goods which the cumbersome central planning system was unable to do.

If China had its own rationales for pursuing economic self-reliance, they were quite different from those that are advanced for other Third World countries. Advocates of a 'food first' policy often argue, eloquently and correctly, that concentration on cash-crop production for export leaves peasants hungry and impoverished. This happens partly because when the poor have to buy rather than produce their own food, they must enter the monetized economy, where they are suddenly subject to wild price fluctuations and to the depredations of speculators or government tax collectors (Lappe & Collins, 1977). It also happens because cash-crop production frequently requires more credit up front than basic food production does, which invites exploitation from usurers (Todaro, 1981, Ch. 10). In China these dangers did not exist. Such poverty as has existed in rural socialist China has not been caused by cash-crop production on unfavourable terms. Indeed, most poor Chinese peasants produce their own food. (The present leadership argues in fact that they are poor in part because they concentrate too much on food production, a point about which they may be right, as we shall see.) Moreover, China eliminated speculators and usurers long before it pursued its 'grain first' policies, and its tax policies were never any danger to the peasantry. So Chinese peasants, unlike their counterparts in many Third World countries, could pursue specialized cash-crop production with much less risk.

Moreover, China is a poor model for many Third World countries of the effects and possibilities of international self-reliance because of the huge size and complexity of its economy, particularly its internal market. Total export earnings made up only 4 per cent of gross domestic product in 1983, very low by comparison with many Third World countries.[18] Thus Chinese agriculture can move toward much greater specialization and export orientation and still not encounter the degree of dependency on external markets and their undependable and exploitative price structures that smaller developing countries lacking extensive internal markets do.

There is good evidence to suggest that the emphasis on local and national self-reliance in foodgrain production did serious damage to agrarian production and income. In many areas key cash crops that were heavily in demand by China's industries and consumers, or that could have earned handsome export earnings, were uprooted so that grain could be planted. Cotton had to be rationed for many years and was in such short supply that it had to be purchased from abroad at relatively high prices—an example of how the emphasis on domestic food production can actually increase import dependency! Production of sugar, oilseed crops and vegetables also suffered (Lardy, 1983, Ch. 2). Meanwhile tremendous pressure was exerted on farmers to expand grain production, which led to double and triple cropping and extensive application of chemical fertilizers. All this damaged the soil in many places and was increasingly cost-inefficient.

Despite criticisms of the previous emphasis on grain production and local self-sufficiency by some present-day leaders and economists, in general there has been relatively little change in overall land use in agriculture. Grain was cultivated on 79.2 per cent of sown area in 1983, compared with 80.3 per cent in 1978. If anything, the decline in grain's share of sown area was greater during the Maoist period: it had been 87.8 per cent in 1952 and 83.5 per cent in 1965. The reasons for this failure of present policy to keep apace with its aims are obscure. One analyst has suggested that Chinese economists simply do not understand the theory of comparative advantage, which would argue that grain production could actually be increased by reducing sown area (in land marginally suited to grain production) and concentrating inputs on the remaining land that is more well suited to it (Lardy, 1983, pp. 200–4). It is also the case that China's transport system remains woefully underdeveloped, possessing the capacity to move limited amounts of goods inefficiently, unreliably and at high cost. No doubt the difficulty in moving toward greater specialization also has to do with fears by regional and local planners that in an emergency they may be unable to obtain needed foodgrain if they do not grow and store it themselves. This fear is partly a cultural imprint of centuries of experience with periodic famine. But it is also understandable in light of the experiences of the Great Leap and probably quite rational an estimate of the capacities of the state and the market in China today to respond to food emergencies.

The present leadership is perhaps most noted outside China for its 'open-door' policies on international economic relations. Foreign trade volume more than doubled from 1978 to 1983 and foreign investments of various kinds have been welcomed. That the post-Mao leadership should have pursued this policy should not be nearly as surprising as it is to many observers. As we have seen, China attempted to take advantage of opportunities provided by its foreign relations in both the early 1950s and the early 1970s to expand its international economic relationships—both times with Chairman Mao's personal imprimatur. In view of this, China's theoretical justifications of international self-reliance seem a flaccid exercise in making a virtue of necessity.

Expanded international economic relationships appear indeed to be in the interest of virtually every major constituency in China. For workers, they mean expanded employment, some directly in the elite export sector and some indirectly in related sectors. For peasants, they could mean some relief from the heavy emphasis on grain production; foodgrain imports have risen sharply since 1978. For both workers and peasants, they mean a greater access to prized foreign goods (though this is still very limited, especially for peasants). For bureaucrats and intellectuals, they also mean access to foreign goods, but even more important they offer expanded contacts with foreigners and the possibility of foreign travel, both of which are important sources of information, social status, resources for career mobility, and material goods.

Indeed, it is in this area that China's 'open-door' policy has provoked the gravest concern both in China and among sympathetic outside observers. A monopoly on foreign contacts and experiences among the bureaucratic and intellectual strata can only serve to widen the social cleavage between them and the rest of the Chinese people. It also poses the danger of an anti-foreign, hyper-patriotic backlash building on China's deep sense of national pride, a phenomenon that has occurred more than once in the past century and a half. It has already provoked a mass campaign against 'spiritual pollution' which drew the support of many Chinese citizens and leaders, including some at the very top. That this campaign seemed out of character with the more general political style of the post-Mao leadership which opposes mass movements, demonstrates the depth of the social and cultural forces being unleashed by the 'open door' to the international economy.

It is also instructive to notice that concern about those policies—both in China and among foreign observers—has not focused on questions of economic dependency and potential underdevelopment. Although much was made in the West of the appearance of Coca Cola in China a few years ago, in fact the prospect of the Chinese economy being sold down the river to multinational corporations, and of Chinese workers ending up working in foreign-owned sweatshops while also contributing to corporate coffers through their consumption of overpriced foreign commodities, seems remote if not impossible. The Chinese government has proved very tough in its negotiations with foreign investors, demanding that only the most modern technologies be used and that they be transferred over specified periods to Chinese firms and technicians. Wages in foreign-owned or joint-venture firms are generally higher, and working conditions better, than in the domestic sector. Continued low incomes combined with tight foreign exchange controls have sharply limited the size of the Chinese market for imported goods. Coca Cola could in fact only be bought by foreigners with dollars and was only sold in shops in foreign hotels and other segregated venues. And many a Western merchant who dreamed just a few years ago of a billion Chinese consumers has had a rude awakening.

Economic Performance

When all is said and done, how well has China's socialist economy performed? Where has it achieved its greatest results, and where do its greatest failures and challenges lie? In general it is impossible to refute the view, widely held among observers of so many ideological stripes, that Chinese socialism has achieved some stunning successes. The 'sick man of Asia', the country that could find no relief under the monarchy or the republic from the economic, social, political and international sufferings that beleaguered it for a full century after the Opium War, only under socialism could 'stand up'[19] and in a few decades restore its position as a major world power as well as a society that could feed, clothe and house the world's largest population at decent standards and afford them some personal and national dignity.

Much of this was achieved during the first decades of socialism, years when the Maoist approach predominated. The official index of living standards (used by the present leadership and its economists) rose 77 per cent from 1952 to 1978. Per-capita grain production rose 11 per cent over the same period, an impressive statistic for a country that began the socialist period with a highly developed traditional agriculture (that had already used up relatively 'easy' sources of growth) and that had to feed one-quarter of the world's population on one-twelfth of the world's arable land. These were also the years when China's basic industrialization began in earnest: industry accounted for 43 per cent of gross output value in 1952 and 72 per cent in 1978. Over this period wages of state employees rose 44 per cent, while peasants' net household income rose 84 per cent. Life expectancy reached 68, compared with a figure well under 60 in the early 1950s. The number of doctors per capita more than doubled, and hospital beds increased more than eleven-fold. All this was accomplished alongside significant gains in economic equality, a stunning achievement in view of the general tendency for inequality to rise during the early phases of economic development (Adelman & Morris, 1973).

Since the advent of the post-Mao period, economic growth has continued, even though the emphasis has shifted from quantitative increases to raising the complexity (that is, specialization and commercialization) and productivity of the economy, the quality of output and the income of the Chinese people. As we have seen, crop specialization has been more pronounced a goal than before, at least for some leaders and economists, but there is no complete consensus on it and concrete results have been very slow. Greater results have been achieved in specialization of the division of labour in the rural areas. By 1983 one hundred million (!) peasants were reported to have left grain production for other lines of (presumably more profitable and productive) work. Only those who can 'specialize' in grain production (which presumably means that they have special knowledge, skill and perhaps resources that make them more efficient) are urged to stay behind in the grain fields—though of course many ordinary peasants will also do so.

Increased labour productivity in agriculture and industry, too, are now major goals. Labour productivity in state-owned industry and construction rose 17 per cent from 1978 to 1983 (though the reforms cannot take all or most of the credit: it rose 24 per cent in the preceding two years, after being relatively stable for the previous six). The post-Mao changes have had their greatest impact on income and standards of living. Indeed, this was one of the major promises made to the Chinese people at the outset of the reform project, and remains one of the most important bases of the present leadership's claim to legitimacy. Rural incomes have risen most dramatically, doubling from 1978 to 1983. Ownership of simple consumer goods like sewing machines, bicycles, wrist-watches and radios have all at least doubled, while the Chinese press regularly delights in reporting on cases it can find of peasants purchasing computers or even aircraft! Wages in the state sector rose 34 per cent from 1978 to 1983.

The darker side of China's economic performance since 1978 has been the undeniable though still largely unquantified rise in income inequality. The present leadership admits this has happened and adopts postures ranging from resignation—arguing that increased inequality is an inevitable result of development, which always occurs unevenly—to laudation—arguing that inequality promotes incentives. Deng Xiaoping himself is reported by foreign scholars who met him to have replied to a question about growing class stratification in the countryside by expectorating into the nearest spittoon and then stating that perhaps this would get the poorer ones to work harder.

For the future China has more than once taught those who would study it that there can be safety only in questions. One set concerns future economic growth. Can household-sized plots provide the basis for further expansion of agriculture based on specialization, mechanization and use of modern agrarian technologies? Can they promote the reductions in the agrarian labour force which the present leadership wants to encourage in order to raise labour productivity? Can the investments that are still needed in infrastructure development be planned, carried out, and ultimately managed in the absence of the collective framework that existed and had meaningful achievements in this area in the past? Can the political tensions that are built into the assignment of collective property for individual use and into the growing economic inequalities and exploitative relationships (such as wage labour and illicit rental relationships) be contained? Can the contradictions between growing market forces and the continued existence of state planning be reconciled? Are the increases in production and particularly in income that have been achieved since 1978 mainly the result of pent-up forces that were let out all at once—and only once—in a short period, or do they signal the start of new forms of growth based on new economic structures? Can consumer expectations that have been fanned by the new leadership be met or reversed?

And in larger terms, there are the questions about the nature of Chinese socialism. China has been the greatest iconoclast in the socialist world, a world with perhaps too many icons and too little capacity for flexible application and critical evaluation of them. In that sense the present course in China has served a very useful purpose, though the achievement is mixed since it, too, has relied on new icons to smash old ones. Still, one can take heart from the fact that the present leadership seems to have passed through its phase of vilifying its past enemies and has preoccupied itself with the tasks at hand over which it has shown a marked willingness to countenance a limited range of debate. China continues to forge new directions—for example, in agriculture—which challenge the ability of students and practitioners of socialism to characterize them and to think creatively about the possibilities that exist under the increasingly broad rubric of socialist praxis.

7 Domestic and Foreign Policy in the Age of Modernization

At the watershed Third Plenum of the party's Eleventh Central Committee, which met in December 1978 and marked the accession to power of the Dengist leadership, a key change was the shift in the main orientation of state policy from political transformation to economic development. As the communiqué of that historic meeting said:

[N]ow is an appropriate time to . . . close the large-scale nationwide movement to expose and criticize Lin Piao [*sic*] and the 'gang of four' and to shift the emphasis of our Party's work and the attention of the people of the whole country to socialist modernization. [*Beijing Review*, 29 December 1978.]

Not one but 'four modernizations'—of industry, agriculture, science/technology and the military—were now to have the highest priority. In Marxian terms, raising the level of the productive forces was to be the paramount task. Political change was no longer to be 'in command', but was reconceptualized (and de-emphasized) as a superstructure whose development could only proceed from that of the economic base. In practical terms, economic development was to be the paramount objective of policy in all areas. This new orientation affected policy in all areas.

Education

Educational policy is now to serve economic modernization in two general ways. First, it is to produce students with the various levels of technical expertise—from simple literacy for machine operators to the complexities of nuclear physics for scientists—needed to foster the development of the economy as the present leadership has defined that process. Second, it is to contribute to social control by inculcating certain political views and cultural and ideological predispositions, including deference to authority, acceptance of discipline, an orientation to and sense of responsibility for self and family, and the legitimacy of certain degrees of social inequality. These views and predispositions are needed, the leadership now believes, for two reasons: to promote effective labour incentives, and to prevent political movements and activities of the sort that interfered with economic modernization during the

Maoist period. (Actually, it would be more accurate to say that these values are to be resuscitated, since they formed basic elements of traditional Chinese culture in imperial days.) The educational system fosters them both directly, through substantive emphasis in curricula, and indirectly through the 'hidden curriculum' comprising classroom organization, teacher expectations, indicators of success, methods of advancement, and modes of social control.

As early as kindergarten, students are now given standardized examinations, on the basis of which some are selected for special 'keypoint' primary schools. Admission to these is essential for those with high educational aspirations, since it is nearly impossible to gain admission to a 'keypoint' secondary school from an ordinary primary school. (In turn, the 'keypoint' secondary schools are practically the only path to formal tertiary education.) Even those left behind are separated into fast, average or slow classes. Students learn early, then, the value of studying hard and paying attention not only from teachers but also, and perhaps more importantly, from parents who have high aspirations for their children. (Parental pressure is only intensified by the one-child policy.) The early appearance of tracking also introduces students in the initial stages of the formation of their value systems to the existence of inequality as a simple fact, thereby fostering its legitimacy or at least acceptance.

'Keypoint' primary schools are the first step in training the technical and scientific intelligentsia that is to make so important a contribution to the modernization programme. Accordingly, these schools are favoured in several ways. Compared with ordinary primary schools, 'keypoint' primary schools have longer programmes (six years rather than the usual five), more academically intensive and advanced curricula, and better teachers and facilities. Besides producing educational inequality, they also reproduce social inequality, since they are almost all found in towns and cities and therefore do not accept students from rural families.

China's leaders believe that the country should have a population who can all at least read simple instructions and public information. Accordingly, the major goal of general primary education now is the eradication of illiteracy, which ran at 34 per cent of the adult population in 1983 and 25 per cent among those between 12 and 45 years of age in 1982. A goal of universal primary education by 1990 has been set. Under a centralization of educational administration, primary curricula and textbooks are to be standardized nation-wide, and are to consist overwhelmingly of training in language and mathematics. Primary school enrolments as a percentage of the applicable age cohort have been rising slightly in recent years. Chinese primary schools now enrol 93 per cent of their age cohort, but in 1980 the drop-out rate was 40 per cent. This high figure was due mainly to peasants pulling their children out of school, either because of their low estimation of the benefits of education and/or the high opportunity cost of keeping children in school under the responsibility systems that tie household income directly to its production. Here, then, is a contradiction between specific reform policies.

There have been two major changes in secondary education. First, the number of students has dropped dramatically, from 60,248,000 in 1979 to 47,548,000 only three years later. All of this drop occurred in the general secondary schools, which shed 7,250,000 at the junior-middle school level (15.7 per cent of the 1979 student body) and 6,515,000 (a full 50 per cent!) at the senior level. Specialized secondary schools engaged in technical and teacher-training lost another 160,000 students (13 per cent). But vocational secondary schools gained 478,000 which amounted to more than a tripling of their size (Bastid, 1984, pp. 196-7).

This reorientation toward vocational training was the second change in secondary education. A goal of having 40 per cent of all senior-middle school students in vocational programmes by 1987 has been set. This is to be accomplished partly by expanding vocational schools and partly by having other secondary schools place greater emphasis on vocational training in their curricula. Middle schools are also contributing directly to the economy by expanding work-study programmes, already in existence in over 40 per cent of secondary and even primary schools in 1982.

The highest priority is being given to the development of tertiary education, perhaps because it came in for the greatest destruction during the Cultural Revolution. Standardized tests are now used universally for undergraduate admission, to select only the cream of the secondary school crop. Then there is further differentiation of the *crème de la crème* for admission to the roughly 15 per cent of colleges and universities designated as 'keypoint' institutions. Quotas for students' social backgrounds have been dropped or de-emphasized. Curricula have been revamped along lines of Western models and political study has been contracted. Social sciences have been introduced or resuscitated after decades of near banishment. Programmes have been extended to at least four years and more in specialized areas. Graduate study leading to doctoral degrees has been expanded, too.

One major problem with implementing this programme at all levels has been that it must inevitably start with a teaching staff that is a product of the previous educational system and therefore is itself not always well qualified to supervise the attainment of the new educational policy goals. In 1979, the government estimated that 53 per cent of primary teachers—mainly those in schools run by rural collectives—were unqualified, as were 70 per cent of junior- and 50 per cent of senior-middle schoolteachers. College and university faculty suffered from insufficient training—over 90 per cent had less than six years of undergraduate and graduate training themselves—and from being badly out of touch with their fields due to the disruptions of the Cultural Revolution, when all schools were shut for two years and most colleges and universities longer.

Several steps have been taken to upgrade China's teachers. In-service training has expanded. In 1983, 201,000 middle schoolteachers were enrolled in teachers' colleges. Primary and secondary schoolteachers have been urged to take examinations qualifying them for formal certification by the Ministry of Education (and concomitant occupational and economic upgrading), and college and university teachers who graduated during the Cultural Revolution have been required to do so. Teacher-training has been strengthened both at home and by the expansion of opportunities to study abroad. Efforts have been made to attract the very best students into teaching careers. For example, salaries have been raised, better material amenities such as housing have been provided, and leaves, holidays and teaching loads have been specified. Academic rank has been restored in order to provide incentives for and recognition of achievement by college and university faculty. Nowadays conversations between Western academics and their Chinese counterparts are frequently peppered with more detailed and urgently-posed questions from the latter about the operation of career ladders in the West—criteria for tenure and promotion, methods of awarding pay rises etc.—than about teaching and research.

One feature of Chinese education that has drawn great attention in the past is its non-formal institutions, including evening adult literacy classes, short courses for peasants and workers during the Cultural Revolution, and so forth. This is one legacy from the past that remains important in China today, because it is an effective and inexpensive way of reaching many people and giving some satisfaction to the broad, popular demand for education, especially among the many young Chinese who have been closed out of regular educational institutions. In 1983, 479,000 adults were enrolled in the Central Broadcasting and Television University, 272,000 in correspondence and evening universities, and 174,000 in special colleges for cadres, peasants and workers. All these programmes lead to college degrees formally recognized by the government. Trade unions operate special classes in economics, management and law to prepare workers for admission to special branch colleges run by regular colleges and universities, usually located on the facilities of secondary schools.

Culture

Cultural policy in the post-Mao period has involved frequent vacillations between liberalization of cultural expression and continued state control, reflecting a strong Chinese ambivalence towards Western-style modernization that dates back to the nineteenth century. Soon after Mao's death, forces for freer cultural expression burst the dikes that had been holding them back for decades. In literature there was an outpouring of stories and novels which came to be known as 'literature of the wounded' because its main theme was persecution of writers and artists during the Cultural Revolution. Some artists began to hold their own public exhibitions of abstract works, sometimes with the help of local officials in gaining space and permission for their displays, and sometimes just in impromptu street-side exhibits of individual work.

These expressive impulses found expression and created controversy at the pinnacle of state organization as well. For example, in September 1979, the artist Yuan Yunsheng unveiled the mural he had been commissioned to paint for the restaurant of the new international terminal of the Beijing Airport. Yuan had chosen as his subject people of the Dai nationality in Yunnan, using an elongated style inspired by Giacometti and Modigliani, and depicting them bathing naked, as is their custom. The mural drew opposition from state officials in the Ministry of Culture and in charge of the airport. Hua Guofeng attempted to mediate the dispute by inviting representatives of the Dai to come to Beijing and offer their opinions. Their response was not what the critics had in mind. The Dai were honoured to be depicted in so important and prominently displayed a work, and confirmed that since they did indeed bathe naked they were not offended. Their criticisms were restricted to small points: they did not wear their sarongs precisely as the artist had painted them, men wore finery rather than shorts (as depicted) to festivals, and so forth. The dissatisfied critics then shifted tactics by mobilizing Dai supporters to criticize the work. They also argued that since Han people were not usually depicted in such lascivious activity—the mural showed a boy chasing a girl—or in an elongated fashion deemed ugly by the critics, the mural represented discrimination against the Dai. In April the mural was covered. Over the succeeding months, successive closings and openings of the curtain now placed over it reflected the shifting currents of cultural policy. Eventually, though, it was boarded up. Yuan Yunsheng received no more such commissions.

The backlash against less restricted cultural expression reached its height with an official campaign to criticize Bai Hua for his screenplay *Unrequited Love* starting in April 1981. Bai had gone too far, it was argued, in his attacks on the Cultural Revolution, blaming the party itself and the country as a whole rather than just the 'gang of four' as the main culprits. Bai was forced to make a self-criticism. But, unlike the fate of those criticized during the Cultural Revolution, Bai was then considered cleared, and was soon receiving favourable treatment in the press again. Still, the *Wenyi Bao* (*Literary Gazette*) was forced to admit that the criticism of Bai had 'provoked strong [critical] reactions among readers' and 'discussion and speculation in foreign mass media, suspecting that the spring[time] in China's literary world would pass and a biting cold would come'. It dismissed such concerns as 'a misunderstanding' (*Beijing Review*, 19 October 1981).

In 1983, a related but distinct set of concerns motivated official campaigns to combat 'spiritual pollution' and, putting the matter more positively, to build a 'socialist spiritual civilization'. 'Spiritual pollution' referred to the deleterious effects of Western culture on Chinese society, including the spread of pornography, prostitution, jazz, rock and roll, and new sexual mores. The campaign to build a 'socialist spiritual civilization' was designed to combat the tendencies to 'run after things material and ... be interested only in material gains' and to 'lead ... a rich yet spiritually meaningless life which impels [one] to cheat, rob and kill' (*Beijing Review*, 2 May 1983). Literature and art were assigned a specific role in fostering China's 'socialist spiritual civilization'. More recently, China shocked the world by permitting the British rock band 'Wham!' to perform, but then reversed itself and denied the Australian band 'Men At Work' permission to do the same.

Debate over the relationship of Western and Chinese culture, and modern and traditional values, did not begin during the socialist period. It has been going on in various forms since the late nineteenth century, when the impact of the West began to be felt seriously in China. Now, as before, it reflects deep controversy in Chinese society. On one side are writers and artists who hunger for greater latitude in their work and who to varying degrees are influenced by the West, as well as many ordinary citizens who desire a more diverse popular culture. On the other are many state leaders as well as many other writers, artists and citizens who are concerned about the ideological effects of an utterly open cultural environment, particularly in a world where the proliferation of exported Western culture has done great damage to the survival of non-Western cultures.

In the light of this debate the state inevitably faces several contradictory pressures. On the side of allowing a certain liberalization there are two main ones. First, the state needs the support and active participation of intellectuals—especially those engaged in <u>science and technology</u>—in order to achieve modernization of the economy. In turn it must support them by depoliticizing their work and allowing them access to the latest Western achievements in their fields. But the ideological environment it creates for non-scientific intellectuals, including artists and writers, is inevitably related to that which it creates for its scientific and technical intellectuals. For example, it is difficult to tell geologists that they may ignore study of Marx's or Mao's work but still remind graphic artists that they must not. More important, scientific intellectuals look at state policy concerning fellow intellectuals in the artistic and literary fields as a barometer by which to gauge their own activities. Attempts to root out Western bourgeois influence in culture and art cannot but have a chilling effect on the willingness of scientists to keep up with and be receptive to the latest American or European work in their own fields. Since the state leadership is aware of this, it must give artists and writers some latitude to pursue their work free of political interference and even allow them some contact with and influence by Western colleagues.

Second, the present leadership came to power based on an ideological programme, which achieved a definite popularity, aimed at reversing many evils perpetrated during the Cultural Revolution. Perhaps the most unpopular aspect of that period was its strict control of culture. Chinese peasants and workers became bored (if not repelled) by the six 'model operas' that were the only ones approved by Jiang Qing, the cultural tsarina of the Cultural Revolution left, for public performance for many years. Chinese readers also showed little interest in the novels and short stories of the day, with their wooden characters, predictable plots and puerile political moralizing.[1] The reversal of the draconian political control of culture has been broadly popular: new literature is snapped up from bookstore shelves, and attendance at films, plays and operas is up dramatically. As a result, the state must continue to limit its regulation of culture, lest it incur the anger of artists, writers and ordinary citizens.

On the other side of the forces for greater latitude in the cultural sphere are those that lead toward a certain regulatory role. First, in general the liberal tradition is very weak in China's historically formed political culture. Unbridled individual expression has never been actively promoted by any regime or significant political movement or guaranteed in any constitution or legislation. Indeed, the Chinese word for 'individual' (*geren*) has a pejorative connotation with undertones of selfishness or self-absorption. So claims advanced by artists and writers for utterly free expression simply cannot be understood by many Chinese citizens and leaders. Second, the influence of Marxism, with its emphasis on the material basis of culture, and of the Maoist rendering of this into a doctrine that in a socialist revolution and state literature and art ought to serve the needs of revolution and social-ism, only reinforce the historically-based Chinese lack of receptivity to free cultural expression. Third, the proliferation of Western ideas is offensive to China's strong and very widely held patriotism. Fourth, Chinese culture has had little exposure to many controversial expressive elements and forms in modern Western culture, such as abstraction, surrealism, atonality in music, and sexual frankness. It is thus hostile to the unfamiliar and unorthodox in ways that echo to some extent the responses these cultural inventions often received in their countries of origin. (This is worth remembering when frequent claims are advanced about stubborn Chinese traditionalism and conservatism.) Fifth, unrestricted space for cultural expression plays into the hands of opponents of the Dengist reform programme, who argue per-suasively that it has brought China all manner of new social problems ('spiritual pollution').

To be sure, these disagreements within the state, cross-pressures on it from society, and contradictions posed by the needs of modernization have imparted a certain dilemma concerning cultural policy and produced frequent reversals. Yet it would be a mistake to see cultural policy as merely a consequence (and a rather irregular one at that) of these opposing vectors. There is also an underlying consistency in cultural policy informed by a positive objective: to fashion a cultural policy suited to the development of the four modernizations. For example, although the mass campaign against 'spiritual pollution' was closed down relatively quickly because it held out the prospect of more mass campaigns, the state has periodically shown its concern about the substantive problems raised in the campaign in order to mollify ideologically and culturally conservative elements in the state who harbour deep suspicions about reform. Accordingly, it has in general kept a tighter rein on artists and writers than on scientists and technicians. It has established the primacy of the 'four basic principles'—adherence to the social-ist road, the people's democratic dictatorship, leadership of the Communist Party, and Marxism–Leninism–Mao Zedong thought—as bench-marks of ideological rectitude. Within them cultural expression has been given some-what greater latitude than in the past, but the boundaries remain. The major difference now is that, while during the Cultural Revolution culture was actively required to promote these goals as conceived by the left leadership, now the state contents itself with less specific concepts of these goals, direct-ing writers and artists simply not to obstruct them though they need not always actively serve them. Since none of this poses a serious threat to the scientists and technicians who are the real intellectual constituency of the present leadership, and since it meets the objections of the Chinese leaders and citizens with more traditional views about modern culture, it has proved to be a politically tenable compromise.

Religion

In a similar vein, restrictions on religious organization and observance have been partially lifted. Article 36 of the 1982 State Constitution guarantees freedom of religion and forbids the state to discriminate on the basis of religion. Monasteries and churches have been restored and reopened, religious works have been published, and spiritual leaders have been ordained.

This has served the post-Mao leadership and its modernization programme in at least two ways. First, it has been a convenient way by which to score political points against the radical left, and hence build popular support for the present leadership among some of those who had been most disaffected by the course of Chinese socialism. (This is especially ironic and even hypocritical since the attacks on religion during the Cultural Revolution were largely fomented by the more conservative leaders—many of whom are now back in power—as a way of deflecting the left's attacks against them.) Second, since the more tolerant posture toward religion has achieved wide recognition outside China, it has proved to be a useful way of communicating to foreigners that the new leadership is prepared to moderate its position on other issues.

The new tolerance toward religion has also had relatively few shortcomings for the present leadership. The main danger is that religion will become a focus for political opposition. But the potential threat is reduced by the fact that most Chinese are not believers in formal, organized religions anyway. Rather, for most Chinese, religious observance takes the form of ancestor reverence and various kinds of local animism. To help ensure that organized religions like Buddhism and, especially, Catholicism (with its internationally centralized authority structure) do not threaten the state, specific measures have been taken. The state has given recognition to a series of quasi-official religious associations, such as the Chinese Patriotic Catholic Association, the Chinese Buddhist Association, the Chinese Islamic Association, the Chinese Christian Council, and so forth. It has provided them with financial resources and a certain autonomy to conduct religious observances and ordain religious officials. But it has also used them as a means of controlling and monitoring the religious movements they represent. For example, the state has argued that there is no need for the Holy See to try to incorporate the Chinese Catholic Church and has persuaded the Chinese Patriotic Catholic Association to concur publicly. In places where religious believers dominate the population of a particular locality, such as Tibet or Muslim areas, the state has retained regional political authority for itself, while at the same time making a great public show of its efforts to grant religious freedom and even to nurture religious institutions and believers.

Military Affairs

The modernization project of the post-Mao leadership has led to serious contradictions in the area of military affairs and defence. On the one hand, it has sought to modernize the military for several reasons: its view that China could not defend itself, much less advance its foreign policy interests, by primary reliance on the 'people's war' guerrilla strategy;[2] its general propensity toward modern technology and organization; and its political opposition to Maoists who were ensconced heavily in the armed forces. On the other, because economic modernization was its highest priority, thorough technical modernization of the military would be very expensive (roughly $50 billion), and national economic resources have been in such short supply, the military was given the lowest priority among the four modernizations, after industry, agriculture and science/technology. Defence spending declined absolutely by one-quarter from 1979 to 1981, and continued to drop as a percentage of state budgets through 1983, when it reached the lowest level (13.7 per cent) since 1961, the nadir of the crisis caused by the Great Leap.

The strains of military modernization, and the contradiction of this goal with the low budgetary priority accorded the military, were but one source of potential military opposition to the post-Mao leadership. Another had to do with the fact that the agrarian reforms have favoured households with large amounts of labour power and with technical and entrepreneurial skills. Families whose bright, assiduous and ambitious young men had joined the army—which had been a magnet for such people for many years when it was one of the very few ways to get ahead—were therefore put at a relative disadvantage when the reforms opened up new opportunities that had not existed when the decision to join the military had been made. This contributed to a serious morale problem among the rank-and-file and even some junior officers. Finally, the armed forces, as in other countries a repository of China's strongest nationalist sentiments, represented a centre of opposition to the 'open-door' approach of the post-Mao leadership to international relations and economic development.

If the military had good reason to oppose the modernization project and the reform-minded leadership, it was also, by virtue of its effective monopoly over state coercive power, precisely the sector best organized to oppose them.[3] This was one important reason why Deng Xiaoping, who gave the leading posts in all other areas to his supporters, kept both military port-folios—the chairs of the Party Military Affairs Commission (MAC) and the government Central Military Commission—for himself.

Lacking much in the way of material resources with which to transform the army from a radically inclined guerrilla force into a modern, professional and less politically minded one, the post-Mao leadership has relied mainly on political and organizational methods. First, Deng moved quickly after the watershed Third Plenum (of December 1978), when he consolidated his leadership in the party, to get control over the armed forces. Within a little more than a year he had replaced ten of the eleven regional military commanders, and by 1982 he had the central command under his control and his supporters in key positions there. Second, the command structure was streamlined and simplified, so that dual command structures (from the heads of the military regions and the central service commanders) were abolished. Commands now flowed directly from the regional headquarters (now toler-ated because the regional commanders were loyal Dengists). The number of such regions has been reduced from eleven to seven, a further simplification. Third, the size of the army has been trimmed by one-quarter to around four million, with further reductions still slated.

Fourth, the technical qualifications of the officer corps have been upgraded. Curricula at officer training schools have been changed to de-emphasize politics and guerrilla strategy and to stress instead science and technology. A new military academy directly under the MAC has been estab-lished, and its faculty is being encouraged to develop contacts with military academics abroad. Meanwhile older, less well-educated (and presumably more politically hostile) officers are encouraged to resign or retire through material inducements such as generous pensions, housing allowances, and continued provision of other perquisites of office such as chauffeured cars. To this has been added administrative pressure in the form of graded age limits for various ranks (which also encourages those at lower ranks to upgrade their skills to receive promotions before they become over age for their level).

This is not to say that the military has received no new resources at all. Purchases of military equipment from abroad have begun. Living conditions for soldiers have been standardized, a rise above the meagre Y10 per month is predicted, and uniforms and basic military hardware have been upgraded.

Nevertheless, the recent exposés of military complicity in 'economic crimes' indicate that there is still much to be done.

But such extra-military activities by the armed forces are not the result only of economic hardship in the ranks. These are crimes of opportunity as well as motive. The army has been asked to participate in the economic modernization effort directly by starting its own factories and enterprises. It is hoped that the profits they earn will help finance military modernization while at the same time contributing to overall economic production. Meanwhile, such profits are helping to subsidize the incomes of at least the more unscrupulous or desperate officers and soldiers who are well placed to use local contacts, transport facilities, administrative authority (at borders), and even coercive authority (to exact levies from those transporting goods along isolated roads) for illicit trade, smuggling or extortion.

Modernization and professionalization of the armed forces has also meant a marked reduction in the role of the people's militias, which at one time had over 200 million members. They are now much smaller and under the direct supervision of the armed forces rather than local production units as in the past. In the event of attack they are charged with strictly auxiliary functions such as troop support and information-gathering—they are not relied on to do much fighting. Public security functions have been taken away from the militias (thus assisting in the effort to regularize the legal process). One objective of these changes is a marked reduction in the capacity of ordinary citizens to challenge the state with armed force, as the left did during the Cultural Revolution.

Finally, the military's influence in national politics has been curtailed. In the wake of the chaos caused by the Cultural Revolution, the army has been called upon as the only institution capable of restoring order and reconstituting state power. One-third of the members of the Eleventh Party Central Committee, elected in 1977, were military representatives, and 89 per cent of those were active military commanders. By contrast, less than one-quarter of the Twelfth Central Committee, elected in 1982, were from the army. Personnel aside, it is equally important that the top positions of state power overseeing the military are held by men loyal to Deng Xiaoping and committed to the civilian control of the military and to giving military modernization a decidedly lower priority than economic development.

Foreign Policy

There has been much enthusiasm abroad about the foreign policy offensives of the post-Mao leadership: by 1984, China had diplomatic relations with

129 countries, belonged to nearly one hundred international organizations, and reached another new peak in foreign-trade volume. This activity was related directly to China's modernization effort in several respects. First, the emphasis on production specialization and pursuit of comparative advantage led to an increased emphasis on foreign trade. Second, the post-Mao leadership has sought to base modernization of the economy partly on the use of imported capital and technology, which necessarily requires extensive international diplomatic and legal relationships, market information, and hard currency that can be earned only through exports. Third, because the modernization drive has, as we have seen, exerted downward pressure on military budgets, China's leaders have redoubled their efforts to increase the country's national security through diplomatic means.

As a result of the close association of the modernization and foreign policies in the post-Mao period, as well as the present leadership's repeated emphasis on the need for an 'open door' to the world, it is often assumed that socialist China was basically closed off from the world before the present leadership came to power. This alleged insularity is linked to traditional Chinese xenophobia and to Maoist self-reliance.

These views are distorted in significant ways. First, the economic modernization drive of the 1950s was also associated with a foreign policy offensive towards the Soviet Union, a country about which the Chinese people—and in particular the Chinese Communist Party—had many reasons to feel suspicious and hostile. At the same time the Chinese government actively sought to expand its relations with other countries. It was Zhou Enlai who literally extended his hand to greet US Secretary of State John Foster Dulles at the 1954 Geneva Conference, a gesture which Dulles pointedly refused to reciprocate. The following year, China played a leading role at the historic Bandung Conference of Non-Aligned Countries.

Second, the self-reliance policy associated with Mao in fact was partly an instance of making a virtue of necessity. Relations with the West got off to a poor start because of the Korean War, into which China was drawn somewhat unwillingly by forces beyond its control. The Cold War, which had produced, and in turn been re-produced by, the Korean War, scuttled any hopes for better relations with the West which China had entertained. When relations between the Soviet Union and China began to deteriorate in the late 1950s, China was left with nowhere to turn. In contrast to the common argument that China's self-reliance policy was the result of domestic factors such as Maoist ideology and developmental policies that did not require foreign economic relations, it has been suggested by some scholars that the reverse is also true: that domestic radicalism was accelerated by foreign threats

(Schurmann, 1968, Supplement). For example, the Great Leap occurred at a time of increased hostility in the Taiwan Straits, and the Cultural Revolution at a time when the Vietnam War was reaching fever pitch. This hypothesis aside, evidence for China's lack of commitment to international isolation comes from the fact that in the early 1970s, when it became clear that the Vietnam War would soon be ending, the Chinese took an active role in improving their relationship with the United States. The theory of Chinese xenophobia or Maoist ideology cannot explain this shift. Indeed, Mao put his personal imprimatur on the improvement of relations with the United States. China also triumphantly entered the United Nations in 1971. So here we have the supposed ideological fountainhead of China's international isolation leading China towards breaking out of that isolation at the earliest possible moment. It appears, then, that China's isolation in the 1960s was less a policy than a necessity forced on it by hostile international circumstances.

Throughout the 1970s there was broad support in China for the improvement of relationships with the United States. The left was happy to use the United States as a counterweight to Soviet influence, which it regarded as the greater potential threat both because of the Soviet Union's proximity and menacing activity—there were border clashes in 1969, and around the same time the Soviet Union is alleged to have approached the United States for its acquiescence in a planned pre-emptive nuclear strike against China's own nuclear installations—and also because of its ideological belief that capitalism in the United States and elsewhere was in long-term decline anyway. More politically centrist elements in the state viewed the opening to the United States as having potentially salutary effects on their incipient plans for economic modernization. Intellectuals yearned for opportunities to expand contacts with colleagues abroad. Many Chinese peasants and workers welcomed the revival of contacts with overseas relatives and/or the appearance of Western consumer goods. And most Chinese hoped that improved relations with the United States would speed up reunification with Taiwan, a deeply felt patriotic goal. Thus the foundations of the 'open-door' policies of the post-Mao period can be found to have been laid down firmly during the Maoist period.

This of course in no way diminishes the rapid expansion of China's foreign relations since 1978. Diplomatic relations with the United States were finally normalized in January 1979, when the meeting halls of the landmark Third Plenum were probably still being swept up. Foreign-trade volumes, which had grown 30 per cent in 1978 (before the Dengist triumph at the Third Plenum), continued to rise very fast—28 per cent in 1979, 24 per cent in 1980, and 27 per cent in 1981. Slow-downs in subsequent years (6.7 per cent in 1982 and 5.4 per cent in 1983) resulted from the need to consolidate trade and stem the previous spending spree, not from any new hostility to foreign trade in principle. In fact, each year the range of China's international economic contacts has expanded to include joint ventures with foreign firms, the establishment of special export-orientated production and trade zones, increased autonomy for provinces and municipalities to deal directly with foreign concerns, and sales of government bonds abroad. Meanwhile, cultural and educational exchanges have proceeded apace. For example, 11,000 Chinese completed overseas study between 1981 and 1985.

Alongside the quantitative expansion of international relationships in recent years has been a strategic shift towards improved relations with the Soviet Union. Continued hostility towards the Soviet Union during the 1970s was based on ideological opposition, especially strong on the left, to Soviet 'revisionism' in domestic policy as well as genuine Soviet threats to Chinese security along their common border in Indochina (where the situation was deteriorating with the Vietnamese invasion of Kampuchea and the Sino-Vietnamese border war of 1979) and in Afghanistan. For many years the Chinese insisted on Soviet withdrawals from the latter two areas as well as a reduction of Soviet troop strength along the Sino-Soviet border as conditions of any improvement of relations.

Yet beyond these exigencies were forces favourable to improved relations. The defeat of the Chinese left removed a serious obstacle to improved Sino-Soviet relations. Normalization of relations with the United States gave the Chinese greater manœuvrability in dealing with the Soviet Union.[4] And the post-Mao leadership and its intellectual and bureaucratic constituency contained many people who had been trained in the Soviet Union, had worked with Soviet technicians in the 1950s, and/or believed in Soviet-style central planning and the value of Soviet technology for China's modernization. Finally, the rise of a reform-minded leadership in the Soviet Union in the post-Brezhnev period has been welcomed by Chinese leaders, who view it in their interest to encourage such change in the world's first and most powerful, but hitherto most economically inflexible, country.

These forces bore fruit by the mid-1980s. As early as 1979, the Chinese signalled change in their approach to the Soviet Union by dropping the epithet 'revisionist' in their references to it. Progress was then blocked for several years by some of the conjunctures in Asian politics mentioned above. But by 1984, as the confidence of the Chinese leadership in its domestic and foreign policies grew, and events in Indochina and Afghanistan cooled down to what appeared to be long-term, but low-level, manageable conflict, movement in Sino-Soviet relations finally began. At the end of the year, Chinese media began to downplay the danger presented by the Soviet Union. A visit by Soviet Deputy Premier Ivan Arkhipov, who had been instrumental in the Soviet aid effort to China in the 1950s, was hosted in December. In May 1985, at the time of the fortieth anniversary of the end of the Second World War, the Chinese began to laud the Soviet contribution to the war effort, while also expanding the presentation of Soviet films and operas. In July, Vice-Premier Yao Yilin repaid the Arkhipov visit, travelling to Moscow to sign a five-year trade agreement. A March 1986 agreement provided for Soviet experts to return to China.

China has also gone on the diplomatic offensive in regional politics in recent years. The 1979 invasion of Vietnam was probably part of an effort by the new post-Mao leadership to enhance its domestic support by appealing to Chinese nationalism. But because Chinese troops put in such a poor showing in the brief border war, and perhaps also because the episode demonstrated an aggressiveness that was not functional for other regional objectives, such adventures have not been repeated. Since then, Chinese foreign policy has projected a decidedly moderate posture, especially on the key questions of Taiwan and Hong Kong.

China regards both these territories as part of China, a point on which it finds agreement with the Taiwan and British authorities. Thus China has always stated publicly that the issues of reunification are actually internal affairs, not matters of foreign policy. As such, it could deal with them in any way it saw fit, including the use of force—which could be justified as the legitimate exercise of state power within its territory, not an act of war. In the 1980s China has not formally renounced this position. Indeed, it cannot, since doing so would amount to the admission that Hong Kong and Taiwan were not part of China, something which no Chinese leadership could ever say without doing great damage to the legitimacy of its claim to represent the country.

But, in a significant change, it has chosen to downplay this position. Taiwan and Hong Kong are now viewed not just as *terrae irredentae*, but also as places that can make great contributions to China's economic modernization. For them to be able to do so the reunifications most occur peacefully. Thus China, which could easily absorb Hong Kong by force any time it chose to do so—by sending in troops or denying the territory needed lifelines such as water and food supplies—and which in any event will absorb most of Hong Kong when the lease runs out in 1997, chose instead to enter into protracted negotiations with Great Britain to ensure a smooth transitional period in the decade preceding 1997. In fact, China agreed to a transitional process that extends beyond 1997.

The Hong Kong solution was important not only in its own right, but also as a harbinger of the resolution of the more important and complex Taiwan problem. Throughout the 1980s, China made repeated overtures to Taiwan for an agreement on peaceful transition. It even offered to allow Taiwan to remain capitalist and to retain its own armed forces. The 1982 State Constitution included an unprecedented provision (Article 31) for the creation of 'special administrative regions' as a way of linking Taiwan and Hong Kong to the state more loosely than other parts of the country. To be sure, Taiwan authorities were unimpressed by verbal guarantees, as the Chinese leadership must have known they would be. Thus the latter took great care to demonstrate China's reasonableness and commitment to peaceful, gradual resolution of the Hong Kong reunification.

In other regional affairs too, China has adopted a much less aggressive posture than in the past. This change flows from its concern with economic modernization in at least two respects. It seeks first to create a climate suitable to regional trade and second to help assure its security through diplomatic rather than more costly military means. Thus support for communist insurgencies in South-East Asia has been drastically decreased in some cases, and dropped completely in others. Overtures for reconciliation with Vietnam have been made and support for the Khmer Rouge downplayed. Chinese leaders have regularly visited their Asian counterparts. A quiet but clear diplomatic offensive toward South Korea has been launched.

Thus by the mid-1980s Chinese foreign policy had reached a new threshold of maturity, complexity and balance. For the first time China was able simultaneously to deal with both superpowers on an increasingly normal basis. It made great progress in recovering parts of the country that had become separated from it, an issue that has repeatedly been a major stumbling-block to improved relations with the West. It has become an increasingly respected and congenial member of the East Asian community of nations. Its foreign trade and diplomacy have grown world-wide. That all this could be accomplished in a relatively short period of time, starting from a point of considerable international isolation and hostility, in a country with deep and in many ways understandable historical and cultural ambivalence about the outside world, is a major achievement. After regarding itself for centuries as the centre of the world—during which time it condescended to foreign countries, ignoring those far away and dominating those nearby—and after enduring a century of defeat and degradation made all the more humiliating by its former greatness and haughtiness, China in the 1970s and 1980s has at least begun to carve out for itself a position as a great nation which at last is confident enough to learn to deal with other nations large and small, great and not so great, in ways that promise to benefit all of them.

Notes

Chapter 1

1. See Moore, 1966. The situations in England and France were, of course, quite different from each other.
2. The case of Sheng Xuanhaui is instructive. See Feuerwerker, 1958.
3. Moore, 1966, p. 183. Skocpol makes the controversial case that in France the state rather than the bourgeoisie played the major role in the transformation to industrial capitalism. See Skocpol, 1979, Ch. 5.
4. The Qing Dynasty was founded by Manchus, an ethnic group distinct from the predominant Han Chinese.
5. This is not to deny the considerable differences among these regimes, or between them and the Guomindang. Barrington Moore summarizes the major reasons why the Guomindang ought not to be considered fascist, though it had affinities with fascism. See Moore, 1966, pp. 196–201.
6. Interestingly, history would later show that the Communist Party did not also conclude from this débâcle that it ought never again to conclude a marriage of convenience with the Guomindang. In fact it did so just ten years later. But by then the CCP had its defences up, in the form of the Red Army.
7. The Guomindang to this day relishes the epithet 'communist bandits' (gongfei).
8. His major statement on the matter is his famous essay, written to criticize Moscow-trained cadres who had no experience in the field of actual revolutionary action, entitled 'On Practice' (Mao, 1967, Vol. I, pp. 295–310).
9. At the time of this writing (July 1985), Li Xiannian is paying the first visit in history by a Chinese head of state to the United States. But the major motif which the American press is assigning to Li is not this; rather, it is that he is a survivor of the Long March.
10. In CCP categorizations, the national bourgeoisie consisted of honest capitalists who were patriotic (i.e., anti-Japanese) and not closely tied to the Guomindang (which would place them in the category of 'bureaucratic capitalists') or to foreign economic interests.
11. That helps explain why the party and the revolutionary movement it led came close to destruction not once but twice in the short span of a decade after 1927.
12. 'Moral economy' theory, which stresses the reciprocity of the landlord–peasant link—such as the provision by landlords of tools, needed services, and mechanisms of social insurance for risk-aversive peasants—has not proved particularly applicable to the Chinese case. See Ralph Thaxton, *China Turned Rightside Up: Revolutionary Legitimacy in the Peasant World*, New Haven, Yale University Press, 1983.

13. Theda Skocpol has pushed this line of argument—especially on the latter two points—to its limits (Skocpol, 1979, pp. 246, 252 and *passim*).

14. Skocpol comes close to such a position in the following statement: 'Precisely because this military strategy [of popular, peasant-based guerrilla warfare] was the only one possible in the circumstances, the Chinese Communist Party after 1927 was forced to come to terms with the peasantry in a way far different from what happened in France and Russia' (Skocpol, 1979, p. 252). But how do we know that this was the only strategy possible? Or that, if it was, the CCP adopted it because it knew this?

15. Skocpol, 1979, p. 4. I have left out the word 'rapid', used by Skocpol, because it does not fit the protracted nature of the Chinese revolution—something which she takes into account in her analysis but not in her definition.

16. It is interesting to note also that this is not a lesson which could be learned directly from the Russian revolution. The Bolsheviks organized the Tsarist armies from within, and ultimately took them over. The need for revolutionaries to have their own military forces is, then, a contribution to revolutionary practice made first by the Chinese revolution.

Chapter 2

1. The best study of the Chinese land reform, depicting both the range and complexity of problems as well as the triumphs, is William Hinton's eyewitness account *Fanshen* (Hinton, 1966).

2. See Chapter 5 for a fuller discussion of gender and family policies and issues.

3. Another way of transferring resources out of the countryside was through a price structure unfavourable to the rural sector. This became important in the 1950s as the countryside began to consume more industrial inputs and sell its output, including that of rural collective enterprises, to urban buyers and the state; but it was not a major source of rural outflow yet in the mid-1950s, when the countryside was less fully articulated to the urban economy (see Lardy, 1983, p. 144 and *passim*).

4. See Chapter 6, note 9.

5. For a perceptive and moving first-hand account of the effects of piece-rates in a state socialist factory, see Haraszti, 1978.

6. The 15.5 per cent figure is calculated from Xue, 1982, p. 960.

7. Today the Dengists view the early and mid-1950s as a golden age of economic growth, even though they have sought to depart from it as a model of economic development.

8. This speech was not published in China until after Mao's death, another signal of the ambivalence and possible controversy swirling around the First Five Year Plan.

9. The terms 'cooperative' and 'cooperativization' are used in this book to refer to

the collective units established in the mid-1950s; it is the standard translation of the term *he zuo she*, which is the Chinese used for them.

10. Of course, former landlords were also excluded, but more for political reasons than out of concern with economic exploitation; the landlords had little property to contribute anyway.

11. The speech was entitled 'On the Correct Handling of Contradictions Among the People.' (see Mao, 1977, pp. 384–421). This version contains important changes made later as a result of the political movement which the original speech unleashed, discussed below. The version cited here in fact notes this, stating in a footnote on page 384 that Mao 'went over the verbatim record and made certain additions before its publication in the *People's Daily* on June 19, 1957'.

12. The term 'brigade' (*shengchan dui*) has military overtones in Chinese as in English, reflecting the militaristic imagery of the day. This kind of imagery was also evident in the subsequent appellation of the production groups (*zu*) as 'teams' (*xiao dui*). It stuck even after the commune period settled down in the mid-1960s.

13. 'Private Plot' is an inaccurate though common translation of *ziliudi*, which literally means 'self-retained plot'. It was not privately owned, in the sense of being property which peasants could purchase, sell or rent. Rather, it was a piece of the collective's land which was allocated temporarily to individual households on a per-capita basis, the product of which was not subject to taxation or collective distribution. It was, then, a sphere of private production and consumption, but not private ownership. The plots were reallocated every three years to make adjustments for changes in household size.

14. The translation has been altered slightly here to improve grammar only.

15. The most seminal statement of the mass line is found in Mao's 1943 essay, 'Some Questions Concerning Methods of Leadership', in Mao, 1965, Vol. III, pp. 117–22.

Chapter 3

1. The substantive details are discussed in Chapter 6, pp. 179–80.

2. Yet they are also reproduced by that leadership. For example, though iconoclastic in so many ways, the Dengists have done little to pursue the structural changes of the Leninist party system—such as brooking party competition and abolishing the principle of democratic centralism—needed for real democratization.

Chapter 4

1. A terminological inconsistency extant in Western political science should be noted here. In much of the literature, particularly general theoretical work (including Marxist and non-Marxist approaches), the term 'state' refers to the structural totality of political institutions, including the party or parties. But in the sub-field of socialist and communist studies, the term 'state' is often used to refer to government institutions such as ministries, bureaux, commissions, etc. In the interests of consistency with the broader literature of political science, and because the term 'government' is more precise a way of referring to the ministerial and administrative organizations of the country, it is used in this book with that denotation, while the term 'state' is reversed to refer to the totality of political institutions in China, including the party, government and mass organizations.

2. On the varied methods of political solicitation, see Blecher, 1978 and 1983.

3. That is not to deny that Lenin and even the early Stalin did recognize the problem of party democracy in theory. See Hammond, 1978, p. 22.

4. It has also reduced its power *vis-à-vis* non-party government and professional organs, which we will take up below, pp. 117 ff.

5. Between NPC sessions, its affairs—including elections to and the convening of future sessions—are handled by a Standing Committee of 100-odd delegates. From the time when the presidency—formerly held by Liu Shaoqi—was abolished until its re-establishment in 1983, the Chair of the Standing Committee was the closest thing China had to a head of state.

6. During the first five years of the People's Republic of China, this role was played by the Chinese People's Political Consultative Congress (CPPCC), which includes delegates of non-communist parties as well as the Communist Party. This was part of the Communist Party's united front policy, which reflected the continuing diversity of political forces in China even after 1949. The CPPCC still exists, and since the Cultural Revolution has undergone something of a resuscitation. Then, as now, its existence does not represent a serious challenge to the primacy of the Communist Party. Rather, it signifies a particular strategy—of limited openness and of cooption—of party rule. See pp. 127–8.

7. In one county, for example, 70 per cent of the 80,000 contracts signed in 1984 were found to be legally invalid, acording to the Chinese press. (*Xinhua News Bulletin* (Hong Kong), 10 September 1985, p. 14).

8. One small but poignant and ironic example of this problem occurred during Ronald Reagan's visit to China in 1985. The Chinese government wanted to publicize the existence of free markets by having the President shop at one. Unfortunately, none existed along his planned travel route. So one was built near the Great Wall. In Dengist China, it can require the power of the state to create a free market!

9. This argument has recently been extended by official Chinese scholars and some

Western scholars to the higher stage of cooperativization. It has even been likened to the Stalinist collectivization (Selden, 1982). This evaluation remains controversial, though, at least among Western scholars.

10. There were also problems of policy, of course: the Great Leap was simply unworkable in most important respects. This is related to its political problems, of course. As argued below, a form of democratic politics more like that of earlier periods might have helped prevent the débâcle.

11. It is unclear whether the mass organizations and other parties could nominate candidates on their own, or only endorse candidates put forward by the Communist Party.

Chapter 5

1. Some distinctions were made between the former exploiters themselves—known as 'class elements' (*jieji chengfen*)—and their offspring—known as people with 'class origin' (*jieji chushen*). But even the children of former 'exploiters' were often treated with opprobrium or were discriminated against in distribution of scarce resources. This reached its extreme in the rise of 'blood theory', explained below, p. 219.

2. The question of private ownership is discussed in Chapter 6.

3. For two case studies in which this process is described in detail, see Blecher & White (1979) and Hinton (1983).

4. Aspects of this line of theorization have been explored by several authors. Perhaps the clearest statement of the approach as a whole is Selden, 1985.

5. Though the term 'economic endowment approach' is not used there, various aspects of this approach are discussed in Blecher, 1985a and 1985b.

6. The dependency ratio is the ratio between the total number of household members and the number capable of full-time work.

7. This point was suggested by Vivienne Shue, personal communication.

8. This is the Dazhai-Xiyang model, discussed in Chapter 6, pp. 179–80.

9. Actually, efforts were made in the 1970s, under the Dazhai/Xiyang agricultural development programme, to enlarge them by amalgamating teams and accounting at the brigade level, which would have equalized rich and poor teams. These efforts were, by and large, resisted in most localities.

10. The Chinese data were supplied to the author by officials of the Hebei provincial government. (They were also supplied to Keith Griffin and Ashwani Saith, who report them in full and offer some discussion in Griffin & Saith, 1981, pp. 18–21). The comparative data for the Third World are calculated from data on the twenty-four Third World countries (Argentina, Bangladesh, Brazil, Chile, Costa Rica, Egypt, Fiji, Honduras, India, Iran, Kenya, Republic of (South) Korea, Mexico, Nepal, Panama, Peru, Philippines, Sierra Leone, Sri Lanka, the Sudan, Tanzania, Trinidad/Tobago, Venezuela and Zambia) contained in a

world study of income distribution conducted by the International Labour Organization (ILO, 1984). The Chinese and ILO data are not strictly comparable. The latter include urban inequality, and the basic unit of measurement in the Chinese data is the county, but in the Third World data it is the household. But the upward adjustment required to make the Chinese data comparable would still not bring them above or even very close to the average Third World data.

11. Foot-binding was a traditional custom in which, at a very early age, girls' feet were wrapped in bandages, with the toes bent under, and subsequently rewrapped throughout their lives. It resulted in virtual crippling: women could hobble about slowly but could not traverse long distances easily on foot. The practice was justified on the aesthetic grounds of the beauty of small feet. Its practical effects were, of course, the physical multilation and pain experienced by women and restriction of their movements to the house and village.

12. The concept of the family wage refers to the phenomenon of paying women less than men on the presumption that men are the main income earners, with women's income being supplemental only.

Chapter 6

1. Of course, applying the experience of the Chinese case—or for that manner any case—to another country must be done with great care. Indeed, there is much to be learnt from the ways in which the 'lessons' of the Chinese case have been drawn and applied in other countries in the past. In some instances, particular elements of the Chinese case have been singled out for adoption and made into a fetish, as in the emphasis on labour mobilization for agricultural development in Kampuchea under the disastrous policies of the Khmer Rouge government. In other cases, one-sided or simplistic conclusions have been drawn to suit particular ideological needs or proclivities: this is now happening with the argument advanced by devotees of capitalism and some socialist sects alike to the effect that China has 'gone capitalist'. Too credulous an attitude towards the post-Mao criticisms of collective agriculture now runs the risk of inducing other countries to give up on it prematurely.

2. These statistics, and many others used in this chapter, are drawn from State Statistical Bureau, 1984.

3. The complex and controversial question of the nature of ownership under the responsibility systems in the countryside is considered below, pp. 182 ff., where it is argued that these systems still involve collective ownership in many respects.

4. These two types of decentralization are very different in form and implications, as we shall see. The pioneering discussion of this is in Schurmann, 1968, pp. 175–8, 196–9 and *passim*.

5. During this period capitalist industrial and commercial firms were being

nationalized and new factories and commercial firms were created. Meanwhile agriculture was cooperativized, which left it a definite operational autonomy (though it was also subject to limited crop planning through state quotas). In this period rural industry had not yet got seriously under way.

6. See the discussion of economic performance, pp. 189–91.

7. It was actually affirmed in November 1957.

8. Economic development requires an accumulation rate in the range of 12–20 per cent or more. See Kuznets, 1966, cited in Cheng, 1982, p. 420.

9. The Chinese term for this system was *yi zhang zhi*, which literally means direction or rule by one head person. Thus it is not sexist in Chinese. Since the universal translation into English is, unfortunately, the sexist term 'one-man management', it has been adopted here, regrettably and with this proviso.

10. On political solicitation in the countryside, see p. 130.

11. The term is my own coinage. See Blecher, 1985b.

12. Higher levels of the commune structure—the production brigade or the commune level—owned small plots of land for offices, warehouses or experimental plots, and also certain productive resources—such as large tractors or waterworks—which were beyond the capacity of the team to finance or use profitably by itself.

13. See p. 73.

14. At times they were subjected to political pressure to use certain systems. For example, during the early 1970s, under a national campaign—discussed below (pp. 179–80)—to emulate the model village of Dazhai, teams were encouraged to use Dazhai's work-point system of time rates which took one's level of collective consciousness into account.

15. For example, in Jiujie Brigade of Xinji Commune (Shulu County, Hebei Province), brigade-level accounting was seen as natural largely because the annual income from brigade-run industries in 1978 was Y345,697, compared with agricultural income (from the former teams) of only Y48,202. Even if there were significant inequalities among teams in agriculture, those were dwarfed by the size of brigade industry, in which they all had an equal share. Although at the time I visited this brigade (in 1979) brigade-level accounting was coming under attack in national policy, the brigade officials asserted in the most definite tones (in the presence of provincial officials!) that they would never return to team accounting, because doing so made no economic sense and would receive no support from the peasants who were benefiting from the large brigade income.

16. This is not to say that economic results under high collectivism were very poor. As we shall see below, (pp. 189 ff.) they were not. Steady growth of output, at least keeping up with population growth, was maintained—no mean achievement. But results in productivity and income were less impressive.

17. This, too, is my own coinage; see Blecher, 1985b.

18. To give just a few examples, in 1977 the figure for Ghana was 32.3 per cent, Kenya 30.8 per cent, Sri Lanka 27.1 per cent, Zaïre 29.4 per cent, and Taiwan 47.6 per cent. See Todaro, 1981, p. 339.

19. The phrase is adapted from Mao's famous intonement, uttered from the podium atop Tiananmen Square in Beijing on 1 October 1949, the day the People's Republic was declared, that 'China has stood up'.

Chapter 7

1. Cultural Revolution-inspired movements for popularization of cultural production, for example by having workers and peasants create their own graphic art, proved much more popular, though.
2. This was made evident by the poor showing of Chinese forces during China's brief border war with Vietnam in 1979.
3. Recall also that Mao's major opponent in 1958 and 1959 was Peng Dehaui, the head of the People's Liberation Army.
4. It was frequently argued that China would play its 'Russia card' against the United States in the 1970s. In fact it seems to have done the reverse, by playing the 'US card' against the Soviet Union. Chinese leaders may have calculated that the 'Russia card' could not be played effectively until normalization with the United States had been accomplished, since before then the Soviets, knowing that the Chinese were in a relatively weak position, could exact a higher price from them.

Bibliography

Books and Articles

Adelman, C. and Morris, C. 1973. *Economic Growth and Social Equity in Developing Countries*. Stanford, Calif., Stanford University Press.

American Rural Small-Scale Industry Delegation, 1977. *Rural Small-Scale Industry in the People's Republic of China*. Berkeley, University of California Press.

Andors, S., 1977. *China's Industrial Revolution*. New York, Pantheon.

Barnett, A. D., with a contribution by Ezra Vogel, 1967. *Cadres, Bureaucracy, and Political Power in Communist China*. New York, Columbia University Press.

——, ed., 1969. *Chinese Communist Politics in Action*. Seattle, University of Washington Press.

——, 1979. *China and the World Food System*. Washington, D.C., Overseas Development Council.

Bartke, W. & Schier, P., 1985. *China's New Party Leadership*. Armonk, N.Y., M. E. Sharpe.

Bastid, M., 1984. 'Chinese Educational Policies in the 1980s and Economic Development', *China Quarterly*, no. 98.

Baum, R. & Teiwes, F., 1968. *Ssu-Ch'ing: The Socialist Education Movement of 1962-1966*. Berkeley, University of California.

Belden, J., 1973. *China Shakes the World*. Harmondsworth, Penguin.

Bennett, G., 1978. *Huadong: The Story of a People's Commune*. Boulder, Co., Westview.

Bianco, L., 1971. *Origins of the Chinese Revolution, 1915-1949*.Stanford, Stanford University Press.

Bilancia, Philip R., 1981. *Dictionary of Chinese Law and Government*. Stanford, Stanford University Press.

Blecher, M., 1976. 'Income Distribution in Small Rural Chinese Communities', *China Quarterly*, no. 68.

——, 1978. *Leader-Mass Relations in Rural Chinese Communities: Local Politics in a Revolutionary Society*, Ph.D. dissertation, University of Chicago.

——, 1979. 'Consensual Politics in Rural Chinese Communities', *Modern China*, vol. 5, no. 1.

——, 1983. 'The Mass Line and Leader-Mass Relations and Communication in Basic-Level Rural Communities' in G. Chu and F. Hsu (eds), *China's New Social Fabric*. London, Kegan Paul International.

——, 1985a. 'Inequality and Socialism in Rural China', *World Development*, vol. 13, no. 1.

—, 1985b. 'The Structure and Contradictions of Productive Relations in Socialist Agrarian "Reform": A Framework for Analysis and the Chinese Case', *Journal of Development Studies*, vol. 22, no. 1.

Blecher, M. and White, G., 1979b. *Micropolitics in Contemporary China: A Technical Unit During and After the Cultural Revolution*. White Plains, NY, M. E. Sharpe.

Blecher, M. *et al*. (forthcoming). *Town and Country in a Developing Chinese County: Government, Economy and Society in Shulu Xian*.

Blunden, Caroline & Elvin, Mark, 1983. *Cultural Atlas of China*. New York, Facts on File.

Bo Y., 1952. 'Three Years of Achievements of the People's Republic of China' in *New China's Economic Achievements, 1949–52*. Beijing, China Committee for the Promotion of International Trade; cited in V. Lippit, 1974. *Land Reform and Economic Development in China*. White Plains, NY, International Arts and Sciences Press.

Bulletin of Concerned Asian Scholars, ed., 1983. *China From Mao to Deng*. Armonk, N.Y., M. E. Sharpe.

Burns, J., 1978. 'The Election of Production Team Cadres in Rural China, 1958–1974', *China Quarterly*, no. 74.

Cell, C., 1977. *Revolution at Work: Mobilization Campaigns in China*. New York, Academic Press.

Chan, A., *et al*., 1984. *Chen Village*, Berkeley, University of California Press.

Chang, C., 1962. *The Income of the Chinese Gentry*. Seattle, University of Washington Press.

Chen, C. (ed.) and Ridley, C. (trans.), 1969. *Rural People's Communes in Lien-Chiang*. Stanford, Calif., Hoover Institution Press.

Chen, J., 1973. *A Year in Upper Felicity*. New York, Macmillan.

Cheng, C., 1982. *China's Economic Development*. Boulder, Co., Westview.

Cheng, Peter, 1983. *China*. Oxford, Clio Press.

Chesneaux, J., 1979. *China: The People's Republic, 1949–1976*. New York, Pantheon.

Chesneaux, J., *et al*., 1977. *China from the 1911 Revolution to Liberation*. New York, Pantheon.

Chu, G., & Hsu, F., eds, 1983. *China's New Social Fabric*. London, Kegan Paul International.

Croll, E., 1981. *The Politics of Marriage in Contemporary China*. Cambridge, Cambridge University Press.

—, 1982. *The Family Rice Bowl: Food and the Domestic Economy in China*. Geneva, UNRISD.

—, 1983. *Chinese Women Since Mao*. London, Zed.

Crook, I. & D., 1979. *Ten Mile Inn*. New York, Pantheon.

Dittmer, L., 1974. *Liu Shao-ch'i and the Chinese Cultural Revolution*. Berkeley, University of California Press.

Donnithorne, A., 1967. *China's Economic System*. New York, Praeger.

Eckstein, A., 1977. *China's Economic Revolution*. Cambridge, Cambridge University Press.

Eckstein, A. ed., 1980. *Quantiative Measures of China's Economic Output*. Ann Arbor, Mich., University of Michigan Press.

Elvin, M., 1973. *The Pattern of the Chinese Past*. Stanford, Stanford University Press.

Esherick, J., 1981. 'Number Games: A Note on Land Distribution in Prerevolutionary China', *Modern China*, Vol. 7, no. 4.

Fei, H., 1953. *China's Gentry*. Chicago, University of Chicago Press.

Feuchtwang, S., & Hussain, A., eds, 1983. *The Chinese Economic Reforms*. Beckenham, Croom Helm.

Feuerwerker, A., 1958. *China's Early Industrialization*. Cambridge, Mass., Harvard University Press.

Gittings, J., 1967. *The Role of the Chinese Army*. London, Oxford University Press.

Gray, J., & White, G., eds, 1982. *China's New Development Strategy*. London, Academic Press.

Griffin, K., ed., 1984. *Institutional Reform and Economic Development in the Chinese Countryside*. Armonk, N.Y., M. E. Sharpe.

Griffin, K., & Saith, A., 1981. *Growth and Equality in Rural China*. Geneva, International Labour Office.

Gurley, J., 1976. *China's Economy and the Maoist Strategy*. New York, Monthly Review.

Hammond, E., 1978. 'Marxism and the Mass Line', *Modern China*, vol. 4, no. 1.

Haraszti, M., 1978. *A Worker in a Worker's State*. New York, Universe Books.

Harding, H., 1981. *Organizing China: The Problem of Bureaucracy*. Stanford, Calif., Stanford University Press.

Hinton, C., 1986. *All Under Heaven* (film: Distributor: New Day Films).

Hinton, H., 1980. *The People's Republic of China. 1949-79: A Documentary Survey*. Wilmington, Del., Scholarly Resources.

Hinton, W., 1966. *Fanshen*. New York, Vintage.

—, 1983. *Shenfan*. New York, Random House.

Ho, P., & Tsou, T., eds, 1969. *China in Crisis*, vol. 1. Chicago, University of Chicago Press.

International Labour Office (ILD), 1984. *World Labour Report*. Geneva.

Johnson, C., 1962. *Peasant Nationalism and Communist Power: The Emergence of Revolutionary China, 1937-1945*. Stanford, Calif., Stanford University Press.

Johnson, G., 1986. 'The Fate of the Communal Economy: Some Contrary Evidence from the Pearl River Delta', paper presented at Association for Asian Studies Annual Meeting, Chicago 1986.

Johnson, K., 1983. *Women, the Family and Peasant Revolution in China*. Chicago, University of Chicago Press.

Kelliher, D., 1986. 'The Changing Pattern of Peasant–State Relations in the 1980s', paper presented at the Association for Asian Studies Annual Meeting, Chicago 1986.

Kim, I., 1973. *The Politics of Chinese Communism: Kiangsi Under the Soviets*. Berkeley, University of California Press.

Kraus, R., 1981. *Class Conflict in Chinese Socialism*. New York, Columbia University Press.

Kuznets, S., 1966. *Modern Economic Growth*. New York, Norton.

Lamb, Malcolm, 1984. *Directory of Officials and Organizations in China, 1968-1983*. Armonk, N.Y., M. E. Sharpe.

Lappe, F., & Collins J., 1977. *Food First*. New York, Ballantine.

Lardy, N., 1978. *Economic Growth and Distribution in China*. Cambridge, Cambridge University Press.

—, 1983. *Agriculture in China's Modern Economic Development*. Cambridge, Cambridge University Press.

Lee, H., 1978. *The Politics of the Chinese Cultural Revolution*. Berkeley, University of California Press.

Lewis, J., 1963. *Leadership in Communist China*. Ithaca, N.Y., Cornell University Press.

Li, F., 1955. 'Report on the Five-Year Plan for Development of the National Economy of the People's Republic of China in 1953-57', in R. Bowie and J. Fairbank (eds), 1962. *Communist China, 1955-1959: Policy Documents With Analysis*. Cambridge, Mass., Harvard University Center for International Affairs and East Asian Research Center.

Li, V., 1978. *Law Without Lawyers*. Boulder, Co., Westview Press.

Lippit, V., 1978. 'The Development of Underdevelopment in China', *Modern China*, vol. 4, no. 3.

Lipton, M., 1976. *Why Poor People Stay Poor*. Cambridge, Mass., Harvard University Press.

Lötveit, T., 1973. *Chinese Communism 1931-1934*. Lund, Sweden, Studentlitteratur.

MacFarquhar, R., 1974. *The Origins of the Cultural Revolution, I: Contradictions Among the People, 1956-1957*. New York, Columbia University Press.

—, 1983. *The Origins of the Cultural Revolution, Vol. 2: The Great Leap Forward, 1958-1960*. New York, Columbia University Press.

Madsen, R., 1984. *Morality and Power in a Chinese Village*. Berkeley, University of California Press.

Maitan, L., 1976. *Party, Army and Masses in China*. London, New Left Books.

Mao Z., 1967. *Selected Works*. Beijing, Foreign Languages Press.

—, 1969. *Mao Zedong Sixiang Wansui [Long Live the Thought of Mao Zedong]*. N.P.

—, 1977. *Selected Works, Volume V*. Beijing, Foreign Languages Press.

Marriage Law of the People's Republic of China, 1950, in A. Blaustein (ed.), 1962. *Fundamental Legal Documents of Communist China*. South Hackensack, NJ, Fred. B. Rothman & Co.

Marx, K., 1959. 'Theses on Feuerbach' in Lewis Feuer (ed.), *Marx and Engels: Basic Writings on Politics and Philosophy*. Garden City, N.Y., Anchor/Doubleday.

Maxwell, N., & McFarlane, B., eds, 1985. *China's Changed Road to Development*. Oxford, Pergamon.

Meisner, Maurice, 1977. *Mao's China: A History of the People's Republic*. New York, Free Press.

Meisner, Mitch, & Blecher, M., 1982. 'Administrative Level and Agrarian Structure, 1975-80: The County (W)as Focial Point in Chinese Rural Development Policy', in Gray and White, eds., 1982.

Moore, B., 1966. *Social Origins of Dictatorship and Democracy*. Boston, Beacon Press.

Moulder, F., 1977. *Japan, China and the Modern World Economy*. Cambridge, Cambridge University Press.

Murphey, R., 1980. *The Fading of the Maoist Vision: City and Country in China's Development*. New York, Methuen.

Myers, R., 1970. *The Chinese Peasant Economy*. Cambridge, Mass., Harvard University Press.

Myrdal, J., 1965. *Report from a Chinese Village*. New York, Signet.

Nee, V., & Mozingo, D., eds, 1983. *State and Society in Contemporary China*. Ithaca, N.Y., Cornell University Press.

Oi, J., 1986. 'From Cadres to Middlemen: The Commercialization of Rural Government', paper presented at Association for Asian Studies Annual Meeting, Chicago 1986.

Oksenberg, M., ed., 1973. *China's Developmental Experience*. New York, Praeger.

Parish, W., ed., 1985. *Chinese Rural Development: The Great Transformation*. Armonk, N.Y., M. E. Sharpe.

Parish, W., & Whyte, M., 1978. *Village and Family in Contemporary China*. Chicago, University of Chicago Press.

Pepper, S., 1970. 'Educational and Political Development in Communist China', *Studies in Comparative Communism*, Vol. 3, nos. 3–4.

Perkins, D., 1975. 'The Growth and Changing Structure of China's Twentieth-Century Economy', in D. Perkins, ed., *China's Modern Economy in Historical Perspective*. Stanford, Stanford University Press.

Perry, E., & Wong, C., eds, 1985. *The Political Economy of Reform in Post-Mao China*. Cambridge, Mass., Harvard University Press.

Potter, S., 1983. 'The Position of Peasants in Modern China's Social Order', *Modern China*, vol. 9, no. 4.

Putterman, L., 1983. 'A Modified Collective Agriculture in Rural Growth-with-Equity.' *World Development*, Vol. 11, No. 2.

Rawski, T., 1979. *Economic Growth and Employment in China*. Oxford, Oxford University Press.

Richman, B., 1969. *Industrial Society in Communist China*. New York, Random House.

Saich, T., 1981. *China: Politics and Government*. New York, St. Martin's.

—, 1983. 'Party Building Since Mao—A Question of Style?' *World Development*, vol. 9, no. 8, pp. 747–66.

Scherer, John L. *China Facts and Figures Annual*. Academic International Press.

Schram, S., 1966. *Mao Tse-tung*. New York, Simon and Schuster.

—, 1973. *Authority, Participation and Cultural Change in China*. Cambridge, Cambridge University Press.

—, ed., 1979. *Mao Tse-Tung Unrehearsed*. Harmondsworth, Penguin.

Schran, P., 1969. *The Development of Chinese Agriculture, 1950–1959*. Urbana, IL, University of Illinois Press.

Schurmann, F., 1968. *Ideology and Organization in Communist China* (second, enlarged edition). Berkeley, University of California Press.

Selden, M., 1971. *The Yenan Way in Revolutionary China*. Cambridge, Mass., Harvard University Press.

—, ed., 1979. *The People's Republic of China: A Documentary History of Revolutionary Change*. New York, Monthly Review.

—, 1982. 'Cooperation and Conflict: Cooperative and Collective Formation in China's Countryside', in M. Selden and V. Lippit (eds.), *The Transition to Socialism in China*. Armonk, NY, M. E. Sharpe.

—, 1985. 'State, Market and Sectoral Inequality in Contemporary China', in Peter Evans, Dietrich Rueschmeyer and Evelyn Huber Stephens, eds., *States Versus Markets in the World-System*. Beverly Hills, Sage Publications.

Shue, V., 1980. *Peasant China in Transition: The Dynamics of Development Towards Socialism, 1949-56*. Berkeley, University of California Press..

Sigurdson, J., 1977. *Rural Industrialization in China*. Cambridge, Mass., Harvard University Press.

Skinner, G. W., 1964-5. 'Marketing and Social Structure in Rural China', *Journal of Asian Studies*, vol. 24, nos. 1-30.

Skocpol, T., 1979. *States and Social Revolutions*. Cambridge, Cambridge University Press.

Smedley, A., 1956. *The Great Road*. New York, Monthly Review Press.

Snow, E., 1961. *Red Star Over China*. New York, Grove Press.

Solinger, D., 1985. '"Temporary Residence Certificate" Regulations in Wuhan, May 1983'. *China Quarterly*, No. 101.

Starr, J., 1979. *Continuing the Revolution: The Political Thought of Mao*. Princeton, Princeton University Press.

State Statistical Bureau, 1984. *Statistical Yearbook of China, 1984*. Hong Kong, Economic Information and Agency.

Stavis, B., 1974. *People's Communes and Rural Development in China*. Ithaca, N.Y., Center for International Studies, Cornell University.

—, 1978. *The Politics of Agricultural Mechanization in China*. Ithaca, N.Y., Cornell University Press.

Szajkowski, B., ed., 1981. *Marxist Governments: A World Survey*. Vol. 2. New York, St. Martin's Press.

—, 1982. *The Establishment of Marxist Regimes*. London, Butterworth.

Tawney, R. H., 1932. *Land and Labour in China*. London, George Allen & Unwin.

Thaxton, R., 1983. *China Turned Rightside Up*. New Haven, Conn. Yale University Press.

Thurston, A., 1977. 'The Revival of Classes in Rural Kwangtung: Production Team Politics in a Period of Crisis', unpublished paper.

Todaro, M., 1981. *Economic Development in the Third World*. New York, Longman.

Townsend, J. & Womack, B., 1985. *Politics in China*, 3rd ed., Boston, Little Brown.

Tsou, T., Blecher, M., & Meisner, M., 1982a. 'National Agricultural Policy: The Dazhai Model and Local Change in the Post-Mao Era', in M. Selden and V. Lippit, eds., *The Transition to Socialism in China*. Armonk, N.Y., M. E. Sharpe.

Tsou, T., Blecher, M., & Meisner, M., 1982b. 'The Responsibility System in Agriculture: Its Implementation in Xiyang and Dazhai', *Modern China*, vol. 8, no. 1 (January), pp.41–104.

Union Research Institute (URI), 1971. *Documents of Chinese Communist Party Central Committee, Vol. 1*. Hong Kong, Union Research Institute.

Vogel, E., 1969. *Canton Under Communism: Programs and Politics in a Provincial Capital, 1948–1968*. Cambridge, Mass., Harvard University Press.

Walker, K., 1965. *Planning in Chinese Agriculture: Socialization and the Private Sector*. Chicago, Aldine.

Watson, A., 1983. 'Agriculture Looks for "Shoes That Fit"': The Production Responsibility System and Its Implications', *World Development*, vol. 11, no. 8.

White, L. III, 1978. *Careers in Shanghai: The Social Guidance of Personal Energies in a Developing Chinese City, 1949–1966*. Berkeley, University of California Press.

Whyte, M., 1974. *Small Groups and Political Rituals in China*. Berkeley, University of California Press.

—— & Parish, W., 1984. *Urban Life in Contemporary China*. Chicago, University of Chicago Press.

Womack, B., 1982. 'The 1980 County-Level Elections in China', *Asian Survey*.

——, 1984. 'Modernization and Democratic Reform in China', *Journal of Asian Studies*, vol. 43, no. 3.

Xu, D., *et al*., 1982. *China's Search for Economic Growth*. Beijing, New World Press.

Xue, M., 1981. *China's Socialist Economy*. Beijing, Foreign Languages Press.

—— (ed.), 1982. *Almanac of China's Economy, 1981*. Cambridge, Mass., Ballinger Publishing.

Yao, W., 1975. *On the Social Basis of the Lin Piao Anti-Party Clique*. Beijing, Foreign Languages Press.

Yahuda, M., 1983. *Towards the End of Isolationism: China's Foreign Policy After Mao*. New York, St. Martin's.

Yu, G., ed., 1984. *China's Socialist Modernization*. Beijing, Foreign Languages Press.

Zhang, C., 1975. *On Exercising All-Round Dictatorship Over the Bourgeoisie*. Beijing, Foreign Languages Press.

Periodicals

Asian Survey
Australian Journal of Chinese Affairs
Beijing Review
Bulletin of Concerned Asian Scholars
China Quarterly
Far Eastern Economic Review
Journal of Asian Studies
Journal of Contemporary Asia
Journal of Developmental Studies

Modern China
Pacific Affairs
Social Sciences in China
World Development
Xinhua News Bulletin.

Basic Data Reference Works

State Statistical Bureau, People's Republic of China. *Statistical Yearbook of China*. Hong Kong, Economic Information and Agency, annual.

White, Gordon, Murray, Robin, & White, Christine (eds), 1983. *Revolutionary Socialist Development in the Third World*. Brighton, Harvester.

World Bank, *World Development Report*. Oxford, Oxford University Press, annual.

Xue Muqiao (ed.), 1982. *Almanac of China's Economy, 1981*. Cambridge, Mass., Ballinger Publishing.

Index